MW01436502

# Commercial Liability Insurance and Risk Management

Volume 2

# Commercial Liability Insurance and Risk Management
## Volume 2

**Donald S. Malecki, CPCU**
Chairman, Donald S. Malecki & Associates, Inc.

**Ronald C. Horn, Ph.D., CPCU, CLU**
Professor of Insurance Studies (Retired)
Baylor University

**Eric A. Wiening, CPCU, ARM, AU**
Assistant Vice President
American Institute for CPCU

**Arthur L. Flitner, CPCU, ARM, AIC**
Senior Director of Curriculum Design
American Institute for CPCU

Third Edition • 1996

American Institute for CPCU
720 Providence Road, Malvern, Pennsylvania 19355-0770

© 1996
American Institute for CPCU

*All rights reserved. This book or any part thereof may not be reproduced without the written permission of the publisher.*

*Third Edition • October 1996*

Library of Congress Catalog Number 95-77152
International Standard Book Number 0-89463-071-7

♻ *Printed in the United States of America on recycled paper.*

# *Dedication*

The American Institute for CPCU dedicates this volume of *Commercial Liability Insurance and Risk Management* to the memory of Dr. Richard deRaismes Kip, CPCU, CLU, distinguished educator in the field of insurance and risk management. During his fifty-year career, Dr. Kip held professorships at three major universities and earned an enviable reputation as a gifted teacher, a skilled writer and researcher, and an effective academic administrator.

Dr. Kip received his CPCU designation in 1948. In the early 1950s, he served as Assistant Dean of the American Institute for CPCU, where he developed the new curriculum in insurance that became the Insurance Institute of America's Program in General Insurance (INS). To date, well over 125,000 insurance practitioners and university students have completed this series of courses.

Dr. Kip taught insurance and finance courses at the University of Pennsylvania for twenty years while also serving as Committee Chairman for the Ethical Guidance of Students. Later, he served as a tenured professor of risk and insurance at Florida State University and at the University of North Florida. Dr. Kip also taught all parts of the CPCU Program in classes sponsored by local CPCU Society chapters in Tallahassee and Jacksonville. From 1943 until 1993, he served as a prominent member of the American Institute for CPCU's national examination committee. His fifty years of writing and reviewing CPCU national examinations exceeded by far the length of service of any other member of the body that sets and maintains the high standards of professional achievement representing the CPCU designation.

# *Preface*

This volume contains the principal study material for Assignments 9 through 15 for CPCU 4, one of the courses in the curriculum leading to the Chartered Property Casualty Underwriter designation. A complete list of required study materials for CPCU 4 is shown in the CPCU 4 Course Guide. Persons planning to take the CPCU 4 exam can make sure they have all of the CPCU 4 study materials, including the current course guide, by calling the Institute's Customer Service Department at 1-800-644-2101.

This seven-chapter volume is the retitled third edition of Volume 2 of *Commercial Liability Risk Management and Insurance*, first published in 1978 and revised in 1986. The current volume has been retitled (*Commercial Liability Insurance and Risk Management*) to indicate more clearly that the principal subject of the CPCU 4 text is *insurance*—viewed within the context of risk management.

The present volume continues the examination of the various lines of commercial insurance that began in Volume 1 of the text. The types of insurance covered in Chapters 9 through 13 of the present volume are workers compensation and employers liability, professional liability, environmental liability, and excess and umbrella liability. Chapter 14 examines surety bonds, and Chapter 15 surveys advanced risk management techniques that some organizations use instead of, or in combination with, commercial insurance.

Many contributing authors and reviewers enriched the first two editions of the text. Although the acknowledgments that follow are limited to naming those who actively participated in the third edition, we express our enduring gratitude to the contributing authors and reviewers of the first two editions.

With regard to the current edition, we would first like to thank five contributing authors: Ellen L. Barton, David J. Dybdahl, Rodney Taylor, Pete Ligeros, and Richard G. Rudolph, who are acknowledged more fully on the

Contributing Authors page that follows this preface. The particular role performed by each contributing author is described below, along with acknowledgment of those who assisted the contributing authors.

- Ellen Barton wrote significant portions of Chapter 10, "Professional Liability Insurance."
- David Dybdahl and Rodney Taylor wrote Chapter 12, "Environmental Insurance," assisted by S. Richard Heymann, J.D., Foley & Lardner; and Nora Vrakas, CPCU, ARM, Assistant Vice President, Willis Corroon.
- Pete Ligeros co-wrote significant portions of Chapter 13, "Excess and Umbrella Liability Insurance," with Donald Malecki.

Richard Rudolph adapted Chapter 15, "Advanced Risk Management Techniques," from the larger work, *The Alternative Market*, published in 1994 by International Risk Management Institute, Inc., Dallas, TX.

*The Alternative Market* is a research project of the Golden Gate Chapter of the CPCU Society. The Chapter's research committee for the project consisted of Donn P. McVeigh, Chair, CPCU, ARM, Creative Risk Concepts International; Robert L. Wilkinson, Co-Chair, CPCU, ARM, Risk Management Consultant; Barbara Goodwin, CPCU, ARM, Minet, Inc.; Erin A. Oberly, CPCU, ARM, Risk Management Consultant; Richard V. Rupp, CPCU, Calco Insurance Agents & Brokers; David Warren, CPCU, Risk Management Consultant; and Ted O. Hall, J.D., CPA, Consulting Accountant.

Each individual recognized below performed the essential task of reviewing one or more chapters of the manuscript to verify that the material was correct, complete, and at an appropriate educational level for CPCU studies. The authors thank the reviewers for their many useful suggestions for improving the manuscript.

Thomas M. Brennan, CPCU, ARM
Master Underwriter
CIGNA Excess Casualty

Richard G. Clarke, CPCU, CIC
Vice President
Palmer & Cay/Carswell

John W. Crocker, CPCU, AFSB
Senior Vice President
Willis Corroon

Michael W. Elliott, CPCU, AIAF
Assistant Vice President
American Institute for CPCU

David L. Hixenbaugh, CPCU, AFSB
Vice President, Bonds
Employers Mutual Casualty Company

Maureen C. McLendon, CPCU, ARM
Senior Research Analyst
International Risk Management Institute, Inc.

Meike Olin, CPCU, CIC
Editor
Standard Publishing Corporation

S. Wesley Porter, Jr., CPCU, AIM, AFSB
Director of Fidelity and Surety Education
American Institute for CPCU

Dennis E. Wine
Vice President, Surety
Surety Association of America

Finally, the authors thank the members of the Institute's Publications Department, whose talents were instrumental in producing the new volume. In particular, we would like to recognize Michael J. Betz, who provided intensive editing and rewriting assistance; Yvette Stavropoulos, who copy edited and indexed the text; and Barbara Skey and Esther Underhill, who typeset the text and created the graphics for its exhibits.

The constructive comments of CPCU 4 course leaders and students on the first two editions of the text were useful in planning this latest edition. We therefore invite you to help shape the next edition of the text by sending us your comments on the current edition. Please address your comments to the Curriculum Department of the American Institute for CPCU.

Donald S. Malecki<br>
Ronald C. Horn<br>
Eric A. Wiening<br>
Arthur L. Flitner

# Contributing Authors

The American Institute for CPCU and the authors acknowledge with deep appreciation the work of the following contributing authors:

Ellen L. Barton, J.D., CPCU, DASHRM
President
Neumann Insurance Company

David J. Dybdahl, CPCU, ARM
Managing Director
Willis Corroon

Pete Ligeros, J.D.
Pete Ligeros & Associates

Richard G. Rudolph, Ph.D., CPCU, ARM, ARP, APA, AIAF, AAM
Principal
Seaver, Rudolph & Associates, Inc.

Rodney Taylor, J.D., P.E., CPCU, CLU, ARM
Senior Vice President
Willis Corroon

# Contents

## 9 Workers Compensation and Employers Liability Insurance   1

    Employers Liability Under the Common Law   2

    State Workers Compensation Laws   4

    Federal Compensation Laws   15

    The Workers Compensation and Employers Liability Policy   21

    Summary   37

## 10 Professional Liability Insurance   39

    Overview of Professional Liability Exposure and Insurance   40

    Physicians Professional Liability Insurance   48

    Accountants Professional Liability Insurance   61

    Architects and Engineers Professional Liability Insurance   68

    Summary   76

## 11 Professional Liability Insurance, Continued   77

    Directors and Officers Liability Insurance   78

    Employee Benefits and Fiduciary Liability Insurance   93

    Employment Practices Liability Insurance   104

    Summary   109

## 12 Environmental Insurance   111

    Legal Basis for Environmental Liability   112

    Environmental Risk Management   128

    Pollution Exclusions   132

    Types of Environmental Insurance Available   139

    Application Process for Environmental Insurance   163

    Summary   165

## 13 Excess and Umbrella Liability Insurance  167

Need for Excess or Umbrella Liability Coverage  167

Basic Characteristics of Excess and Umbrella Liability Policies  170

Excess Liability Insurance  172

Umbrella Liability Insurance  175

Structuring the Liability Insurance Program  195

Summary  198

## 14 Surety Bonds  201

Surety Bond Fundamentals  202

Contract Bonds  207

Federal Noncontract Surety Bonds  216

License and Permit Bonds  217

Public Official Bonds  220

Judicial Bonds  222

Financial Guarantee Coverages  228

Summary  229

## 15 Advanced Risk Management Techniques  231

Self-Insurance  232

Large Deductible Plans  238

Captive Insurers  240

Fronting  243

Retrospective Rating Plans  247

Summary  254

## Bibliography  257

## Index  259

# Chapter 9

# Workers Compensation and Employers Liability Insurance[1]

**Workers compensation** is a comprehensive term used to refer to the statutes that provide for fixed awards and medical reimbursement to employees or their dependents in cases of employment-related injuries and diseases. Those awards are granted without regard to negligence or fault on the employer's part, thus differentiating the compensation system from the more traditional common-law system. Workers compensation laws are intended to benefit the employee *and* the employer. These statutes have created a "no-fault" system whereby the employee loses the right to sue for common-law damages in return for the employer's strict liability for work-related accidents.

Workers compensation *laws* and workers compensation *insurance* are so closely interrelated that many people incorrectly use these two terms interchangeably. Actually, workers compensation insurance is but one method by which an employer can demonstrate the ability to satisfy obligations imposed by the workers compensation laws. Some state workers compensation statutes do not require insurance for those who can self-insure. However, most employers purchase workers compensation insurance to protect themselves from liabilities imposed by state workers compensation laws.

Despite the existence of workers compensation laws, employers can in some instances be sued as a result of employee injury or disease. Consequently, the

1

standard insurance policy used to provide workers compensation coverage in most states includes so-called employers liability coverage to protect employers against such suits.

The major topics examined in this chapter include the following:

- The liability of employers for employment-related injuries under the common law
- Common features of state and federal workers compensation laws
- The standard workers compensation and employers liability policy and important endorsements

# Employers Liability Under the Common Law

Before workers compensation statutes were enacted, courts applied common-law concepts to the disposition of occupational injury and disease claims by an employee against an employer.

Understanding the common-law concepts applicable to employers liability is important for two reasons:

1. Workers compensation laws made an extraordinary departure from the common law that based responsibility for an injury on fault. This departure resulted from the inadequacies in common law that prevented it from dealing adequately with work-related injuries.
2. The various workers compensation laws have exceptions for certain employments or circumstances. When a worker is outside the scope of workers compensation laws, he or she retains the right to sue the employer under the common law. In some cases, even an employee who is covered by workers compensation may be able to sue.

## Employer's Duty of Care

Under the common law, an employer is bound to exercise a reasonable degree of care for the employee's safety. The following specific duties have been abstracted from this general duty of care:

1. Provide a safe place to work
2. Provide an adequate number of competent fellow employees
3. Provide safe tools and equipment
4. Warn the employee of inherent dangers
5. Make and enforce rules for the safety of all employees

The failure on the part of the employer to exercise such care as the circumstances require constitutes negligence. If such negligence is the proximate cause of an employee's injury, the employer is answerable in damages, in the absence of a valid legal defense. In all cases, the burden of establishing the employer's negligence is on the employee. Unless the employee can sustain that burden, the employee may not recover under the common law.

## Common-Law Defenses

If the failure of the employer to meet one or more of its duties causes injury to an employee, the employee would have a cause of action for damages against the employer. However, the employer is protected by three common-law defenses: assumption of risk, contributory negligence, and the negligence of a fellow employee. Under certain modern compensation laws, if an employer fails to provide security for its workers compensation obligations, its employees may elect their common-law rights, while the employer is barred from asserting the defenses described below.

### Assumption of Risk

The assumption-of-risk defense can be applied if two conditions are present:

1. The employee knows or is aware of the existence of the risk and has a corresponding appreciation of the extent of the danger.
2. The employee voluntarily exposes himself or herself to the danger.

The employee is expected to have knowledge of a danger that is open and apparent. If the employee accepts employment under such circumstances, he or she will be deemed to have voluntarily exposed himself or herself to the danger and may not recover for any resulting injury. The same is true when an employer fails to meet a duty and an employee who is aware of this failure continues to work. The employee will be held to have assumed the risk of injury.

However, the employee cannot be held to have assumed a risk of which he or she was unaware. For example, if, unknown to the employee, radioactive materials are used in another section of the plant, and the employee suffers an injury from exposure to radiation, it cannot be said that the employee assumed this risk since he or she was not aware of it in the first place.

### Contributory Negligence

Under the common law, everyone is required to exercise care for his or her own safety. If an employee fails to exercise such care, he or she will be deemed to be contributorily negligent even though the negligence of the employer was also a contributing cause of the injury. The common-law rule is that if the employee's contributory negligence is responsible *to any degree* in causing the accident, the employee is barred from recovery. Thus, under the common law, a momentary lapse in behavior on the part of the employee could defeat recovery even though the negligence of the employer contributed to a much greater degree to the occurrence of, or the extent of, the injury.

The contributory negligence defense has been largely replaced by the comparative negligence defense. *Comparative negligence* is based on the principle that the contributory negligence of the employee is not a complete defense. Instead, the negligence of the employee is taken into account in reducing the amount of recovery. Comparative negligence laws enable employees to recover a portion of their damages even when they are substantially at fault.

Assumption of risk is sometimes regarded as another form of contributory negligence. However, certain comparative negligence statutes do *not* eliminate the defense of assumption of risk. If the comparative negligence statute does not specifically include assumption of risk within its definition of contributory negligence, then the assumption-of-risk defense is still available to the defendant.

### Negligence of a Fellow Employee

The employer is not liable for an injury caused solely by the negligence of a fellow employee. This is an exception to the general rule of *respondeat superior*, under which the negligence of an employee acting within the course and scope of his or her employment is imputed to the employer. In general, courts have been reluctant to apply the fellow-employee defense (also known as the fellow-servant rule).

## State Workers Compensation Laws

Before workers compensation laws were enacted, the harshness of the common law was only slightly modified. For example, some courts rejected the assumption-of-risk defense in regard to safety violations by the employer. A number of legislatures enacted employers liability statutes that restricted or eliminated the fellow-servant rule, restricted the assumption-of-risk defense, or applied comparative negligence in lieu of contributory negligence. All of these efforts were negligible compared to the changes in the law brought about by workers compensation legislation.

The Wisconsin workers compensation statute, effective in 1911, is the oldest comprehensive compensation law in the United States. By 1920, all but a few of the states had passed workers compensation laws. Today, all fifty states, the

## Chapter 9 / Workers Compensation and Employers Liability Insurance

District of Columbia, Puerto Rico, Guam, the U.S. Virgin Islands, and all the Canadian provinces have such laws. Modern workers compensation law makes a significant break from the principles of the common law and employers liability statutes.

## *Principles of Workers Compensation Law*

Workers compensation involved an entirely new legal concept: employer liability without regard to fault. Under this concept, the cost of occupational injury and disease was to be assessed against the employer even if the employer was neither negligent nor otherwise responsible under common law or employers liability statutes. The various state investigatory commissions in the beginning of the century developed a consensus that under modern industrial conditions, the employment relationship alone was ample reason for assessing the employer for the cost of occupational injury. Industrial accidents were recognized as one of the inevitable hazards of industry, not necessarily the result of a lack of skill, but rather related to the nature of the industry, characterized by long hours, new and complex processes, untrained workers, mechanization, repetitive operations, speed, and the use of toxic materials. The cost of industrial accidents and diseases was regarded as a legitimate cost of production.

The workers compensation laws balanced the interests of both employer and employee. Workers gave up their existing legal remedy, the right of a tort action for negligent injury against the employer. In so doing, workers gave up the right to recover damages for pain and suffering or inconvenience. The employer gave up various defenses and became obligated to respond to the employee's injury in accordance with the terms of the compensation act. The law provided relative certainty as to the amount of benefits to be paid for specified injuries. The general purpose of the compensation legislation was to alleviate the plight of the worker. All of the following have been stated as specific objectives of the workers compensation system:

1. Prompt payment of adequate benefits, according to a fixed and predetermined schedule, to injured employees or their dependents.
2. Elimination of the delays and costs of litigation to the employee and to society.
3. Establishment of a guarantee of benefit payment; benefits to be secured by a form of "insurance."
4. Promotion of industrial safety and industrial hygiene; employers would observe the relationship between accident prevention and the reduced cost of workers compensation benefits.
5. Payment for medical care services.

Other benefits anticipated from workers compensation legislation included the reduction of friction between the worker and the employer, and the easing of public and private relief.

Workers compensation statutes were intended to cure the defects of the common law and employers liability statutes and to present simple and rational provisions devoid of legalisms. The relief provided was to be certain and immediate. Injury schedules attempted to make payments largely automatic, resulting in few occasions when adversarial proceedings would be required. The remedial and beneficial purpose of compensation legislation is often cited as a justification for extending coverage in close or doubtful cases. This attitude has the support of legal scholars of workers compensation and is enacted in practice by compensation hearing officers and judges.

## Common Features of Compensation Laws

The following features are particularly important in the workers compensation laws of the United States:

1. Choice of law
2. The description of persons and employments covered
3. The description of injuries and diseases covered
4. The benefits provided
5. The methods of financing benefits
6. The procedure for obtaining benefits
7. Administration

### Choice of Law

In any given case of an employment-related injury, the laws of numerous states may apply if the circumstances of employment occur in different states. The following are such circumstances: the place of injury, the place of hire, the place of employment, the location of the employer, the residence of the employee, and any state whose compensation laws are adopted by contract. In general, the laws of the states where the injury occurred, where the employment usually occurs, and where the employee was hired *all* apply to a loss. The employee cannot receive duplicate benefits but can select the state with the most generous benefits.

### Persons and Employments Covered

Because the original workers compensation laws were directed toward addressing a specific social problem, the only industries that were initially affected were those whose operations were considered to be "hazardous," as defined in the particular law. Today, workers compensation statutes cover most public and private employments whether or not they are "hazardous" in the traditional sense of the term. Some statutes include within the scope of their coverage civilian workers such as volunteer firefighters, auxiliary police officers, and civilian defense workers. Some of the earlier statutes covered only employments carried on for pecuniary gain. Such a provision would eliminate all public employees such as police officers, firefighters, and sanitation workers, as well as those employed by a charity, since none of these workers are employed by profit-making enterprises. A few laws still retain this provision. The workers compensation laws of some states exclude domestic and farm workers, who therefore retain their common law rights of action against their employers.

As a general rule, an employer's legal obligations for occupational injury or disease extend to employees only, not to independent contractors. The distinction between an employee and an independent contractor is therefore an important one. It is best expressed in terms of the extent of the employer's right to direct and control the work-related activities of each:

- An *employee* is one for whom the employer typically fixes the hours of employment, provides the tools with which to do the work, and defines and supervises the results of the work, as well as methods and means of doing the work.
- An *independent contractor* is one for whom the employer does not typically fix the hours of employment and may or may not provide the tools with which to do the work. The employer defines the *results* of the work, but perhaps most important, does *not* define and supervise the *methods and means* of doing the work.

The essential distinction between employees and independent contractors is that the employer has the right to control and direct the activities of an employee, not only as to the result to be accomplished but also as to the methods and means by which the result is obtained.

The workers compensation statutes of many states contain an important exception to the general rule that an employer's workers compensation obligations do not extend to independent contractors. These statutes consider the employees of independent contractors to be "statutory" employees of the principal (the entity hiring the independent contractor) if the independent contractor has not maintained workers compensation insurance covering such employees. Thus, if an employee of the uninsured independent contractor sustains a compensable injury, the principal can be held liable to provide workers compensation benefits to the injured employee. However, after paying benefits to a statutory employee, the principal ordinarily has the right to seek recovery from the independent contractor.

A principal's obligation to provide workers compensation benefits to statutory employees applies also to a general contractor that has hired a subcontractor. That is, the employees of an uninsured subcontractor can be deemed statutory employees of the general contractor.

Because of the provisions regarding statutory employees, a principal that hires independent contractors should obtain certificates of insurance from its independent contractors before they begin their operations for the principal. Moreover, because a certificate of insurance does not guarantee that the insurance will be in effect on a date later than that when the certificate was issued, the principal should also maintain valid workers compensation insurance in case the contractor does not have insurance when a loss actually occurs.

### *Injuries and Diseases Covered*

It has always been the purpose of workers compensation to provide benefits only for *occupational injury*—injury arising from the worker's employment. It would be difficult to rationalize coverage for nonoccupational injuries and diseases under a program financed exclusively by the employer.

A compensable injury or disease must be occupational in nature as defined by the law. The most obvious losses are caused by industrial accidents. Hence, early compensation laws often referred only to "accidents" occurring within the scope of employment; they contained no provision with regard to occupational disease. Even today, it is necessary to define by statute what is an occupational disease and the proof required to qualify both injuries and occupational diseases for coverage. Not all occupational diseases are covered, and the requirements to prove compensability for injury and disease differ.

With regard to injuries, an employee seeking workers compensation benefits must show that (1) he or she suffered an injury caused by accident, (2) the accident arose out of employment, and (3) the accident occurred in the course of employment. To be compensable, (1) a disease must be covered by the statute as one that normally results from the nature of the employment, and (2) the exposure to the disease must arise from employment.

The laws of the great majority of the states define an occupational injury as one that "arises out of and in the course of employment." The framers of this definition wanted to be assured of a causal connection between employment

## Chapter 9 / Workers Compensation and Employers Liability Insurance

and injury. To be compensable, the injury must not only occur while the employee is at work, but it must also be related to that work.

- The words "arising out of the employment" refer to the origin or the cause of the injury; the accident, in order to be compensable, must arise out of some risk reasonably incidental to the employment.
- "In the course of employment" refers to the time, place, and circumstances under which the injury took place. The employee must have been doing something that he or she was employed to do, and the accident must have occurred while the employee was so occupied.

For compensation to be awarded for injury, most jurisdictions require that the injury be accidental. Generally, an *injury* may be defined as trauma to the body and such disease or infection as may naturally or unavoidably result therefrom. This definition of injury excludes internally produced systemic conditions and damage to property including clothing and prosthetic devices. The courts have defined *accident* as an event that takes place without foresight or expectation—an undesigned, sudden, and unexpected event. Hence, a person who willfully injures himself is not entitled to workers compensation, because the injury is not "accidental" in the sense indicated. The compensation statute will often further define accidental injury by stipulating that injuries arising from certain causes are not covered, such as injuries caused by intoxication, willful failure to use a safety appliance or observe safety regulations, or failure to perform a duty required by statute.

## Benefits Provided

There are four types of workers compensation benefits:

1. Indemnity payments for time lost from work
2. Payments for medical services
3. Rehabilitation services
4. Death benefits

The two most important are indemnity payments for time lost from work and payments for medical services. Rehabilitation services consist partly of medical services, but ideally they extend well beyond them and are thus considered apart from medical services. Likewise, death benefits are considered apart from medical and indemnity payments.

### Indemnity Payments

Indemnity payments are designed to compensate for lost wages. In all jurisdictions, benefits are payable to disabled workers only after a "waiting period" that ranges from three to seven days after the injury. This feature is designed to reduce compensation costs and to discourage malingering. However, in most states, benefits are retroactive to the date of the injury if the injured worker is unable to work for a specified period of time. The majority of job-related disabilities are of very short duration and do not involve indemnity benefit payments, yet they can nevertheless account for substantial aggregate medical benefits.

Disability extending beyond the waiting period is classified for benefit purposes as *temporary* or *permanent,* and *partial* or *total. Temporary total disability* payments are made to a worker who cannot work at his or her usual occupation during the period of recovery. Permanent disabilities resulting from more serious injuries are classified for statistical purposes by the severity of the disabling condition as minor permanent partial, major permanent partial, and permanent total disability. *Permanent total disability* involves injuries that prohibit further employment.

The duration of the payments for a given permanent partial disability varies greatly from state to state. States also differ on the relative duration of payments for different disabilities. For example, two states may not only provide different benefits for the loss of a hand, but the relative value of those benefits compared to some other injury, such as loss of an arm, may also differ.

### Payments for Medical Services

During the early development of workers compensation laws, only limited provisions were made for medical benefits. Today, however, almost all states cover 100 percent of necessary medical expenses. This liberalization in medical benefits has been the greatest single improvement in workers compensation.

### Rehabilitation Services

The most promising of recent benefit developments is the growth of provisions for physical and vocational rehabilitation. Under early workers compensation laws, after the medical care called for by law had been provided, there were no further services regardless of the extent of recovery from disability. When treatment ran out or no further benefit from it was apparent, permanent total disability became an acceptable condition. With advances in physical and rehabilitative medicine, paramedical services, and vocational training facilities, permanent total disability can no longer be accepted as the final result in every case of serious injury.

Rehabilitation programs are a means to reduce the seriousness and, thus, the cost of disabling injuries. They do so, in part, by providing vocational or physical assistance to the injured so that they can return to gainful employment. Although considered an integral part of complete medical treatment, rehabilitation may go much further and include such services as vocational training or training to drive a specially equipped car.

Although only some states include specific rehabilitation provisions in their workers compensation laws, rehabilitation is allowed and provided in all states even if unspecified in the law. Many insurers have been leaders in conducting rehabilitation programs for disabled workers, often providing rehabilitation benefits well beyond those required by the law. This often reduces the ultimate loss costs because the rehabilitated workers are able to seek gainful employment. Equally important is the social benefit of making disabled workers feel that they are a meaningful part of society.

### Death Benefits

Like disability payments, death benefit payments to surviving spouses and dependents vary from jurisdiction to jurisdiction. In over half the jurisdictions, these income replacement benefits to dependents are limited in time. Both the amount and the duration of the weekly benefit typically depend on whether there are minor children. Benefits may also be limited or terminated if the surviving spouse remarries. As is true for permanent total disability benefits, about one-fourth of the states adjust death benefits annually to match all or part of the increase in prices or wages. In addition to income replacement benefits, all states pay a burial allowance.

## Methods of Financing Benefits

Most workers compensation statutes require employers to demonstrate financial ability to pay any claims that may arise. Possible methods of meeting this obligation include the following:

- Private insurance
- Insurance through assigned risk plans
- Insurance through state funds
- Qualified "self-insurance" plans
- Excess insurance

However, every state does not allow all of these methods.

### Private Insurance

An employer can meet its workers compensation obligation by purchasing insurance from a private insurer licensed to write workers compensation coverage in the state. In return for the premium, the insurance company promises to pay the benefits and assume most administrative duties required by law for work-related injuries.

### Assigned Risk Plans

Some businesses cannot obtain private insurance because they do not meet insurers' underwriting criteria. Because of the compulsory nature of workers compensation, a firm without insurance could be forced out of business because of the penalties imposed. For this reason, assigned risk plans exist to make insurance available. An employer rejected by private insurers can apply to the plan in the appropriate state to obtain coverage.

### State Funds

In twenty-two states, state funds provide workers compensation insurance. Territorial funds are in effect in Puerto Rico and the U.S. Virgin Islands. Although controlled by the state government, these state and territorial funds operate in essentially the same manner as private insurance companies. The most significant differences are that they accept any good-faith applicant for insurance in the state and that no assigned risk plan is necessary. In most jurisdictions, the fund competes with private insurers. In a few other jurisdictions, only the state fund may provide workers compensation coverage.

**Competitive State Funds** In sixteen states, state funds sell workers compensation insurance in competition with private insurance companies and are thus called **competitive state funds**. An employer in these states can purchase insurance from either a private insurer or the state fund.

**Monopolistic State Funds** Six states (Nevada, North Dakota, Ohio, Washington, West Virginia, and Wyoming) plus Puerto Rico and the U.S. Virgin Islands require all workers compensation insurance to be placed with the state or territorial fund. (Nevada will allow private insurance as of July 1, 1999.) Because no private insurer is licensed to write workers compensation coverage in these jurisdictions, the state or territorial funds have no competition and are thus known as **monopolistic state funds**. Workers compensation coverage, but not necessarily employers liability coverage, is available from these funds.

### Self-Insurance

Almost all states allow employers to retain the risk of workers compensation losses if they demonstrate the financial capacity to do so by meeting certain requirements.

To qualify as a "self-insurer," an employer must post a surety bond or other collateral with the workers compensation administrative agency of the state to guarantee the security of benefit payments. In addition, most states require evidence of an ability to administer the benefit payments and services mandated by the law. Self-insurance is usually practical only for large employers.

Most states also allow self-insured groups, usually a group of employers that are in the same or a similar business. The requirements for self-insured groups are similar to those for individual self-insurers.

### Excess Insurance

An employer that qualifies for self-insurance may still decide to purchase excess insurance to cover catastrophic losses. Some states may require excess insurance above a permitted self-insured retention level. Excess insurance will be described in more detail in Chapter 13.

## Procedure for Obtaining Benefits

The compensation laws require the worker to notify the employer of an injury within a certain period of time (often thirty days) in order to obtain benefits. Notice must be given to the employer, supervisor, or someone in a managerial position. A failure to give notice is generally excused when the employer witnessed or heard about the occurrence of the accident, or when the failure to give notice did not prejudice the employer's right to investigate and verify the details of the accident.

Compensation laws require the employee or his or her survivors to file a claim for compensation within a designated time, usually one year. Failure to file a claim within the statutory period renders the claim unenforceable even if it has merit. The statute of limitations, together with the notice requirement, recognizes that the employer should not be required to respond to claims that cannot be investigated and defended and that might result in an accrued liability for which the employer had not planned.

## Administration

Broadly speaking, the traditional objective of workers compensation claim administration has been to ensure that the injured worker knows his or her rights and receives the benefits to which he or she is entitled. The principal administrative objective is to provide a simple, convenient, and inexpensive method of settling the claims of injured workers and their dependents. Full and prompt payment when due is the essential virtue of the compensation system. If payments are not made, the system must provide a speedy and effective method of settling controversies.

State compensation administration for the settlement of disputes is largely a quasi-judicial function. In general, two bodies administer benefits in the

United States—the courts and special commissions. In all states, the courts serve as an appellate forum for workers compensation claims. However, in a few states, the courts conduct the initial administration of workers compensation claims. These courts hear workers compensation claims, determine compensability, and issue judgments in exactly the same way as they would in any other type of case.

The administration of workers compensation by a commission or compensation board is far from perfect but is usually better than court administration. The majority of jurisdictions have created quasi-judicial bodies for the administration of workers compensation claims, variously called a *workers compensation board* or an *industrial accident commission*. These bodies supervise the administration of the workers compensation law and hear and determine disputes that arise under it. The decisions of the board are usually conclusive as to questions of fact, and an appeal to a court may usually be made only on questions of law.

## Third-Party Claims

When an employee who is eligible for workers compensation benefits is injured by the tort of a third party, the employee has a choice of remedies. The employee may (1) sue the third party and reject his or her workers compensation remedy, (2) accept compensation and forgo his or her remedy against the third party, or (3) accept compensation and also sue the third party.

- *Sue the third party.* If the employee selects the alternative of suing the third party, the employee must bring the action at his or her own expense (although the fee of the plaintiff's attorney, under the usual contingent fee arrangement, would be payable only in the event of a recovery). If unsuccessful, the employee may enter his or her claim for compensation at that time. The fact that he or she did sue the third party will not affect the right to statutory compensation, even though the compensation claim will be deferred pending the outcome of the third-party action.

- *Accept compensation.* The employee may decide to accept compensation and take no interest in pursuing his or her remedy against the third party. However, the employer or the employer's insurer is subrogated to the rights of the employee against the third party and may bring an action at its own expense against the third party. In the event of a recovery, the employer will first reimburse itself for the compensation and medical payments made (or for which it is liable), together with the costs of the action. If the insurer recovers more than its expenditures in the third-party action, any excess will be paid to the employee on a percentage basis.

- *Accept compensation and sue the third party.* If the employee chooses this alternative, the employer or the employer's insurer has a lien on the proceeds of the employee's recovery to the extent of the workers compensation payments made. The employer or the insurer may intervene in the employee's suit as a party plaintiff. In the event of recovery, most state laws provide that the employer's lien attaches only to the employee's net recovery after the payment of costs and attorney fees has been made.

# Federal Compensation Laws

A large percentage of the work force is eligible for state workers compensation benefits. Nevertheless, state workers compensation laws do not apply to all employees. Many employees are covered by the federal laws discussed below and summarized in Exhibit 9-1. An employer's obligation to provide the benefits required (or to pay the damages allowed) by these laws can be insured by adding various endorsements to the standard workers compensation and employers liability insurance policy. The sections that follow focus on the laws themselves; a later section in this chapter describes the corresponding insurance methods in more detail.

## Federal Employers' Liability Act

The **Federal Employers' Liability Act (FELA)**, which applies only to employees of interstate railroads, predates the first workers compensation law in the United States. Intrastate railroads that connect to interstate railroads by way of sidings or interchanges are deemed to be instruments of interstate commerce and are thus also subject to FELA. Enacted in 1908 and still in effect, FELA allows employees (or the survivors of deceased employees) to sue their employers for occupational injuries resulting from the employer's negligence. FELA provides that contributory negligence reduces but does not bar recovery (thus applying comparative negligence), and it also eliminates assumption of risk as a defense in suits subject to FELA. FELA makes the employer liable for the negligence of all its officers, agents, and employees, thus eliminating the fellow-employee defense as well. In short, FELA permits injured employees to sue their employers without the traditional employer defenses.

## Longshore and Harbor Workers' Compensation Act

Congress enacted the **Longshore and Harbor Workers' Compensation Act (LHWCA)** in 1927 in response to a Supreme Court ruling that federal admiralty jurisdiction was supreme and state compensation laws inoperative in cases of accidents on the navigable waters of the United States. The

**Exhibit 9-1**
Federal Compensation and Employers Liability Laws

| Employees Subject to Law | Statute | Nature of Remedy |
|---|---|---|
| Employees of interstate railroads | Federal Employers' Liability Act (FELA) | Negligence suit against employer |
| Maritime workers, with some exceptions (such as the master or crew of a vessel) | Longshore and Harbor Workers Compensation Act (LHWCA) | No-fault benefits as defined by the statute |
| (1) Civilian employees at U.S. military bases acquired from foreign governments<br>(2) Civilian employees working overseas under contracts with agencies of the U.S. government | Defense Base Act | Same as LHWCA |
| Workers on fixed offshore drilling and production platforms on the Outer Continental Shelf of the U.S. | Outer Continental Shelf Lands Act | Same as LHWCA |
| Civilian employees of "nonappropriated fund instrumentalities" on U.S. military bases, such as stores and theaters | Nonappropriated Fund Instrumentalities Act | Same as LHWCA |
| Members of a vessel's crew | Jones Act | Same as FELA |
| Members of a vessel's crew | Death on the High Seas Act | Survivors may sue employer for death occurring beyond a marine league from the shore of any state. |
| Migrant and seasonal farm workers | Migrant and Seasonal Agricultural Worker Protection Act | Suit against employer |
| Nonmilitary employees of the U.S. government | Federal Employees' Compensation Act | No-fault benefits as defined by the statute |

## Chapter 9 / Workers Compensation and Employers Liability Insurance

immediate effect of this ruling was to leave longshore workers without compensation. (A longshore worker is a person employed to load and unload vessels. The term "stevedore" is also used to describe such an employee.)

To address the problem, Congress enacted the LHWCA, modeling it after state workers compensation statutes. Thus, workers subject to the LHWCA lost the right to sue in return for gaining the right to collect medical, disability, and death benefits as defined in the statute. The statute was amended in 1972 and 1984 to address various problems that had arisen over the years, such as judicial expansion of the employees eligible for benefits.

### Workers Covered

The purpose of the LHWCA is to provide compensation benefits to persons who are engaged in longshoring or other maritime employment, such as the building, repairing, or dismantling of vessels. Courts interpreted "maritime employment" broadly, however, so as to extend the LHWCA to a wide range of workers as long as they were injured while working upon "navigable waters." The 1984 amendments to the LHWCA were aimed in part at defining the scope of employees who can qualify for LHWCA benefits (see below).

Although the LHWCA provides essentially the same *types* of benefits as are generally provided by state workers compensation laws, the *amounts payable* under LHWCA are often higher. Thus, in any case when an employee might be able to recover either LHWCA benefits or state workers compensation benefits, the employee can be expected to choose the compensation system that provides the better benefits. Because of the "gray area" between state workers compensation laws and the LHWCA, many employers obtain insurance for both exposures.

### Injury Must Occur Upon Navigable Waters

The LHWCA requires that the injury occur upon the navigable waters of the United States, including any adjoining pier, wharf, dry dock, terminal, building way, marine railway, or other adjoining area customarily used by an employer in loading, unloading, repairing, dismantling, or building a vessel. The LHWCA does not define "navigable waters of the United States," but the term is generally construed to include any bodies of water (including rivers, canals, lakes, harbors, and even the high seas) capable of being used for commerce between states or between the United States and foreign countries.

### Excluded Employees

The LHWCA specifically excludes the following types of employees:

- A master or member of a crew of any vessel. Crew members have several possible remedies for occupational injuries, as described below.
- Any person engaged by a master of a vessel to load or unload or repair any small vessel under eighteen tons net.
- An officer or employee of the United States or any agency thereof or of any state or foreign government or of any subdivision thereof.

In addition, the following persons are excluded from receiving LHWCA benefits *if they are subject to coverage under a state workers compensation law*:

1. Office clerical, secretarial, security, or data processing employees
2. Employees of a club, camp, recreational operation, restaurant, museum, or retail outlet
3. Marina employees who are not engaged in construction, replacement, or expansion of the marina, except for routine maintenance
4. Persons who possess all of the following attributes:
   - They are employed by suppliers, transporters, or vendors.
   - They are temporarily doing business on the premises of a maritime employer.
   - They are not engaged in work normally performed by employees of the maritime employer.

   An example of an employee who meets these conditions is a truck driver who has made a delivery to an ocean cargo terminal or a shipyard.
5. Aquaculture workers
6. Persons employed to build, repair, or dismantle any recreational vessel under sixty-five feet in length

The six classes of employees listed immediately above can qualify for LHWCA coverage if they are not subject to coverage under a state workers compensation law. For example, an office worker at a shipyard might be injured while walking on a pier at the shipyard, thus satisfying the requirement that he or she was injured while on navigable waters. Similarly, workers in a maritime museum, a floating restaurant, or a boat dealership might be injured while working on navigable waters. If these employees are not subject to coverage under a state workers compensation law, their employer can become legally obligated to provide LHWCA benefits. It is thus desirable for organizations whose employees could be eligible for LHWCA benefits to have LHWCA coverage in case it is needed. LHWCA coverage can be added by endorsement to the standard workers compensation and employers liability insurance policy.

The LHWCA also excludes employees of facilities certified by the Secretary of Labor as being engaged in the business of building, repairing, or dismantling exclusively "small vessels." As defined in the LHWCA, a "small vessel" is (1) a commercial barge that is under 900 light-ship displacement tons or (2) a commercial tugboat, towboat, crew boat, supply boat, fishing vessel, or other work vessel under 1,600 tons gross. However, employees of such facilities are covered under the LHWCA when any of the following is true:

1. The employee is injured while upon the navigable waters of the United States or while upon any adjoining pier, wharf, dock, facility over land for launching vessels, or facility over land for hauling, lifting, or dry-docking vessels.
2. The facility receives federal maritime subsidies.
3. The employee is not subject to coverage under a state workers compensation law.

## Extensions of the LHWCA

Some federal statutes extend the benefits of the LHWCA to additional classes of employees. Three such statutes are described below.

### Defense Base Act

The **Defense Base Act** applies the benefits of the LHWCA to (1) civilian employees at any military, air, or naval bases acquired by the United States (after January 1, 1940) from foreign governments and (2) civilian employees working at overseas locations under contracts being performed for agencies of the United States government.

### Outer Continental Shelf Lands Act

The **Outer Continental Shelf Lands Act (OCSLA)** extends the benefits of the LHWCA to workers, other than members of a vessel's crew, engaged in the exploration for or production of natural resources on the outer continental shelf of the United States. Typically, employees subject to OCSLA are workers situated on offshore drilling and production platforms. OCSLA defines the outer continental shelf as the submerged lands of the United States adjacent to the coast but outside the area of the state's territorial boundaries. The territorial boundaries of Florida and Texas extend to ten nautical miles from their coastlines, and those of all other coastal states extend to three nautical miles from their coastlines.[2]

## Nonappropriated Fund Instrumentalities Act

The **Nonappropriated Fund Instrumentalities Act** extends the benefits of the LHWCA to civilian employees of "nonappropriated fund instrumentalities," which include various facilities on military bases such as stores, day-care centers, and movie theaters.

# Laws Applicable to Crew Members

The various legal remedies available to the members of a vessel's crew or their survivors were described in Chapter 7 in connection with the loss exposures that can be insured with marine insurance. In summary, those remedies are based on the following:

1. General maritime law, which has been created by legal traditions and court decisions rather than statutes. General maritime law includes the following:
    - The vessel owner's obligation to pay **maintenance and cure** to injured crew members. Maintenance covers the costs of food and lodging, and cure covers the cost of medical treatment.
    - The **vessel owner's warranty of seaworthiness**. General maritime law permits a crew member who is injured as a result of the unseaworthiness of the vessel to sue both the vessel owner and the vessel itself for resulting damages.
    - The so-called Moragne remedy, which permits survivors of deceased crew members to sue the employer for wrongful death occurring in territorial waters or on the high seas and resulting from either the employer's negligence or unseaworthiness of the vessel.

2. The Merchant Marine Act of 1920, better known as the **Jones Act**. This statute extends to crew members of vessels the remedies provided by FELA. Thus, an injured crew member (or the survivors of a deceased crew member) can seek damages from the employer if the injury (or death) was caused in whole or in part by the negligence of the employer or its agents or employees.

3. The Death on the High Seas Act. This federal statute allows survivors of deceased crew members to sue the employer for death occurring beyond a marine league from the shore of any state.

# Migrant and Seasonal Agricultural Worker Protection Act

This statute provides various protections to migrant and seasonal agricultural workers. Among the protections provided to such workers is the right to sue their employers for occupational injury or illness. This right of action applies even though the applicable workers compensation act might contain a provision declaring workers compensation the exclusive remedy for occupational injury or illness of such workers.

## Federal Employees' Compensation Act

The Federal Employees' Compensation Act provides workers compensation benefits for nonmilitary employees of the federal government. The federal government self-insures this exposure.

# The Workers Compensation and Employers Liability Policy

In the United States, workers compensation insurance is provided under a standard form known as the "workers compensation and employers liability insurance policy." This form is maintained and filed in most states by the National Council on Compensation Insurance (NCCI). NCCI is an insurance advisory organization that provides many of the same services for workers compensation insurers that the Insurance Services Office, the American Association of Insurance Services, and the Surety Association of America perform for insurers engaged in other lines of insurance.

The **workers compensation and employers liability insurance policy (WC&EL)** combines coverage for both of the following:

1. Obligations imposed by workers compensation statutes
2. Damages that an employer becomes legally obligated to pay (apart from workers compensation statutes) because of bodily injury by accident or disease to an employee

The policy contains uniform provisions even though workers compensation benefits vary by state. It is possible to use the same policy in various states because the applicable workers compensation laws are incorporated by reference in the policy. Thus, the covered workers compensation benefits are not itemized in the policy. The benefits specified in the applicable statute govern the types and amounts of benefits payable by the insurer.

A complete WC&EL policy consists of the following documents:

1. Information page
2. Policy form
3. Endorsements (if any apply)

These documents are not designed to be included in the ISO commercial package policy format.

## Information Page

The information page is equivalent to the declarations page of other policies. The WC&EL information page is divided into four major parts or items, as shown in Exhibit 9-2.

Item 1 gives essential information about the insured, including the insured's name and mailing address, the type of legal entity, and workplaces other than the insured's mailing address.

Item 2 shows the coverage period. Coverage begins and ends at 12:01 A.M. at the address of the insured given in item 1.

Item 3 summarizes the coverage provided by the policy. Benefits required by the workers compensation law of the state or states listed in item 3A will be paid in the event of an injury to an employee. This space should normally list all states in which the insured has operations and the insurer is licensed to provide coverage. Item 3B shows the limits of liability under the employers liability coverage for bodily injury by accident and by disease. An entry in item 3C indicates that workers compensation coverage will be extended automatically to the additional states listed if the insured expands operation to jurisdictions other than those listed in item 3A. In addition, all endorsements and schedules attached to the policy at inception are listed on the information page or in a schedule attached to the policy.

The information necessary to calculate the estimated policy premium appears in item 4. It includes a description of the classification(s) assigned to the insured's business. This description and the corresponding code number are taken from the appropriate workers compensation manual. Another column contains the insured's estimate of what the remuneration (payroll) will be for the period covered by the policy. The estimated payroll is shown beside each classification.

The next column shows the rate applicable to each classification. Usually the rate is expressed in dollars of premium per $100 of payroll. The last column shows the estimated premium determined by multiplying the estimated payroll by the rate for each classification.

## Exhibit 9-2
### WC&EL Information Page

**WORKERS COMPENSATION AND EMPLOYERS LIABILITY INSURANCE POLICY**

**INFORMATION PAGE**

Insurer:

POLICY NO.

1. **The Insured:** AMR Corporation
   **Mailing address:** 2000 Industrial Highway
   Workingtown, PA 19000

   ___ Individual
   _X_ Corporation or _____
   ___ Partnership

   Other workplaces not shown above:

2. The policy period is from 10/1/96 to 10/1/97 at the insured's mailing address.

3. A. Workers Compensation Insurance: Part One of the policy applies to the Workers Compensation Law of the states listed here: PA

   B. Employers Liability Insurance: Part Two of the policy applies to work in each state listed in Item 3.A. The limits of our liability under Part Two are:

   | | | |
   |---|---|---|
   | Bodily Injury by Accident | $ 100,000 | each accident |
   | Bodily Injury by Disease | $ 500,000 | policy limit |
   | Bodily Injury by Disease | $ 100,000 | each employee |

   C. Other States Insurance: Part Three of the policy applies to the states, if any, listed here:

   All except those listed in Item 3A and ME, NV, ND, OH, WA, WV, WY and OR

   D. This policy includes these endorsements and schedules:

   See Schedule

4. The premium for this policy will be determined by our Manuals of Rules, Classifications, Rates and Rating Plans. All information required below is subject to verification and change by audit.

   | Classifications | Code No. | Premium Basis Total estimated Annual Remuneration | Rate Per $100 of Remuneration | Estimated Annual Premium |
   |---|---|---|---|---|
   | Sheet Metal Shop | 0454 | 300,000 | 11.53 | 34,590 |
   | Clerical Office | 0953 | 275,000 | .49 | 1,348 |
   | | | Experience Modification of 1.382 Applied | | 13,728 |
   | | | Estimated Premium Discount | | (4,869) |
   | | | **Total Estimated Annual Premium** $ | | 44,797 |

   **Minimum Premium** $ 1,273     **Expense Constant** $     140

   Countersigned by _____

WC 00 00 01 A
© 1987 National Council on Compensation Insurance.

## Policy Form

The standard WC&EL policy form includes a general section and six parts, as follows:

- Part One—Workers Compensation Insurance
- Part Two—Employers Liability Insurance
- Part Three—Other States Insurance
- Part Four—Your Duties If Injury Occurs
- Part Five—Premium
- Part Six—Conditions

### General Section

The general section explains the nature of the policy and defines important terms. The first paragraph explains that the policy is a contract and that the parties are "you" (the insured) and "we" (the insurer). The insured is the employer named in item 1 of the information page. The policy states that if that employer is a partnership, coverage applies to the partners only in their capacity as employer of that partnership's employees. If one of the partners is also involved in an enterprise other than the entity named in the policy, and that enterprise also has employees, there must be a separate workers compensation policy or self-insurance plan.

Paragraph C of the general section defines "workers compensation law" to mean "the workers or workmen's compensation law and occupational disease law of each state or territory named in item 3A of the Information Page." Any amendments in effect during the policy period are included, but any provisions of a statute that relate to nonoccupational disability benefits are not included within this definition. Moreover, the definition is limited to *state* laws. The United States Longshore and Harbor Workers' Compensation Act and other federal laws are not included.

According to paragraph D, the term "state" means any of the fifty states or the District of Columbia. Coverage for the workers compensation law of a United States territory applies only when item 3A of the information page explicitly names that territory.

Covered locations are defined to include all workplaces listed on the information page and all of the insured's workplaces in states listed in item 3A unless other insurance or self-insurance applies.

### Part One—Workers Compensation Insurance

The coverage provided by Part One obligates the insurer to pay all compensation and other benefits required of the insured by the workers compensation law or occupational disease law of any state listed in item 3A of the information page. The employer automatically receives coverage for all benefits required by that state's workers compensation law for all locations, operations, and employees as designated by the law. The policy applies to all operations of the employer except those otherwise insured or specifically excluded by endorsement.

The coverage applies to bodily injury by accident and by disease. The accident must occur during the policy period, and the last exposure to conditions causing or aggravating disease in the employment of the insured must occur during the policy period.

According to the policy, the insurer will pay the benefits required by the workers compensation law. The policy shows no dollar limit for these benefits. Any applicable limits would be those found within the law itself. Part One of the policy contains no outright exclusions.

The policy establishes the insurer's right and duty to defend the insured against any claim, proceeding, or suit for benefits payable by the policy. The insurer also agrees to pay the following additional costs as part of any claim, proceeding, or suit the insurer defends against the following:

1. Reasonable expenses incurred at the insurer's request, other than loss of earnings
2. Premiums for bonds to release attachments and appeal bonds in bond amounts up to the amount payable under the insurance
3. Litigation costs taxed against the insured
4. Interest on a judgment as required by law until the insurer offers the amount due under the policy
5. Expenses incurred by the insurer

In some cases, the insurer may, because of misconduct on the part of the insured, have to make workers compensation payments on behalf of the insured in excess of the benefits ordinarily provided by the workers compensation law. When that happens, the policy provides that the insured will reimburse the insurance company for the difference between the benefits actually paid and the benefits that are regularly payable. The policy cites the following examples of situations in which extra benefits might be required:

1. The insured engages in serious and willful misconduct.
2. The insured knowingly hires an employee in violation of law.
3. The insured fails to comply with a health or safety law or regulation.
4. The insured discharges, coerces, or otherwise discriminates against an employee in violation of the workers compensation law.

Subrogation rights of the insurer are reaffirmed in the policy. When the insurer pays compensation or employers liability benefits on behalf of an insured, any right of recovery the insured or the injured employee may have against a third party becomes the right of the insurer.

The policy also recognizes the legal requirements that directly obligate the insurance company to pay workers compensation benefits to any injured employee or, in the event of death, to the employee's dependents. Because the contract is made primarily for the benefit of employees and their dependents, they have a direct right of action against the insurance company.

For the protection of the employee, the policy provides that the obligations of the insurance company will not be affected by the failure of the employer to comply with the policy requirements.

All workers compensation laws covered by the policy become a part of the insurance contract just as if they were written into the policy, and employees have the rights to benefits defined by those laws. If the policy and the applicable workers compensation law conflict, the policy agrees to conform to the law. The policy is automatically amended when there are changes in the law.

## Part Two—Employers Liability Insurance

Part Two of the policy, which provides employers liability coverage, is structured like a traditional liability policy, containing an insuring agreement in which the insurer agrees to pay damages on behalf of the insured.

### Need for Coverage

Employers frequently ask their insurance agents or brokers why they need employers liability insurance. The coverage provided by workers compensation laws is extensive, and generally workers compensation is considered, at least in theory, to be the exclusive remedy for injuries subject to the workers compensation law. Nonetheless, depending to a large degree on the law of the particular state, an employer can be held liable in several ways, apart from workers compensation, to pay damages resulting from occupational injuries. Because these types of claims are not for workers compensation benefits, they are not covered by workers compensation insurance. Employers liability coverage helps to fill some of these gaps in workers compensation insurance.

The employers liability section of the WC&EL policy describes four common types of suits or claims that are covered by employers liability coverage:

1. Third-party-over
2. Care and loss of services

3. Consequential bodily injury
4. Dual capacity

**Third-Party-Over** In the context of third-party-over suits or claims, "third party" refers to a person or organization other than the employer or the employee. If an employee of the insured sues a third party (such as a machine manufacturer) for an occupational injury, the third party can make a "third-party-over" suit against the employer. The suit might allege, for example, that the employer was negligent in maintaining the defective machine and that the employer must therefore indemnify the manufacturer for all or part of the damages the manufacturer had to pay to the employee.

**Care and Loss of Services** Among the damages that the spouse of an injured or deceased person can obtain from the liable party are damages for care and loss of services, also known as loss of consortium. The word "consortium" denotes services, companionship, and affection, including sexual relations. In some states, the law permits the spouse of an injured employee to recover for loss of consortium resulting from the employer's negligence, even though the employee has collected workers compensation benefits. In some cases, the law permits family members other than spouses to make similar claims against a negligent employer.

**Consequential Bodily Injury** Family members of an injured employee can suffer bodily injury as a consequence of injury to the employee. For example, the injured employee's elderly parent might suffer a heart attack upon being informed of the injury. Another example of consequential injury is AIDS contracted by the spouse of a health care worker who contracted AIDS as a result of negligence imputed to the worker's employer. In some states, the family member who has suffered a consequential injury can recover damages from the employer if the employer can be shown to have been negligent in causing the employee's injury or illness.

**Dual Capacity** Dual-capacity suits occur when an injured employee sues his or her employer in a capacity other than as employer. Typically, dual-capacity claims involve products liability. For example, the employee, while working, might be injured by a product manufactured by the employer. Although the law concerning dual-capacity suits varies among the states, such suits may succeed under certain circumstances. In essence, the employee sues the employer in its capacity as a manufacturer rather than in its capacity as an employer.

**Other Types of Suits or Claims Covered** Under a variety of circumstances, some employees and some employers are not subject to workers compensation. For example, some workers compensation laws exclude agricultural workers and domestic servants, and other workers compensation laws do not apply to employers with fewer than a specified number of employees. When an employee or employer is excluded or exempt from workers compensation, an injured employee can ordinarily sue the employer for occupational injury or disease under common-law principles. Generally, such claims are covered by employers liability insurance, subject to the provisions described below.

### Employers Liability Insuring Agreement

The insurer agrees to pay damages that the insured becomes legally obligated to pay because of bodily injury by accident or disease to an employee. The bodily injury must arise out of and in the course of the employee's employment, and the legal obligation must not be covered under a state or federal workers compensation or disability benefits law. The insurer also agrees to defend the insured against claims or suits seeking covered damages.

Another requirement of Part B is that the employment out of which the injury arises must be necessary or incidental to the insured's work in a state or territory listed in item 3A of the information page. This provision is not a requirement that the injury must *occur* in one of the states or territories listed. For example, an employee might be injured after driving into an unlisted state to buy supplies for work being performed in a listed state. Even though the injury occurred outside the listed state, the injury still arose out of employment that was necessary or incidental to the insured's work in a listed state.

Employers liability coverage is subject to the following coverage triggers:

- For bodily injury *by accident,* the policy that is in effect when the *injury occurs* is the policy that applies.
- For bodily injury *by disease,* the policy that is in effect on the employee's *last day of last exposure* to the conditions causing or aggravating the injury is the policy that applies.

### Employers Liability Exclusions

Like most other liability policies, employers liability coverage is subject to many exclusions, which prevent overlapping coverage with other forms of insurance and eliminate coverage not intended by the insurer.

**Statutory Obligations** In keeping with the basic purpose of employers liability coverage, several exclusions are aimed at eliminating coverage for claims that would be covered under various statutes, including the following:

- Any workers compensation, occupational disease, unemployment compensation, or disability benefits law

- The Longshore and Harbor Workers' Compensation Act (LHWCA)
- The Federal Employers' Liability Act
- The Migrant and Seasonal Agricultural Worker Protection Act
- Any other federal workers compensation or occupational disease law

Also excluded is bodily injury to a master or member of the crew of any vessel. Masters and crew members of vessels are not eligible for LHWCA benefits but can pursue remedies described earlier in this chapter.

Various endorsements, described later in this chapter, are available for extending the policy to cover the excluded liabilities.

***Injury Outside the United States or Canada*** Employers liability coverage does not apply to bodily injury that occurs outside the United States, its territories or possessions, and Canada. However, this exclusion does not apply to injury to a resident or citizen of the United States or Canada who is *temporarily* outside the places listed above.

***Liability Assumed Under Contract*** Employers liability coverage basically does not apply to liability assumed under contract—even if the insured has assumed another party's liability for injury to the insured's own employee. (Recall from Chapter 3 that the CGL policy covers liability assumed under an "insured contract," even if the liability assumed is for injury to an employee of the insured.)

The contractual liability exclusion contains one exception: The exclusion does not apply to a warranty that work performed by the insured will be done in a workmanlike manner. Although this exception is not likely to be involved in most employers liability claims, it clarifies that a claim alleging warranty of workmanship would not be excluded if it met all other criteria required for employers liability coverage to apply.

***Other Exclusions*** Employers liability insurance also does not apply to any of the following:

1. Punitive or exemplary damages for injury or death of any illegally employed person
2. Bodily injury to employees employed in violation of the law with the knowledge of the insured or any executive officers of the insured
3. Bodily injury intentionally caused by the insured
4. Damages arising out of employment practices, including (but not limited to) demotion, evaluation, harassment, discrimination, and termination
5. Fines or penalties imposed for violation of federal or state law

### Limits of Liability

Unlike workers compensation coverage, employers liability coverage is subject to limits of liability stated in the policy. The three limits that apply to employers liability coverage are as follows:

1. The "bodily injury by accident" limit is the most that the insurer will pay for bodily injury resulting from any one accident, regardless of the number of employees injured.
2. The "bodily injury by disease—policy limit" is the most that the insurer will pay for all bodily injury by disease, regardless of the number of employees who sustain disease.
3. The "bodily injury by disease—each employee" limit is the most that the insurer will pay for bodily injury by disease to any one employee.

Defense costs, as well as supplementary payments similar to those covered under the CGL coverage form, are covered in addition to the limits of liability. However, the insurer has no duty to pay defense costs or supplementary payments after it has paid the applicable limit of insurance.

## Part Three—Other States Insurance

As discussed earlier in this chapter, an injured employee may be able to qualify for benefits under the workers compensation laws of more than one state. For example, depending on the provisions of the laws involved, an employee who was hired in State A but is currently working in State B might qualify for benefits under the workers compensation law of either state, thus giving the employee the option of choosing the law that will provide the better benefits. If this worker's employer has a WC&EL policy that shows only State A in item 3A of the information page, the policy will only cover the employer for benefits under the law of State A. If the employee chooses to make claim under the law of State B, the employer will not be covered. Thus, an employer should make sure that all states in which it is currently conducting operations at policy inception are listed in item 3A of its WC&EL policy.

Sometimes, however, an employer might commence operations in a new state, not listed in item 3A, at some point after policy inception. To provide a way for the policy to cover obligations under workers compensation laws of states other than those listed in item 3A, the WC&EL policy contains a feature known as **other states insurance**, which is incorporated within the policy form as Part Three. To activate other states insurance, the names of one or more states must be shown in item 3C of the information page. When a state is listed in item 3C, the policy will cover the named insured's obligations under the workers compensation law of that state just as if that state were listed in item 3A.

If the insured has operations in a particular state on the effective date of the policy but that state is not listed in item 3A, the insured must notify the insurer within thirty days or else no coverage will apply for that state. Thus, when operations are *known* to exist in a particular state, that state should be listed in item 3A. When operations do not currently take place in additional states but *could* be extended into those states, those states should be listed in item 3C. States in which the insurer is not licensed to write workers compensation insurance (including those that have monopolistic state funds) should not be listed in either item.

If the insured anticipates operating in a state with a monopolistic workers compensation fund, the insured should obtain workers compensation insurance from the state fund. Because the workers compensation policies issued by monopolistic state funds do not include employers liability insurance, many employers buy a type of employers liability insurance called **stop gap coverage** in order to provide employers liability coverage with respect to employment in monopolistic fund states. This coverage is often provided by the same insurer that provides the insured's general liability insurance.

The WC&EL policy does not require that the injury or illness must *occur* in a state listed in either item 3A or 3C. Rather, workers compensation coverage is restricted to paying benefits required by the workers compensation laws of those states shown in the policy. Thus, the policy could cover injury or illness occurring anywhere. The requirement for workers compensation coverage to apply is that the insured must be required to pay benefits by the workers compensation law of a state listed in the policy.

With employers liability coverage, the employment out of which the employee's injury arises must be necessary or incidental to the insured's work in a state listed in item 3A (or, by extension, listed in 3C). Subject to that requirement, a covered injury or illness could occur anywhere except as otherwise excluded. The employers liability section, as discussed earlier, is subject to an exclusion of injury occurring outside the United States, its territories or possessions, or Canada. (The exclusion does not apply to U.S. or Canadian citizens or residents who are *temporarily* outside those places.) This exclusion applies only to employers liability coverage—not to workers compensation coverage.

### *Part Four—Your Duties If Injury Occurs*

Part Four explains the duties of the insured when a loss occurs. The insured must promptly notify the insurer of any injury, claim, or suit. The insured must also cooperate with the insurer, attend hearings and trials at the request of the insurer, and help secure witnesses. The insured cannot, except at its own expense, voluntarily make any payment, assume any obligation, or incur any expenses except for immediate medical and other services at the time of injury as required by the workers compensation law.

## *Part Five—Premium*

Workers compensation premiums are based on the insured's payroll, which cannot be precisely determined until after the policy expires. Part Five explains premium determination procedures, establishing the role of insurance company manuals in determining premium and stipulating that the manuals and the premium may change during the policy period. The policy tells the insured that the classifications and rates shown on the information page may change if they do not accurately describe the work covered by the policy.

Part Five also defines payroll as the most common premium basis and stresses that it includes the remuneration of executive officers and the payroll of employees of uninsured contractors and subcontractors. The audit provision explains the insurer's right to examine and audit the insured's books and records at any time during the policy period and within three years after expiration insofar as such books and records relate to the policy. It explains why the final premium may be different from the estimated premium and shows how the premium will be determined on cancellation of the policy. The insured must keep records of information needed to compute the policy premium and provide such records to the insurer when requested.

## *Part Six—Conditions*

The policy conditions limit or define the rights and obligations of the parties to the insurance contract. The conditions address insurer inspections, policy years, assignment, cancellation, and who represents the insured.

### *Inspection*

One condition gives the insurer permission to inspect a policyholder's workplaces and operations. These inspections allow the insurer to determine that safe practices are employed and proper precautions taken for the safety of employees.

Although this condition states that the insurer is permitted to inspect workplaces, the policy does not require the insurer to perform inspections. When such services are performed, however, the policy indicates that this does not constitute an undertaking to warrant that any workplaces, operations, machinery, or equipment inspected are safe or healthful.

### Long-Term Policy

If the policy period is longer than one year, each year is considered separate as far as policy provisions are concerned, and premium is computed in accordance with the manual rules and rates in effect for that year. An exception is a three-year fixed-rate policy that would carry an endorsement modifying this provision. Such three-year policies are rarely issued and are used only for insureds with small premiums.

### Assignment

With the written consent of the insurer, the insured can transfer or assign the policy to cover a new interest. For example, if the insured business is sold, its workers compensation policy can be transferred to the new owner if the current insurer agrees in writing. However, it is generally preferable that a new policy be issued and the old policy canceled.

### Cancellation

Cancellation of the policy is generally permitted by law. However, some laws restrict the insurer's right of cancellation. This condition outlines the cancellation rights of the insurer and the insured and is subject in all cases to any requirements of the applicable workers compensation law. In essence, it is possible for the insured to cancel the policy virtually without notice. The insurer, however, must provide at least ten days' written notice before cancellation becomes effective.

### Sole Representative

The first named insured acts on behalf of all insureds for premium payment, refund, cancellation, and other rights and duties under the policy.

## Endorsements

Despite the flexibility offered by the standard workers compensation policy, a number of situations require modification of standard policy provisions by adding an appropriate endorsement to the policy. Some of the more important endorsements are examined below.

## Voluntary Compensation Endorsement

The workers compensation laws of most states exempt some types of employment from statutory workers compensation benefits. The most commonly exempted occupations are farm labor, domestic employment, and casual labor. In some cases, the law does not apply to employers with fewer than a certain minimum number of employees. The workers compensation laws of some states do not apply to partners, sole proprietors, or executive officers. Even when exempt persons are not entitled to workers compensation benefits by law, the same benefits can be extended to them by voluntary action.

The **voluntary compensation and employers liability coverage endorsement** amends the standard WC&EL policy to include an additional coverage called "voluntary compensation." The additional coverage does not make employees subject to the workers compensation law, but it obligates the insurance company to pay, on behalf of the insured, an amount equal to the compensation benefits that would be payable to such employees if they were subject to the workers compensation law designated in the endorsement.

The voluntary compensation endorsement states that if an employee entitled to payment under the endorsement brings a suit under the common law, the coverage provided by the endorsement reverts to employers liability insurance. The insurer will defend the insured against the employee's suit and pay any settlement awarded, subject to the stipulated limits of liability.

The voluntary compensation endorsement covers bodily injury that occurs outside the United States, its territories or possessions, or Canada only if the employee is a United States or Canadian citizen temporarily away from those places. In all other cases—such as an employee who is a U.S. citizen but is assigned indefinitely to a foreign country—the voluntary compensation endorsement will not provide coverage for injury occurring outside the regular policy territory.

## Foreign Voluntary Compensation Coverage

Some insurance companies provide **foreign voluntary compensation coverage** under independently filed forms. The purpose of such coverage is to extend workers compensation benefits to United States citizens who are hired or assigned by their employers to work indefinitely outside the country and who are outside the jurisdiction of any compulsory workers compensation or similar act.

Because foreign voluntary compensation coverage is independently filed, various approaches are used. One approach is to add an endorsement to the standard WC&EL policy that expresses the insurer's promise to pay covered employees the benefits provided under a specified compensation act, which could be that of the state in which the employer is domiciled or even a federal compensation act such as the Defense Base Act or the LHWCA. The endorsement may contain additional benefits, such as coverage for the costs of repatriating an injured employee or the remains of a deceased employee. Coverage may also be included for endemic diseases, such as yellow fever or malaria, that are indigenous or particularly prevalent in certain parts of the world. Injury resulting from war or military action may be excluded.

When an employee is covered under any other foreign workers compensation law and the employer is paying the premiums, the voluntary coverage may state that the insurer is obligated to pay only the difference, if any, between the benefits that would otherwise be provided by the endorsement and those payable under the foreign law.

## LHWCA Coverage Endorsement

The United States Longshore and Harbor Workers' Compensation Act follows the same principles as the state workers compensation laws. In some circumstances, an employer may be subject to both the LHWCA and the state workers compensation law at the same time. Although both of these exposures may be insured, they must be covered and rated separately.

Coverage can be provided by adding the **United States Longshore and Harbor Workers' Compensation Act endorsement** to the workers compensation policy. The endorsement amends the definition of "workers compensation law" to include the LHWCA with respect to operations in any state designated in the endorsement's schedule. (In practice, many WC&EL insurers are unwilling to add LHWCA coverage because of the unfavorable loss experience associated with the LHWCA.)

The LHWCA coverage endorsement does not cover the insured's obligations under any other compensation statutes, including even those that extend LHWCA benefits to various classes of employees: the Defense Base Act, the Outer Continental Shelf Lands Act, and the Nonappropriated Fund Instrumentalities Act. Separate coverage endorsements to the WC&EL policy are available for covering an employer's obligations under those statutes.

## Maritime Coverage Endorsement

Vessel owners normally cover their liabilities for occupational injuries of crew members through protection and indemnity (P&I) insurance, as described in Chapter 7. However, an alternative way of covering such liabilities is by endorsing the standard WC&EL policy with either (1) the **maritime coverage endorsement** or (2) a combination of that endorsement and the **voluntary compensation maritime coverage endorsement**.

Because these approaches provide a narrower scope of coverage than crew coverage under a typical P&I policy, they are more likely to be used by employers who have minor or incidental crew exposures than by shipowners who have regular crews. For example, a building contractor might undertake a project on navigable waters that could involve Jones Act liability for some employees. To cover all possible liabilities, the contractor might want to have both the LHWCA coverage endorsement and the maritime coverage endorsement(s) added to its WC&EL policy.

The maritime coverage endorsement modifies only the employers liability section of the WC&EL policy. The endorsement extends the employers liability section to cover bodily injury by accident or disease arising out of employment necessary or incidental to the maritime work described in the endorsement schedule. The voluntary compensation maritime coverage endorsement obligates the insurer to pay benefits to maritime employees in the same manner as the voluntary compensation and employers liability endorsement discussed earlier in this chapter.

Several important restrictions apply under the maritime coverage endorsement:

- The bodily injury must occur in the territorial limits of, or in the operation of a vessel sailing directly between the ports of, the continental United States, Alaska, Hawaii, or Canada. Thus, the endorsement would provide no coverage for injury occurring between other places, such as a voyage from a U.S. port to a Mexican port.
- The maritime coverage endorsement does not cover bodily injury covered by a protection and indemnity policy issued to the insured or for the insured's benefit—even if the P&I policy does not apply because of an other insurance clause, a deductible, or a similar provision. Thus, the maritime coverage endorsement should not be purchased to supplement a P&I policy.
- The maritime coverage endorsement does not cover the insured's duty to provide maintenance and cure. However, standard WC&EL manual rules allow this exclusion to be deleted for an additional premium.

When any of the above restrictions would pose a coverage problem, the employer should consider obtaining a separate P&I policy.

## *Other Coverage Endorsements*

In addition to the coverage endorsements described above, other NCCI coverage endorsements are available for insuring an employer's obligations under the following statutes:

- Defense Base Act
- Outer Continental Shelf Lands Act

- Nonappropriated Fund Instrumentalities Act
- Federal Employers' Liability Act
- Migrant and Seasonal Agricultural Worker Protection Act
- Federal Coal Mine Health and Safety Act

# Summary

Workers compensation laws evolved out of a common-law system that did not satisfactorily address work-related injuries. Workers compensation laws provide workers with specified benefits and protect employers against tort suits in most cases.

Most employees are covered under state workers compensation laws. Maritime workers, such as those who build, repair, load, or unload vessels, are covered under the Longshore and Harbor Workers Compensation Act (LHWCA), which, like state workers compensation laws, provides defined benefits to injured employees in return for eliminating their right to sue. Crew members of vessels are not covered by the LHWCA but have various legal remedies for their work-related injuries or illnesses.

An employer's obligations under workers compensation laws can be insured under the standard workers compensation and employers liability (WC&EL) policy. The policy expresses the insurer's promise to pay all benefits required by the workers compensation law of any state listed in the policy.

The WC&EL policy also provides employers liability insurance, which covers claims against the insured because of bodily injury by accident or disease to an employee. Although workers compensation laws generally eliminate the right of employees to sue their employers for occupational injuries, some types of suits are allowed in some states. Common examples of claims or suits that might be covered by employers liability coverage are third-party-over suits, suits for care and loss of services, consequential bodily injury suits, and suits based on the dual-capacity doctrine.

Other states insurance, a feature of the WC&EL policy, permits the insured to make sure that the WC&EL policy will cover operations in additional states (listed in item 3C of the information page) if the insured's operations expand into those states during the policy period.

Endorsements can be added to the WC&EL policy to cover the insured's obligations under the LHWCA and various laws that extend the LHWCA to other employments. Coverage for lawsuits by crew members of a vessel can be covered under the maritime coverage endorsement.

When an employer has employees who are not covered under the workers compensation statute, the employer can obtain *voluntary* workers compensation coverage for those employees. It provides the same benefits as if the employee were covered under the workers compensation statute in the specified jurisdiction. An organization that employs U.S. citizens abroad for indefinite periods may want to purchase foreign voluntary compensation coverage.

# Chapter Notes

1. This chapter is based in part on Chapter 1 of James J. Markham, ed., *Principles of Workers Compensation Claims* (Malvern, PA: Insurance Institute of America, 1992) and Chapter 12 of Bernard L. Webb, Arthur L. Flitner, and Jerome Trupin, *Commercial Insurance*, 3rd ed. (Malvern, PA: Insurance Institute of America, 1996).
2. *IRMI's Workers Comp: A Complete Guide to Coverage, Laws, and Cost Containment* (Dallas, TX: International Risk Management Institute, 1995), VII.D.4.

# Chapter 10

# Professional Liability Insurance

The word "profession" was associated historically with the occupations known as the learned professions: law, medicine, education, and the clergy. However, as society has become more complex and specialized, the number of occupations requiring extensive technical knowledge or training has increased dramatically. "Professional liability," therefore, is not restricted to the traditional professions; rather, **professional liability** can be loosely defined as liability for the failure to use the degree of skill expected of a person in a particular field.[1] The list of occupations that have a professional liability exposure is expanding, including such recent additions as computer programmers and management consultants.

Because the occupations requiring professional liability insurance are too numerous to cover in one chapter of this text, this chapter examines the professional liability exposures of, and insurance policies for, three representative types of professionals: (1) physicians, (2) accountants, and (3) architects and engineers.[2]

Although the term **professional liability insurance** has historically been used to describe insurance covering liability arising out of the providing of professional services to others, that term is now also frequently applied to certain coverages that are widely purchased by organizations of all types, regardless of whether they provide professional services to others. Three common examples of these additional types of professional liability insurance are directors and officers liability insurance, fiduciary liability insurance, and employment practices liability insurance, which will be examined in Chapter 11.

# Overview of Professional Liability Exposure and Insurance

The sections that follow discuss three topics that are fundamental to understanding the bulk of this chapter: (1) the general duties of all professionals, (2) the extent to which the commercial general liability (CGL) policy covers professional liability exposures, and (3) common characteristics of professional liability policies. Subsequent sections of this chapter examine in greater detail the legal standards that apply to specific professions as well as the corresponding professional liability policies.

## Duties of Professionals

Professionals are bound by law to (1) perform the services for which they were hired and (2) perform those services in accordance with the appropriate standards of conduct. The first duty is primarily contractual; the second duty arises from the principles of tort law.

### Contractual Duty

When a client hires a professional to perform a service, a contractual arrangement is created. A contract is a promise or a set of promises that the law recognizes as a duty. Most professional contracts are promises to perform services for clients.

When a professional fails to perform contractual obligations as promised and the other party suffers harm as a result, the injured party is entitled to be restored, as nearly as practical, to the position that he or she would have occupied had the contract been performed as promised.

Damages recoverable for breach of contract can be categorized as follows:

1. Compensatory damages—money that will offset the loss sustained
2. Consequential damages—awarded when the professional, at the time of the contracting, was aware of some special or unusual circumstance that might occur as a result of the breach
3. Liquidated damages—damages stipulated in the contract as the amount to be recovered if a breach occurs
4. Nominal damages—such as one dollar, awarded when a breach occurs, but the plaintiff suffers no actual loss or damages

The injured party must make a reasonable effort to avoid or at least minimize damages. Moreover, to recover compensatory damages, the injured party must prove the amount of loss, as well as that he or she suffered the loss as a direct result of the breach of contract. Usually, the breaching party is obligated to pay only damages that would normally result from the breach; however, when the professional was aware that a greater loss would be probable, consequential damages may be awarded.

## *Tort-Related Duty*

Like all members of society, professionals have a duty to follow a recognized standard of conduct in the course of daily activities. The basic standard for both professionals and other members of society is to use reasonable care to avoid causing injury to other persons. Failure to maintain that accepted standard of conduct will expose a professional to liability for any damage caused to another person.

A tort is a private wrong, as opposed to a crime, which is a public wrong. A cause of action for a tort injury arises when a person violates a duty imposed by law. To determine whether an act was wrongful, the test usually applied is whether a prudent person, in the exercise of ordinary care, would have foreseen that the injury or damage would have naturally or probably resulted from the conduct.

## *Contract Versus Tort Actions*

The primary difference between contract and tort actions lies in the nature of the interests protected:

- *Contract actions* are created to protect the interest of the parties in having promises performed; accordingly, contract actions arise because of the intent or conduct of the parties.
- *Tort actions* protect a party's right to freedom from various kinds of harm; the underlying duties of conduct are imposed by law for social reasons.

A professional's violation of a duty owed to a client can result in a contract action, a tort action, or both. If a professional fails to perform the services agreed to, a breach of contract occurs. If the professional does not perform the services in the manner expected, either a contract or tort cause of action may arise. If a professional's performance causes damage or personal injury, a tort action is most likely to result.

## *Professional Corporations*

Most states permit specified classes of professionals to do business as professional corporations (sometimes called "PCs" or "PAs," professional associations). Many states also have statutes permitting professionals to do business as "limited liability companies" (LLCs). Unless PCs or LLCs are authorized, a professional must practice either as a sole proprietor or in a partnership.

Any employee or officer of a PC or an LLC is *personally* liable for his or her own actions. Thus, if a professional's performance fails to meet the standards for professionals of his or her class, the professional may be liable to the injured person, even if the professional practices as a shareholder of a PC or as a member of an LLC. Some states require PCs to buy insurance meeting minimum standards, usually for any act arising out of the rendering of professional services.

## Professional Liability Coverage Under CGL Policies

The liability of some types of professionals would be covered under a CGL policy unless an endorsement excluding professional liability was added. For example, the injury caused by a sponge left in a patient's abdominal cavity is certainly "bodily injury" as that term is used in the CGL policy. Insurers generally do not want to cover such professional liability exposures under their CGL policies. Consequently, when insuring persons or organizations that render certain professional services, insurers routinely endorse their CGL policies to exclude professional liability. The *Commercial Lines Manual* of Insurance Services Office (ISO) advises that various professional liability exclusions be added to CGL policies for numerous occupations, as shown in Exhibit 10-1. Each of these occupations may have a need for professional liability insurance.

As discussed in Chapter 4, the CGL coverage form, even if it is not endorsed with one of the professional liability exclusion endorsements, contains an exclusion that eliminates coverage for any employee for bodily injury or personal injury arising out of that employee's providing or failing to provide *professional health care services.* Because that exclusion applies only to the individual employee, the employer (named insured) is covered for vicarious liability arising out of the employee's providing or failing to provide professional health care services—assuming that an applicable professional liability exclusion has not been attached to the policy.

For example, a shopping mall owner might employ a paramedic to provide first-aid services to members of the public injured on the mall premises. If the mall owner's CGL policy does not contain a medical professional liability exclusion endorsement, the policy would exclude coverage only for the paramedic with regard to claims for injury arising out of professional health care services provided by the paramedic. If the mall owner became vicariously

**Exhibit 10-1**
Some Classifications Requiring Professional Liability Exclusions

| | |
|---|---|
| Ambulance services | Hearing aid stores* |
| Analytical chemists | Inspection or appraisal companies |
| Barber shops | Insurance agents |
| Beauty parlors | Insurance companies |
| Blood banks | Laboratories—research, development, or testing |
| Cemeteries | |
| Computer manufacturers | Marine appraisers or surveyors |
| Cosmetic, hair, or skin preparation stores | Medical offices |
| Crematories | Medical or x-ray laboratories |
| Drugstores* | |
| Electronic data processing operations | Optical goods stores* |
| | Penal institutions |
| Engineers or architects | Saunas and baths |
| Fire departments | Tanning salons |
| Funeral homes or chapels | Tattoo parlors |
| Health-care facilities | Veterinarians or veterinary hospitals |
| Health or exercise clubs | |

\* Professional services exclusion is not required for drugstores, hearing aid stores, and optical goods stores if products liability coverage is included.

liable for injury resulting from the paramedic's professional errors or omissions, the CGL policy would protect the mall owner. This feature of CGL coverage is often referred to as "incidental medical malpractice liability coverage."

The CGL exclusion discussed above applies only to professional *health care* services and thus has no applicability to the rendering of other types of professional services. However, even in the absence of a professional liability exclusion, the CGL policy would not cover many professional liability losses because they would not come within the CGL definitions of "bodily injury," "property damage," "personal injury," or "advertising injury." For example, a lawyer representing a client in a contract dispute might negligently fail to file a suit within the time period allowed by the applicable state law. If the failure to file suit caused a financial loss to the client, the lawyer would probably be liable for the loss. The lawyer's liability would not be covered under the lawyer's CGL policy even if a professional liability exclusion had not been attached to the policy, because the type of injury incurred was not bodily injury, property damage, advertising injury, or personal injury.

## Common Characteristics of Professional Liability Policies

Because the liability exposures of one profession (such as medicine) may differ considerably from the liability exposures of another profession (such as engineering), insurers use different policies to insure members of each profession. In most cases, only a few insurers who specialize in a particular type of professional liability insurance write that type of insurance. Specialization is necessary to develop the skills required to successfully underwrite risks and adjust claims that differ from the usual bodily injury and property damage exposures faced by most insureds.

Although ISO has developed professional liability forms for lawyers, hospitals, physicians, and other medical professionals, most professional liability insurance is written on forms developed by individual insurers. Thus, the provisions of professional liability policies can differ considerably, not only among policies covering different professions but even among policies covering the same profession. The sections that follow describe some of the general similarities and differences among professional liability policies. Professional liability policies for representative professions are described in greater detail in later sections of this chapter.

### Covered Acts and Consequences

Professional liability differs from liability for ordinary business exposures, such as liability for (1) injury to clients who slip and fall on the insured's business premises, (2) injury to a third party caused by the negligent operation of an auto, or (3) injury to a consumer resulting from a defect in a product manufactured by the insured. Professional liability policies are not designed to cover ordinary business exposures such as those covered under a CGL or commercial auto policy, but rather to cover tortious conduct in the rendering of professional services or the failure to render professional services.

Apart from that basic distinction between professional and business exposures, the professional liability coverage needs of particular professionals differ with the possible consequences of their professional acts or omissions. Consequently, as the following examples demonstrate, professional liability policies differ in the types of loss they cover.

The principal consequence of a physician's negligence, for example, is injury (physical or psychological) to a patient. Accordingly, professional liability policies for physicians are principally concerned with covering liability for *injury* resulting from the insured's rendering of professional services. The same is true of professional liability insurance for other medical professionals such as dentists and nurses. In the absence of a policy definition, the word "injury" includes any deprivation or harm, including property damage.

In contrast, policies for professionals such as accountants and attorneys are concerned with covering liability for purely *financial harm* resulting from the insured's errors or omissions in rendering professional services. For example, in 1989, an insurance company that had lent money to a steamship company to buy several vessels filed a $31 million lawsuit against three law firms over an alleged error in which three zeros were dropped from mortgage documents drawn up in connection with the loan.[3] The alleged error of the law firms did not cause bodily injury or damage to tangible property; however, the error allegedly impaired the insurance company's security interest in the mortgaged property. Professional liability policies for accountants and attorneys typically exclude bodily injury and property damage in order to prevent overlaps with other insurance policies, such as the CGL policy.

The consequences of an architect's or engineer's professional acts can range from a client's incurring of additional costs to damages for bodily injury or property damage. A client might have to incur additional costs to redo part of a project that was improperly designed by the insured architect or engineer. In more dramatic cases, a completed building that was designed by an architect or engineer might actually collapse because of design errors, resulting in bodily injury to the building's occupants and damage to the building itself and its contents. An architect's or engineer's professional liability policy should thus be worded broadly enough to cover the range of possible losses for which the insured might incur professional liability.

Some professional liability policies limit their coverage to *negligent* acts, errors, or omissions. This is a narrower form of coverage than that provided by a professional liability policy that simply covers injury or loss arising out of the insured's rendering or failing to render professional services. The former type of policy would only cover against allegations of *negligence*, whereas the latter would cover any allegation of injury or loss resulting from the insured's rendering or failing to render professional services. For example, the latter type of policy could cover allegations of intentional torts, such as defamation or battery, whereas the former type of policy would not. Policies that limit coverage to negligent acts, errors, or omissions are often referred to as **errors and omissions (E&O) liability policies** rather than professional liability policies, but the usage of those terms is inexact. A particular insurer's policy whose name includes the words "professional liability policy" can be limited to covering negligent acts, errors, or omissions. A professional liability policy that does not limit coverage to *negligent* acts, errors, or omissions is (all other things being equal) superior to one that contains that limitation.

## Who Is Covered

Professional liability policies naturally cover the professionals themselves, and most also cover partners, owners, directors, officers, and stockholders of professional organizations. Some professional liability policies also cover the employees of professional organizations (though some require an endorsement to provide this coverage), and some cover the insured's estates, heirs, and legal representatives.

Also covered are professional partnerships or organizations formed by the professionals (such as a law firm or a physicians' group). Rather than providing coverage for organizations, however, some policies only cover an organization's obligation to indemnify professionals who are sued in conjunction with their activities on the organization's behalf. Coverage for organizations can usually be added by endorsement to those policies; since organizations are commonly named in lawsuits, that coverage can be valuable.

## Defense Coverage

In addition to paying claims or settling suits on behalf of the insured, professional liability policies ordinarily pay the costs of defending against claims or suits alleging loss covered under the policy. Defense coverage typically includes the supplementary payments associated with other commercial liability policies. However, policies vary widely in their provision of defense costs. Some common variations are summarized below.

In some policies, the insurer assumes the right and duty to defend, thus reserving the right to appoint defense counsel. In other policies, the insurer agrees to pay defense costs but does not assume the right and duty to defend. In policies taking the latter approach, the insured can select counsel of his or her own choice. Often, however, the policy requires the insured to obtain the insurer's approval of the counsel selected.

In some policies, defense costs are payable in addition to policy limits, as in the CGL policy. In other policies, defense costs are included within limits. When a policy covers defense costs within limits, the insured must take potential defense costs into consideration when selecting limits.

Most commercial liability policies give the insurance company the right and duty to defend *or settle* claims or suits. Some professional liability policies, in contrast, require the insurance company to obtain the insured's consent before settling a claim made against the insured. Thus, the insured can, in effect, require the insurance company to take the often more costly route of defending against a claim instead of settling the claim out of court. Although out-of-court settlements often reduce claim costs, they can also create the public impression that the insured professional is admitting fault. The consent-to-settle provision is a specific recognition that the insured, as a professional, has a reputation to protect that transcends the economic interest of the insurance company to dispose of the claim as inexpensively as possible.

To discourage insureds from unreasonably refusing to let the insurer settle a claim, policies that contain a consent-to-settle clause are often subject to a special provision. This provision states that if the insured withholds consent to a settlement recommended by the insurance company and elects to contest the claim, the insurer's liability for the claim will not exceed the amount for which the claim could have been settled, plus claim expenses incurred up to the date of refusal. Because of the practical difficulties that can arise out of consent-to-settle provisions, many professional liability insurers do not include such provisions in their policies. Rather, such insurers reserve the traditional right to defend or settle at their own discretion.

## Coverage Triggers

Many professional liability coverages develop "long-tail" claims—that is, claims that are presented long after the policy has expired. A classic example involves professional liability of obstetricians. In most states, a statute of limitations provides that negligence claims are barred unless a lawsuit is filed within a specified period, such as two years. In cases involving injury to newborn babies, the time limit does not begin to run until an infant has reached majority (eighteen years in most states). Thus, it is not unusual for an obstetrician who is alleged to have negligently inflicted an injury on a newborn infant to be faced with a claim many years later, after the infant has reached majority. Consequently, insurers prefer to use claims-made professional liability policies in order to more closely match claims with policies currently in force.

The claims-made approach was discussed in Chapter 4 in connection with the CGL policy. A common difference between independently developed claims-made forms and the ISO claims-made CGL form is in the extended reporting period provisions. The ISO form automatically includes a basic extended reporting period, and a supplemental extended reporting period can be added for an additional premium. If the insured purchases the supplemental extended reporting period, there is an unlimited time period to report claims that occurred during the policy period.

In contrast, the claims-made provisions found in professional liability policies often do not contain an automatic extended reporting period. Any extended reporting period must usually be specifically requested and paid for, and few (if any) policies offer an *unlimited* extended reporting period; one to three years is more common. Policies vary as to the circumstances in which the insured is allowed to obtain an extended reporting period. For example, one policy might allow the insured to purchase an extended reporting period if the policy is canceled or nonrenewed by either the insurance company or the insured. Another policy might allow the option only when the insurer has canceled or nonrenewed the policy.

Offsetting to some degree the limitations on extended reporting periods, some professional liability policies contain a provision stating that a claim will be deemed to have been made during the policy period if the insured reports to the insurer during the policy period the circumstances of an incident that could be expected to lead to a formal claim at some later point. Thus, if the actual claim is not made until after the policy expires, the claim will be treated as if it was made during the policy period, even if the policy does not have an extended reporting period. Such a provision is obviously more favorable to the insured than a requirement that a claim will not be considered to have been first made until the insured actually receives a demand for money damages from the third party claimant.

### Coverage Territory

Many professional liability policies provide coverage for acts committed anywhere in the world, as long as suit is brought in the United States or Canada. Some policies provide broader coverage by allowing suit to be brought anywhere in the world, and some provide narrower coverage by requiring that the act be committed in a more restricted policy territory, such as the United States or Canada. When worldwide coverage is needed, underwriters are usually willing to provide it.

### Exclusions

Exclusions vary widely in professional liability policies. Some policies, such as physicians professional liability policies, contain few exclusions. Other policies, such as directors and officers liability policies, often contain many exclusions. The exclusions likely to be encountered in the various types of professional liability policies will be described in the separate descriptions of policies that appear later in this chapter.

## Physicians Professional Liability Insurance

Medical professional liability insurance is a general name that encompasses different policies for a wide range of medical professionals, including (but by no means limited to) physicians, dentists, nurses, therapists, optometrists, emergency medical technicians, and veterinarians. Medical professional liability insurance also encompasses professional liability policies for hospitals and various other medical organizations, such as clinics, nursing homes, laboratories, managed care organizations, and visiting nurses associations.

Professional liability insurance for physicians—commonly known as "medical malpractice insurance"—is the best known type of medical professional liability insurance and is the subject of the discussion that follows. The legal basis for imposing professional liability on a physician is examined first, followed by a review of the policy provisions typically found in physicians professional liability policies.

## Loss Exposure

The law is well established that physicians can be held liable under negligence principles for injuries to their patients. The basic rules that govern other negligence actions also apply in a suit against a medical professional. No higher degree of culpability is required to establish liability against a physician than is required in any other tort action. In each instance, the professional's duty is to use reasonable care to avoid injury to other persons.

In order for a physician to be considered negligent in a medical professional liability case, four elements must be present: (1) a duty owed by the physician to a patient; (2) a breach of that duty by the physician; (3) an injury suffered by the patient; and (4) proof that the patient's injury was proximately caused by the physician's breach of duty.

In nonprofessional cases, jurors can usually evaluate the defendant's conduct in light of their own experience and background. For example, no special knowledge is required to judge whether a driver who failed to stop at a stop sign was negligent. Professional cases are different. Without special knowledge, jurors would often have difficulty in determining whether the professional used the required level of skill and care. Therefore, the jury needs to be informed of the standards that pertain to that particular profession. Integrating this element of proof into court actions against medical professionals has posed problems.

### Standard of Care

The law generally requires that the plaintiff prove the proper standard of care applicable to the medical treatment that was received, as well as the causal connection between the failure to observe the proper standard of care and the resulting injury. Most courts require that expert testimony be produced to establish the appropriate standard of care. Other jurisdictions have found that the proper standard of professional care can be established by authoritative journals or treatises, as well as other secondary or collateral sources. In any event, the court will require the plaintiff to show that some recognized standard was breached.

## Locality Rule

U.S. courts once adhered to the rule that a physician's treatment must be measured by the skill and care used by other physicians in the same community. A variation of this rule broadened the standard to encompass the skill and care exercised by physicians in similar communities. However, this so-called "locality rule" and its variations have been criticized as being outmoded, and in many states, court decisions have repudiated the locality rule.

The rationale for the rule—the presumption that physicians in small or rural communities lack opportunities to keep abreast of advances in the profession and lack up-to-date facilities for treating patients—is, in many cases, invalid. Advances in medical technology are widely disseminated through professional journals and continuing education seminars. In addition, improved transportation and regional referral centers have enabled patients to receive necessary treatment in appropriate facilities. Nevertheless, although the locality in which a physician practices is no longer the determining factor in establishing the applicable level of care, it is still a factor to be considered.

## Specialists and Duty of Referral

Specialists are required to possess and apply that extra degree of skill and care used by prudent specialists practicing in the same field. If a patient's condition requires consultation with or care by a specialist, the attending physician has a duty either to tell the patient about the seriousness of the condition or to refer the patient to a specialist. Physicians are ordinarily not held liable for a specialist's negligence unless they exercise control over the specialist's course of treatment. Likewise, physicians are generally not held liable for the acts of surgeons when the physicians do not assist in the medical procedures. Nor would attending physicians be liable for the acts of substitute physicians, unless an attending physician failed to use reasonable care in the selection of a substitute.

## Delegation

Physicians, like other employers, can be held liable for the negligence of their employees. For example, a physician might employ an office nurse to administer medications. If the nurse commits an error while administering medicine and an injury results, the physician could be held responsible. Likewise, physicians can be held legally liable for the negligence of other physicians with whom they have entered into a partnership or a professional corporation for the practice of medicine.

Less clear are cases in which a doctor delegates a task to an employee of the hospital, particularly during surgery. For years, courts held that a physician could not be charged with the negligence of a hospital employee if delegating the particular task to a hospital employee was customary, unless the physician directly supervised the performance of the work. More recently, however, some courts have imposed liability on a physician in such a situation. They have considered hospital employees to be temporary servants of the operating surgeon and have found surgeons liable for failures that occur under their implied direction and supervision. (This legal theory is known as the "captain of the ship" or "borrowed servant" theory.)

## Diligence and Abandonment

A physician has a duty to be diligent in the treatment of patients. Moreover, a physician has a duty to treat a patient as long as treatment is required. In other words, a physician has a duty not to abandon a patient.

## Informed Consent

In order to perform an operation, a physician must obtain the consent of the patient (or someone legally authorized to give consent), except under emergency conditions or in unanticipated situations. In addition, the surgeon or attending physician must reasonably disclose to the patient or the patient's qualified representative the potential problems associated with the surgery or treatment so that the patient or the representative can decide whether to proceed with the surgery or accept the treatment. To obtain such **informed consent**, a physician is generally required to disclose information to the patient on the following five topics:

1. The nature of the patient's condition or problem
2. The nature or purpose of the procedure or treatment that the physician is proposing
3. The risks associated with the proposed procedure or treatment
4. The anticipated benefits (results) of the proposed procedure or treatment
5. Alternative procedures or treatments and the risks associated with them

## Common Allegations Against Physicians

Professional liability claims against medical professionals are often based on allegations of surgical error, improper diagnosis, improper tests, lack of informed consent, and improper administration of anesthetics and drugs.

### Surgical Error

A surgeon who performs an operation has the duty to exercise the reasonable care, skill, and diligence that prudent surgeons in similar situations usually exercise. For example, failure to remove instruments, surgical sponges, or other foreign substances from the patient's body before the incision has been closed has been held to be negligence on the part of the operating surgeon.

### Improper Diagnosis

One of the fundamental duties of a physician is to make a properly skillful and careful diagnosis of ailments. If a physician fails to bring to a diagnosis the proper degree of skill or care, the physician may be held liable to the patient for any resulting damage. However, a mistake in diagnosis caused by an error in judgment is not actionable if the physician has used the proper degree of skill and care. That is, liability is not imposed on a physician for making an error in judgment, except when the error results from a failure to comply with a recognized standard of medical care that is exercised by prudent physicians in the same specialty under similar circumstances.

### Improper Tests

Physicians have a duty to employ the proper tests and evaluations to determine the condition of a patient about to undergo a proposed treatment or operation. Whether the failure to make such tests or examinations constitutes a lack of due and reasonable care and skill depends on whether the standards of skill and care require such a test or an examination in a particular case.

### Lack of Informed Consent

Failure to disclose in advance the known, significant risks of a particular procedure or treatment may render the physician or surgeon liable. Physicians and surgeons are not, however, expected to disclose every conceivable risk, because excessive disclosure might do patients more harm than good.

### Use and Administration of Anesthetics or Drugs

The duty and liability of a physician in administering an anesthetic or a drug to a patient are substantially the same as those which generally govern the treatment of patients; that is, physicians are bound to exercise the same degree of care and skill that prudent physicians of similar skill and training usually exercise under similar circumstances. In most cases involving the question of negligence, physicians have been held liable for injuries to patients resulting from the administration of the wrong drug or medicine. Related causes of action include the failure to properly sterilize instruments, drugs, or operative fields; breaking hypodermic needles; the use of harmful drugs instead of the proper ones; the improper use of spinal injections; and the death or injury of a patient under excessive or improper anesthesia.

## Other Allegations

Many other allegations can be made against medical professionals. For just a few of many possible examples, an injured patient's professional liability claim might be based on the following:

- A surgeon's failure to continue care after the patient leaves the operating room
- Negligent treatment of an organ donor or donee in connection with organ transplants
- Improper treatment of fractures or dislocations caused by the improper application of a cast or a splint or other treatment
- Transfusions of the wrong type of blood or blood contaminated with serum hepatitis or the human immunodeficiency virus (HIV)
- Improper implantation or insertion of a prosthetic device

# Defenses

The most basic defense to a negligence action made against a medical professional is that no negligence occurred—that the physician exercised the required degree of skill and care and that the method of treatment was appropriate. Other defenses that medical professionals can use to respond to allegations of professional liability are the statute of limitations, Good Samaritan statutes, contributory or comparative negligence, and informed consent.

## Statute of Limitations

A statute of limitations sets forth the period of time within which various types of actions must be brought. Failure to sue within the time set forth in the statute terminates the plaintiff's right to enforce a claim. Generally, most U.S. jurisdictions apply their personal injury statutes of limitations to medical professional liability actions, absent a special statute that creates a limitation for that type of litigation. The time periods permitted by statutes of limitation, which vary by state, are usually one to three years. Generally, a statute does not run against a minor during the period of minority. After attaining the age of majority, the former minor is usually granted an additional period within which a tort action may be initiated. In medical cases, most jurisdictions have ruled that the statute begins to run at the time of the wrongful act, though some courts have held that the statute starts to run at the end of the medical treatment. Moreover, some courts have adopted the discovery rule, which states that the statute begins to run when the injured person either learns of the injury or should reasonably have learned of it.

### Good Samaritan Statutes

Most states have adopted **Good Samaritan statutes**, which exempt from liability physicians and others licensed to treat patients when they provide emergency care without compensation (for example, at an accident scene). Good Samaritan statutes apply only to treatment that is not grossly negligent or reckless.

### Contributory Negligence

If the patient does not exercise the standard of care that he or she is required to exercise for his or her own safety, if that negligence occurs simultaneously with the negligence of the physician, and if it causes an injury that becomes a cause of action, the patient's negligence may either bar recovery or reduce the amount of recovery. For example, a patient's refusal to undergo a treatment that the physician recommends might be grounds for the physician to assert contributory negligence as a defense.

### Informed Consent

As mentioned earlier, except in emergency situations, physicians must obtain consent from the patient or from the patient's representative before performing any procedure. As long as the physician discloses to the patient the benefits or risks of and alternatives to a procedure, it has been held that the patient, in agreeing to the procedure, waives a technical "battery." Obtaining a patient's informed consent does not, however, protect a physician against allegations of professional negligence, because informed consent does not constitute an acceptance of the physician's negligence.

## Policy Provisions

**Physicians professional liability policies** are used to insure physicians and dentists, and they are commonly adapted to cover allied medical professionals, such as nurses and anesthetists. Physicians professional liability policies do not cover general liability exposures. Obtaining professional liability insurance and general liability insurance from the same insurance company, when possible, is generally recommended as a way of avoiding situations in which separate insurers might both deny coverage for a "gray area" occurrence, such as injuries resulting from a patient's falling while attempting to climb down from an examining table without assistance.

## Insuring Agreements

A typical physicians professional liability policy typically includes two insuring agreements, one relating to *individual* coverage and the other to *organization* coverage.

### Individual Coverage

The individual insuring agreement typically covers sums that the individual professional becomes legally obligated to pay as damages because of the following:

1. Professional acts or omissions committed by the insured professional
2. Professional acts or omissions committed by the professional's employees or other persons under the professional's supervision (such as a laboratory technician or nurse) for which the insured professional incurs vicarious liability
3. The professional's service on a formal accreditation board or any similar committee

The third aspect of individual coverage corresponds to the common practice of physicians serving on a hospital committee whose purpose is to consider other physicians' requests for staff privileges at the hospital. If the committee denies staff privileges to a physician, that physician might sue the committee members for damages. A physicians professional liability policy ordinarily protects the insured professional against such suits. Some policies do not cover this exposure. Because physicians serve on these committees at the request and for the benefit of hospitals, some insurers believe that this exposure ought to be covered under the hospital's own professional liability policy.

Although the individual insuring agreement protects the insured physician against vicarious liability for the professional acts or omissions of employees and others, the policy usually does not provide any coverage for the subordinate professional (such as a nurse employed by the insured). Although coverage for such individuals can be added by endorsement to the physician's policy, the coverage can also be provided under a separate policy covering the nurse or other professional employee. The separate-policy approach is often preferred because it provides a separate limit of liability. Thus, in a claim made against both the physician and his or her employee, both parties will not have to share the same limit of insurance for the claim.

### Organization Coverage

The organization insuring agreement covers the insured's professional partnership, association, or corporation for damages resulting from professional acts or omissions committed by anyone for whose acts or omissions the organization is legally liable. For example, one of the insured's patients might sue both the insured and the professional corporation with whom the insured practices medicine. The individual insuring agreement would cover the insured professional, and the organization insuring agreement would cover the corporation.

## Exclusions

Physicians professional liability policies vary considerably in the exclusions that they contain. Typically, such policies contain relatively few exclusions, partly because the restriction of coverage to *professional* liability in the insuring agreements eliminates the need for many exclusions found in other commercial liability policies. Exclusions that might be found in a physicians professional liability policy are briefly described below.

### High-Risk Medical Procedures

Some policies exclude surgical procedures or other treatments that are more likely than others to result in severe liability losses. If a physician specializes in such procedures or treatments, he or she can usually have the applicable exclusion(s) removed from the policy for an additional premium.

### Criminal Acts

Most policies exclude criminal acts committed by the insured, although some policies agree to defend the insured against allegations of criminal acts.

### Sexual Misconduct

Many physicians professional liability policies agree to defend their insureds against allegations of sexual misconduct but exclude any damages payable if the insured is found to have committed sexual misconduct. Some policies exclude both defense costs and damages for sexual abuse or misconduct.

### Proprietary Activities

Physicians professional liability policies often contain an exclusion eliminating coverage for the insured's activities as a proprietor, administrator, officer, stockholder, or member of the board of trustees of any hospital, clinic with bed and board facilities, nursing home, laboratory, or other business enterprise. Coverage for such activities is not contemplated in the rates for physicians professional liability policies. Such activities can be covered under a separate hospital professional liability policy or in some cases by endorsement to the physicians professional liability policy.

### Other Exclusions

A physicians professional liability policy might also exclude any of the following:

- Punitive damages
- Pollution (as might result from hazardous waste generated by a physician's practice)
- Discrimination (as might occur if a physician refuses to treat a particular patient)
- Contractual liability (as might occur if the insured agrees to hold a substitute doctor harmless)

## Other Provisions

Physicians professional liability policies ordinarily are subject to two limits of insurance. One limit applies to each medical incident (or, in some cases, to each person). The other limit is an annual aggregate limit. The annual aggregate limit is usually set at two or three times the per incident limit.

The coverage territory for physicians professional liability policies is often limited to acts occurring in the state in which the insured's practice is located. The reason for this restriction is that the frequency and severity of medical professional liability claims are higher in some states than in others. Before an insurer agrees to cover services rendered in a more hazardous state, it normally wants to be made aware of the increased exposure so that it can charge an additional, appropriate premium.

Physicians professional liability policies usually apply on a claims-made basis, subject to variations as discussed earlier in this chapter.

# Loss Control

Loss control includes all of the measures that can reduce or eliminate hazards. Continuing education, though it certainly provides other benefits, can be the most effective means by which the members of any profession can control liability losses. Courts often accept the failure to make reasonable continuing education efforts as evidence of professional negligence. Indeed, the common law duty to stay current in one's field has been supplemented and underscored by such modern developments as (1) the universal recognition of continuing education as an ethical obligation of all professionals and (2) the trend toward mandatory continuing education as a condition of periodic relicensing or recertification of professionals. Regardless of whether a medical professional is required to complete formalized programs of continuing education, every medical professional who is named as a defendant in a negligence action can expect to be questioned about what he or she has done to stay abreast of the latest techniques and knowledge in the field.

Some medical professionals practice "defensive medicine" by requiring extensive diagnostic tests before rendering opinions or performing services. To the extent that such tests are *medically* unnecessary, they contribute to the spiraling costs of health care. Some medically unnecessary tests, though, are *legally* necessary to prevent and control medical professional liability claims. Furthermore, decisions by physicians to order marginally necessary tests are not entirely self-serving. The tests may prove beneficial to the health of patients, and any increased costs attributable to the tests may be preferable to the alternative—increased costs attributable to increases in medical professional liability claims.

A summary of measures that physicians can use to prevent professional liability claims is presented in Exhibit 10-2.

**Exhibit 10-2**
Summary of Loss Control Measures for Physicians*

1. **Know the Patient**
   Physicians should look for red flags that can alert them to the possibility that the patient is the type who could initiate litigation later. The patient might cause problems if he or she:
   - Does not complete a thorough medical history
   - Is mentally incompetent
   - Complains about other physicians
   - Says the physician is the only one who "understands" him or her
   - Misses appointments without good reason
   - Lies to the physician or the physician's staff
   - Acts contrary to the physician's advice
   - Has a history of filing medical professional liability suits
   - Continually avoids financial responsibility
   - Asks for a guarantee of results

2. **Maintain Communication and Exercise Courtesy**
   Physicians and their staff should:
   - Return patients' phone calls promptly
   - Listen to their patients' concerns about both their cases and their personal lives
   - Communicate with patients' family members
   - Avoid making careless or indiscreet remarks
   - Never lose their temper with patients
   - Never ignore patients
   - Never criticize the work of other physicians
   - Keep their waiting rooms tidy

## Chapter 10 / Professional Liability Insurance 59

3. **Keep Thorough Records**

   To help in a medical professional liability defense, every patient's medical records should contain the following:
   - The patient's medical history, including the patient's own medical history form
   - Personal information about the patient
   - The date, time, and place of every meeting and every medical treatment
   - Results of every examination and test
   - Every diagnosis and reasons for the diagnosis
   - Prognosis and treatment plan, and follow-up instructions
   - Informed consent forms
   - Names of prescription medicines used before, during, and after treatment, with copies of prescription forms
   - Results of medications and treatments
   - Information about drug or other allergies
   - Photographs of the patient taken during the tenure of treatment
   - Information about missed appointments, refused medications and treatments, medical complications, noncompliance or lying, and any unusual occurrences

4. **Avoid Even the Appearance of Negligence**

   Physicians must be especially careful when discharging patients from treatment. They should avoid making statements like "the patient has no medical problems," because every patient will eventually develop some kind of medical problem. They should also avoid saying that they're discharging patients "for financial reasons"; juries are notoriously unsympathetic towards physicians who refuse to see poverty-stricken patients.

5. **Diagnose and Test Thoroughly**

   Physicians should adequately document the diagnoses, particularly negative diagnoses. Diagnoses are often missed because the physician didn't conduct a thorough diagnosis or order enough tests; sometimes the failure to test is a more significant problem than the failure to diagnose. Other diagnosis-related problems can occur when a physician fails to discover or test for drug or food allergies or other conditions that may affect the course of treatment.

6. **Keep Informed About Informed Consent**

   Proper informed consent documentation contains three elements that a physician should obtain before performing medical treatment. Those three elements can be remembered by the acronym "BAR":

*Continued on next page.*

- B is for background—Everything the physician knows about the patient on which the diagnosis is based, including the patient's symptoms and medical history and the physician's recommended treatment or procedure.
- A is for alternatives—The physician must explain what he or she expects will happen if the patient declines to have a treatment or procedure and describe any safe alternatives to the treatment or procedure.
- R is for risks—The patient must clearly understand the risks and possible outcomes, even if they are remote, of the treatment or procedure.

### 7. Know What's Happening at the Hospital

Physicians must be careful when referring patients to the emergency room; if something were to go wrong, they could be found jointly liable for abandonment or an emergency room physician's missed diagnosis. In addition, physicians are responsible for potentially harmful conditions in a hospital if they notice them and fail to take remedying action. Most hospitals also require that discharge orders be made by the patient's physician, so physicians shouldn't delegate that responsibility to anyone else.

### 8. Don't Take on Too Much Work

When physicians spread themselves too thin, they can adversely affect their relationships with patients by causing the patients to think that they don't care enough to spend sufficient time with them. In addition, physicians shouldn't handle cases outside of their own areas of training and expertise; rather, they should refer patients to qualified specialists for treatment. Physicians must remember, though, that even when they refer a patient to another physician for treatment, they still have responsibility, and thus liability, to the patient.

### 9. Monitor Partners and Staff

Careless comments by office assistants can lead to lawsuits, especially if the comments pertain to a patient's finances, sexual matters, emotional problems, pregnancies, and abortions. Nurses and other staff members who aren't licensed physicians should refrain from diagnosing illnesses and treating patients. When physicians share space, staff, and expenses, they also share liability, and assets of the partnership could be liquidated to cover damages resulting from the negligence of any past or present partner.

### 10. Prevention Is the Best Defense

More and more doctors are practicing "defensive medicine," in which every patient is appraised as a potential litigant. The goal of these physicians is to prevent the mistakes that can later lead to a medical professional liability suit.

This exhibit is summarized from "Ten Procedures for Avoiding Medical Malpractice," published by the St. Paul Fire and Marine Insurance Company (originally published by Promedion Professional Education).

# Accountants Professional Liability Insurance

This section examines (1) the professional liability exposure of accountants, (2) the typical provisions of accountants professional liability insurance, and (3) applicable loss control techniques.

## Loss Exposure

Many accountants do not have their own clients but are salaried employees of commercial entities. These "private" accountants owe essentially the same duties to third parties as does any other employee. This discussion will focus on the professional liability exposures of "public" accountants who hold themselves out to the public as professionals who are willing to perform professional services, for a fee, as independent contractors (or employees, partners, or shareholders thereof). Most public accountants are Certified Public Accountants (CPAs) who have met experience and educational requirements, have passed required examinations, and are bound by a comprehensive and strictly enforced code of professional ethics.

Public accountants perform a variety of services. Each task that public accountants perform carries exposure to liability. The three conventional theories of recovery against public accountants are breach of contract, tort, and statutory violations.

### Breach of Contract

The contract theory of liability against accountants is based on the contractual relationship between accountants and their clients. This relationship serves as the "foundation of the accountants' responsibilities and rights."[4]

A client can assert breach of contract against an accountant if the client suffers damage because of his or her accountant's negligent or otherwise improper or incomplete performance of engagement. Under certain circumstances, a third party can also assert breach of contract if the third party can prove that he or she was an "intended beneficiary" of the contract between the accountant and the client. For example, an investor who relied on a misleading financial statement including the opinion of an accountant could assert that the accountant breached the contract with the organization whose statement was involved.

### Tort Liability

As members of a skilled profession, public accountants are liable for their failure to perform with reasonable professional care and competence. In the absence of a contract that describes the respective parties' duties and rights, the conventional law of torts governs the potential liability of accountants.

### Statutory Liability

Accountants must comply with certain statutory requirements. Primary among those requirements are those imposed by federal and state securities laws. Another area of accountant liability based on statutory duties concerns the Employee Retirement Income Security Act of 1974 (ERISA).

## Common Allegations Against Accountants

Claims against accountants arise from many aspects of accounting practice, with new areas of potential liability developing constantly. This section will discuss tax services, audit services, accounting services, client counterclaims, failure to detect embezzlement, securities laws, business and investment advice, breach of fiduciary duties, and management advisory service.

### Tax Services

Claims arising out of tax services include allegations that an accountant is responsible for the late filing of returns, claims of underpayment of estimated tax obligations, and claims based on governmental disallowance of the treatment anticipated by the accountant and reported on a tax return prepared by the accountant. Resulting damage can include payment of penalties and interest and other financial harm to the client.

Taxation is a broad and complex field that requires both accounting and legal expertise. Accountants must remain current with the Internal Revenue Code and with regulatory changes. Every legislative and regulatory change to the code creates a new element in the standard of professional due care against which the performance of tax practitioners will be judged.

### Audit Services

Accountants engaged to perform audits undertake three distinct tasks: (1) the investigation and gathering of data, including studying the client's operations and industry; (2) the analysis of the collected data to draw inferences and reach conclusions; and (3) the presenting of conclusions in the form of an opinion or a certificate.[5]

Courts tend to measure an auditor's potential liability in light of various duties. The duty to audit is generally considered to be a duty to provide accurate, reliable information for those who will or may rely on the audited financial statements. Another duty, the duty of independence from the client, is considered to be essential and virtually inviolate. The duty to adhere to generally accepted accounting principles (GAAP) and generally accepted auditing standards (GAAS) requires maximum fairness and accuracy in the auditor's presentation of all financial information. Adherence to GAAP or GAAS, however, does not always provide a successful defense.

Claims can also arise from the auditor's duty to detect fraud or inquire into suspicious circumstances, illegality, or abnormal activities. Finally, the auditor's duty of disclosure is a potential source of claims.

## *Accounting Services*

Claims involving accounting services are generally based on allegations of improper execution of what is called compilation and review (that is, unaudited) work. When performing a compilation or review, the accountant usually acknowledges that no audit was undertaken but that nothing the accountant noticed indicated that entries were not made according to GAAP. The accounting profession has instituted standards for unaudited accounting and review services. Failure to follow these standards may result in liability.

## *Client Counterclaims*

If an accountant sues a client in an effort to collect fees, the client may countersue to defeat or diminish the accountant's claim. Client counterclaims involve all types of substantive issues, including claims based on tax services, audit services, accounting services, management advisory services, and business and investment advice. The only reasonably effective deterrent to the commencement of client counterclaims is for accountants to bill for services promptly and regularly, thereby minimizing the later need to sue for unpaid fees.

## *Failure To Detect Embezzlement*

Claims arising because of an accountant's failure to detect embezzlement during an audit or another engagement often involve demands for severe damages. Accountants have long been subject to liability for failing to discover embezzlements by a client's bookkeeper by failing to compare checks drawn by the bookkeeper with invoices. Accountants have also been held liable for an inadequate review of delinquent accounts to discover embezzlement by municipal employees such as a city treasurer and for the failure to detect check forgery or alteration schemes.

The courts have acknowledged the limits on accountants' ability to discover client employee dishonesty. However, claims against accountants based on client employee dishonesty often include allegations that the accountant had recommended, selected, or approved the employee, or that the accountant had failed to warn the client that the client's internal control system was inadequate.

### Securities Laws

Securities-related claims often involve high-dollar liabilities and defense costs. Complaints based on securities statutes may include claims of violations of rules that prohibit false or misleading statements willfully or recklessly made in connection with the offer or sale of securities; in registration statements and prospectuses; and in documents required to be filed with the Securities and Exchange Commission (SEC). Allegedly false and misleading statements upon which such claims are based can appear in financial statements, projections, or tax opinions.

### Business and Investment Advice

Claims based on accountants' allegedly negligent business and investment advice arise out of audit or accounting services and tax and management advice, and they generally involve business acquisition evaluations and projections. Also involved are services in which the accountant has advised on such matters as a suitable mix of portfolio investments for business funds or is consulted by potential lenders or sureties.

### Breach of Fiduciary Duties

Claims may be brought against accountants for breaches of fiduciary responsibilities under ERISA or under the judicially expanded definition of "fiduciary" in the SEC's Rule 106. Because many large accounting firms have actuaries on staff, liability potential for accounting firms arising from work with pension plans has expanded beyond the risks inherent with being a fiduciary. Given the nature of actuarial science and pension plans, these claims could involve lengthy time lapses between an alleged negligent act or omission and the discovery of the alleged harm.[6]

### Management Advisory Services

Claims of this type concern allegations that an accountant gave bad advice to a business on how to improve its efficiency or to make maximum use of its resources. As in any professional service, accountants who present themselves as qualified to advise on management matters, efficiency, resource use, economic planning, or computer systems represent to their clients that they have the skill required to perform the service. Such accountants are then bound to exercise reasonable care and to comply with the provisions of their contracts.

## Policy Provisions

There is no standard form for **accountants professional liability insurance**. Policy provisions can vary considerably among insurers. The discussion that follows describes the major provisions typically found in representative policies.

### Insuring Agreement

The insuring agreement of an accountants professional liability policy ordinarily provides that the insurer will pay on behalf of the insured all sums that the insured becomes legally obligated to pay for damages resulting from the insured's professional services. The policy definition of "professional services" can vary from policy to policy. Typically, the definition is rather broadly worded to include services performed or advice given in the conduct of the insured's practice as an accountant. Occasionally, the broad scope of the definition is modified by an endorsement or other policy provisions to eliminate coverage for specified high-risk accounting activities.

As accounting firms broaden the scope of their management advisory services offered (which, for example, might include computer systems assistance), the possibility arises that an insurer might consider some of the firm's management advisory services to fall outside the definition of professional accounting services. Accordingly, when applying for professional liability insurance, an accounting firm should disclose to the insurer the nature of all services it offers and, if necessary, seek to modify the policy language to ascertain that the policy covers all such services for which coverage is wanted.

An accountants professional liability policy ordinarily covers the costs of defending against claims, including false or fraudulent claims, alleging damages that would be covered under the policy. However, most accountants liability policies pay defense costs *within* the policy limits.

A claims-made coverage trigger normally applies to professional liability policies. The claims-made provisions vary along the lines described earlier in this chapter.

### Who Is Insured

In addition to covering the named insured, accountants professional liability policies typically cover past and present officers, directors, partners, stockholders, and employees for professional services performed within the scope of their duties on behalf of the named insured. Heirs, executors, administrators, and legal representatives of an insured are also usually covered because an accountant can be held personally liable for professional errors or omissions. If the accountant dies or becomes bankrupt or incapacitated, the plaintiff may be able to make a claim against the accountant's heirs, executor, administrator, or legal representative.

## Exclusions

The most important differences between two prospective accountants professional liability policies are often in their exclusions. Thus, the exclusions of any prospective policy should be carefully reviewed before accepting the policy to ascertain that the policy will provide adequate coverage for the insured's activities.

### Bodily Injury and Property Damage

Most accountants professional liability policies exclude claims for bodily injury or damage to tangible property, for at least two reasons: (1) the usual consequence of an accountant's malpractice is simply financial harm to the client or other party harmed, and (2) excluding bodily injury and property damage is an efficient way of eliminating coverage for claims covered under more ordinary commercial insurance policies such as the CGL and business auto policies.

In most cases, the exclusion of bodily injury and property damage does not pose any problem. However, it is possible to imagine a case in which a businessowner might allege that he or she became physically ill because of bad business decisions based on faulty advice or inaccurate information provided by the accountant. If the accountant's CGL policy did not contain a professional services exclusion, such bodily injury could be covered under that policy. If the accountant's CGL policy *did* contain a professional services exclusion, the insured could offer to pay the professional liability insurer an additional premium to modify the bodily injury and property damage exclusion so that it would allow coverage to apply for bodily injury resulting from professional services.

### Dishonest or Criminal Acts

Accountants professional liability policies exclude acts that are dishonest, fraudulent, or criminal. However, an important aspect of this exclusion is the extent to which the policy provides exceptions to the exclusion. Prospective policyholders generally seek two such exceptions, as follows:

1. That the policy will cover the cost of *defending* against claims alleging dishonest, fraudulent, or criminal acts, even though the policy will not pay any damages if the insured is actually found guilty of such acts.
2. That the policy will defend and pay damages on behalf of *innocent* insureds who are sued or held legally liable because of the dishonest, fraudulent, or

criminal acts of another insured. Although an appropriately worded severability of interests provision might provide the same result, many insureds would prefer to have a specific grant of coverage for this important exposure.

### Other Exclusions

Many other exclusions might be found in an accountants professional liability policy. Some of these exclusions can sometimes be deleted for an additional premium. The exclusions include, but are not limited to, the following:

- Punitive damages
- Liability assumed under a contract
- Incidents reported to a prior insurer
- Claim made by one insured against another insured
- Investment advice

### Limits and Deductible

An accountants professional liability policy usually has a per claim limit and an annual aggregate limit. The policy deductible ordinarily applies to each wrongful act. Thus, under a policy with this provision, if several claims were made because of one wrongful act, the deductible would apply only once to all payments for the related claims.

## Loss Control

Measures that public accountants can use to minimize the frequency and severity of their professional liability losses include the following:

- Engagement letters or similar documents that explain the rights and responsibilities of the parties should reflect any change in the relationship. For example, if the statement is being changed from an audited statement to an unaudited statement, the change should be documented. This documentation is important to a defense because of the varying standards that are applied to the rendering of different types of services.

- In most states, continuing education is now a mandatory precondition of periodic recertification for CPAs. It is also a good loss prevention measure that allows accountants to learn about developments in the accounting profession that may affect the standards to which they will be held.

- Accounting firms should develop in-house guidelines and standards, and their accountants should observe them. An in-house quality control manual may provide additional checks.

- Accountants should avoid positions that might involve a conflict of interest. They should not develop relationships with clients that could jeopardize the independence of the auditing function.
- Specialization can minimize or help to control professional liability exposures. Like physicians, accountants should not hesitate to consult with their peers or refer clients to specialists for matters beyond their competence.

# Architects and Engineers Professional Liability Insurance

Architects and engineers in private practice have exposures to professional liability claims from aggrieved clients and third parties. Architects and engineers frequently perform similar tasks, including designing and drafting plans for a wide variety of structures. They may also supervise the actual construction. Both are exposed to substantial liability in the course of their work. This section will treat architecture and engineering as one profession, since the law applies similarly to both and the same professional liability policies are used to insure both.

## Loss Exposure

Like the other professionals discussed in this chapter, architects and engineers are required to adhere to an applicable standard of care. Likewise, architects and engineers are subject to liability based on contracts, the common law of torts, and the violation of applicable statutes regulating construction and design.

Actions based on contracts are generally governed by the contract law of the state in which a contract is executed or performed. Contracts are thus extremely important and should be drafted with care.

To prevail in a tort action, a plaintiff is required to show that the architect or engineer owed him or her a duty, that the architect or engineer breached that duty by his or her conduct, and that as a result of the breach the plaintiff sustained injury, measurable in money damages, for which the plaintiff requests relief.

Failure to comply with applicable statutes regulating construction and design is another basis for architects and engineers professional liability. These statutes include local ordinances specifying such requirements as the number of fire doors and the level of reinforced concrete for any subsurface construction.

## Common Allegations Against Architects and Engineers

Common allegations against architects and engineers include practicing beyond the scope of the license, breach of contract, negligent preparation of plans or designs, negligently performed site surveys, negligent selection of materials or equipment, increased construction costs, negligent supervision of construction, conflict of interest, and negligent performance as an arbitrator.

### Practicing Beyond the Scope of the License

States require architects and engineers to register and to be licensed before entering practice. Practicing beyond the scope of a license—which would occur, for instance, if an engineer drafted architectural plans—not only violates a statute but could also be used as persuasive evidence against the engineer in a civil action for damages.

### Breach of Contract

The American Institute of Architects publishes a model contract that architects use widely to govern their relationships with clients. A breach of any of the conditions in the contract between an architect and his or her client may give rise to a claim for damages by the client. For example, if an architect contracts to supply drawings by a certain date and fails to do so, the architect may be liable to the client for any resulting increased costs. The architect may also be liable to suppliers and workers idled by the delay. Similarly, if an architect is hired to draft plans for a building not to exceed a certain cost of construction, the architect may be liable for overruns beyond the costs contemplated in the plans.

### Conflict of Interest

When an architect or engineer is hired, an agent-principal relationship is established. As an agent who owes a duty of loyalty to the principal, the architect or engineer cannot engage in activities counter to the interest of the client. For example, the architect or engineer should not have a financial interest in a contractor or supplier for a project unless this fact were disclosed to the client/project owner. An architect with such a conflict of interest would be liable to the principal for damages based, at least in part, on the architect's profit.

### Negligent Preparation of Plans or Designs

A significant exposure to liability comes from allegations that an architect or engineer was negligent in the preparation of plans or in the design of a particular structure. Although many courts have held that an architect's work, in the absence of a special agreement, does not imply or guarantee a perfect plan, architects are obligated to prepare plans and drawings that conform to the ordinary expertise and skill of architects. Some cases clearly show negligence, such as when a floor or roof collapses because the design did not provide for adequate structural support. Other cases inevitably involve highly subjective determinations.

In cases involving negligence of design, damages can be measured in two ways. First, if the defect in the building is minor, damages are usually measured by the cost of repairing the defect. Second, if the defect is major, damages are usually measured by the difference between the value of the building as it was built and the value it would have had if it had been built according to the correct plans and specifications.

### Negligently Performed Site Surveys

Claims made against architects and engineers also arise in connection with site surveys and profiles of soil conditions. These exposures are particularly troublesome because determining negligence is not always possible. The negligent party may be the project owner who supplied the information, the contractor who performed additional survey work, or the architect who modified the information provided. The architect or engineer can seldom escape liability because a contractor cannot construct a structure without a plan for which an architect or engineer is usually responsible.

### Negligent Selection of Materials or Equipment

Even if the architect does not warrant the quality of building materials to be used, the architect is still required to select the type of materials to be used. Most claims alleging negligent specification of materials or equipment are between professionals and their clients, but if a third party brings a claim against the project owner, the project owner may bring the architect or engineer into the litigation.

### Increased Construction Costs

Construction costs may be higher than the architect or engineer anticipated, and consequently the project owner may make a claim against the architect or engineer for one or more of the following reasons:

- The quantities shown on the plans and specifications were wrong, or the design was defective.
- The designated construction procedures cost the contractor too much money.
- The architect or engineer will not approve the work, the estimate, or the materials or equipment that the contractor has installed.

### Negligent Supervision of Construction

The architect's liability concerning the duty to supervise construction is separate and distinct from the liability of those engaged in the actual construction. The architect's obligation is not inherent in the architect-project owner relationship but is often established by contract. Originally, courts held that the duty to supervise was limited to ensuring that the construction conformed to the specifications and materials contemplated by the plans. More recently, some courts have held that the duty to supervise, once accepted, may include overseeing the construction techniques and procedures. This duty carries with it the responsibility to condemn unfit work. In jurisdictions with structural work laws, this exposure can be significantly increased.

### Liability to Other Parties

At one time, architects and engineers were responsible only to project owners. However, now third parties who are injured or who suffer property damage as a proximate result of an architect or engineer's negligence are potential plaintiffs.

### Negligent Performance as an Arbitrator

Architects are often required by a three-way contract to arbitrate differences between owners and contractors. Generally, claims against architects that arise from their performance as arbitrator can be defended successfully. Architect-arbitrators have a kind of limited immunity in their role as an intermediary.

## Defenses

The defenses ordinarily available in negligence cases are also available to architects. The statute of limitations defense may be used, even though the applicable statute may begin to run only upon discovery of a defect by the project owner. Acquiescence in acceptance of faulty plans may provide a contract defense, as will contributory or comparative negligence and assumption of risk in a tort case. In addition, the architect or engineer may respond to a plaintiff's allegations by asserting the following:

- No duty was owed to the plaintiff.
- No breach of duty to the plaintiff occurred.
- There is no causal connection between the architect or engineer's acts and the plaintiff's injury.

## Policy Provisions

There is no standard form for providing **architects and engineers professional liability insurance** (also known as design professional liability insurance).

Insurers offering the coverage draft their own policies, develop their own rates, and make their own underwriting rules. Nonetheless, the coverage provisions of the different policies tend to be similar.

## *Insuring Agreement*

The insurer generally agrees to pay on behalf of the insured all sums that the insured becomes legally obligated to pay as damages because of liability arising out of the insured's rendering or failing to render professional services as an architect or engineer. In some policies, the term "professional services" is defined to include only specifically described professional services. The insured's agent or broker should ascertain that any definition or description of professional services in the policy is broad enough to meet the insured's particular needs.

In many cases, the policy also specifically covers the insured for professional acts, errors, or omissions of the insured's subcontractors. Because an architect or engineer can be held liable for professional errors or omissions of its subcontractors, this extension of coverage can be very important to the insured. Typically, the extension does not protect the subcontractor unless the subcontractor has been named as an additional insured. Thus, the insurer may have the right to subrogate against the subcontractor after paying a claim on behalf of the insured because of the subcontractor's negligence.

Architects and engineers professional liability policies almost always provide for defense, settlement, and supplementary payments in much the same way as general liability policies do. However, in many architects and engineers policies, defense costs are payable within the limits of liability. Thus, the insured needs to take probable defense costs into consideration when requesting policy limits from the insurer.

Virtually all architects and engineers policies are written on a claims-made basis, subject to variations along the lines of those described earlier in this chapter.

## *Who Is Insured*

The named insured of an architects or engineers professional liability policy can be either an individual professional or an architectural or engineering firm. The policy typically covers, in addition to the named insured, the named insured's principals, partners, directors, officers, stockholders, and employees *while acting in their capacities as such*. The named insured's policy would not, for example, cover an architect employed by the named insured with regard to "moonlighting" work the employee performed as an independent contractor.

The policy, in addition to covering present principals, partners, employees, and so on, often covers individuals who *formerly* occupied those positions. When that is the case, those individuals are covered only with respect to claims for professional services performed on behalf of the named insured *before* the employment (or other) relationship was terminated.

Architectural and engineering firms often enter into joint ventures to accomplish particular projects. Insurers are generally not willing to insure undeclared joint ventures that the insured might enter into, because the insurer will not have had the opportunity to underwrite the other members of the joint venture. Accordingly, architects and engineers professional liability policies typically exclude professional services performed by the insured as part of a joint venture unless that joint venture is named in the policy.

## Exclusions

Architects and engineers professional liability policies usually contain numerous exclusions. Some of these exclusions are of the sort found in other types of professional liability policies, such as exclusions of claims for discrimination, punitive damages, or dishonest or criminal acts. Other exclusions are designed to eliminate overlaps with other policies, such as the insured's CGL and umbrella liability policies. Still other exclusions are aimed at exposures more directly related to the hazards peculiar to architects and engineers.

Unlike some professional liability policies, such as those for accountants and attorneys, architects and engineers professional liability policies do not contain a flat exclusion of claims for bodily injury and property damage. Such an exclusion would be inappropriate because, in many cases, an architect's or engineer's professional negligence results in building defects that can damage property or injure people. Nevertheless, architects and engineers professional liability policies typically contain other, more specific exclusions to clearly eliminate coverage for liability exposures that are routinely covered under other commercial liability policies. Representative exclusions of this type eliminate coverage for the following:

- Employers liability and workers compensation obligations.
- The design of goods sold by the insured. (This exposure is covered by products liability coverage under the CGL policy.)
- The discharge or release of pollutants.
- The ownership, maintenance, or use of automobiles, aircraft, or watercraft.
- Projects for which any construction is performed wholly or partially by the insured, a subsidiary of the insured, or a subcontractor of the insured. (Bodily injury or property damage resulting from negligent construction is covered, to some extent, by the CGL coverage form.)

Other exclusions eliminate coverage for acts or omissions related specifically to the architects and engineers professional liability exposure. Common examples of such excluded acts or omissions are as follows:

- Failure to complete drawings, specifications, or other instruments of service on time
- Express warranties or guarantees made by the insured
- Advising, requiring, or maintaining of any type of insurance or bond, or failure to do so
- Providing of or revising cost estimates, or failure to do so

### Other Provisions

Architects and engineers professional liability policies are ordinarily subject to a per claim limit and an annual aggregate limit. The policy deductible normally applies to each claim.

The coverage territory provision should always be broad enough to encompass the locations of all possible projects in which the insured might be involved during the policy year. If a policy form does not contain a worldwide coverage territory, the policy can usually be modified by endorsement to provide the needed coverage territory.

## Loss Control

Important measures that can be used to control the professional liability losses of architects and engineers can be categorized as (1) management and personnel support, (2) record keeping, (3) quality control, and (4) performance responsibilities.

### Management and Personnel Support

No loss control program can succeed unless both management and the operating personnel support it. Design firms therefore need to establish a written policy on the objectives of their loss control program. Many firms have a formal statement that assigns responsibility for each risk management task, including maintaining safety, providing security, training employees, purchasing insurance, and establishing retention levels.

### Record Keeping

Good records can help an architectural or engineering firm to (1) identify the program's costs and benefits, (2) determine the sources of loss and their underlying causes, (3) determine retention levels, and (4) defend against professional liability claims or suits.

## Quality Control

Procedures must be established that will help to reduce or prevent the chance that plans, specifications, and surveys will be negligently prepared or performed. Quality control techniques can help to fulfill that objective. For example, experienced senior members of the firm should check the work of junior staff members. To a degree, quality control is required by various government regulations and laws, such as the Occupational Safety and Health Act, which requires compliance to standards concerning the safety of operations and materials.

## Performance Responsibilities

Architects and engineers should explain the performance responsibilities of design professionals to their clients. In addition, architects and engineers should not accept oral changes to orders. Reasonable performance schedules should be established. Ambiguous contract language should be avoided. Written reports should be prepared for clients as work progresses. Architects and engineers should require completion statements from clients upon completion of the work. A contract provision should stipulate that the firm will not be responsible for delays or default in the performance of design services that are beyond the firm's control.

## Noninsurance Transfers

Historically, architects and engineers have used hold harmless and indemnity agreements to transfer their liabilities to other parties. Architects and engineers once required others, particularly contractors, to assume all liability arising from operations, including losses caused by the architects and engineers themselves and other losses over which the contractors had no control. Many states have enacted statutes that hold such broad agreements to be unenforceable.

The American Institute of Architects has since developed standard loss-transfer provisions, such as indemnification agreements, that are not as stringent as they once were. These contract provisions transfer the potential contingent liability of architects and project owners to those whose negligence results in a claim or suit. For example, the agreement could require a contractor to indemnify and hold harmless the owner and architect from all claims, losses, and expenses that arise out of the performance of work and that are caused in part or in whole by the contractor's negligence. A firm that contractually transfers the financial consequences of its liability may also want to require various types and amounts of insurance and certificates or other evidence that acceptable insurance is being maintained.

## Summary

Professional liability can be loosely defined as liability for the failure to use the degree of skill expected of a person in a particular field. Once confined to a few occupations, professional liability insurance now encompasses many.

When an insurer issues a commercial general liability (CGL) policy to any of a long list of professional persons or firms, the insurer normally adds an exclusion eliminating coverage for liability arising out of the insured's rendering of professional services. Thus, the insured usually purchases a separate professional liability insurance policy to cover such professional services. For example, a CGL policy covering a doctor's office will cover routine premises liability claims but will not cover claims arising out of the doctor's professional medical services (such as injury resulting from the doctor's failure to diagnose a serious illness).

To illustrate the vast professional liability insurance field, this chapter focused on the following representative professions: physicians, accountants, and architects and engineers. The discussion of each encompassed (1) the legal basis for professional liability claims against each type of professional, (2) the provisions commonly encountered in policies used to insure those professionals, and (3) measures commonly used to control each type of professional liability.

## Chapter Notes

1. "Professional Liability and Claims Made Coverage" (St. Paul, MN: St. Paul Fire and Marine Ins. Co., Rev. 6-94), p. 1.
2. For further reading on the liability exposures and insurance treatment of these and other professions, see Robert A. Bregman and Jack P. Gibson, *Professional Liability Insurance* (Dallas, TX: International Risk Management Institute, updated periodically).
3. "Prudential Sues Law Firms," *Journal of Commerce*, October 2, 1989, p. 8-B.
4. S. Levy, *Accountants' Legal Responsibility* (New York, NY: American Institute of Accountants, 1954), p. 9.
5. The scope and depth of these audit activities vary by engagement. One engagement may require only an examination of financial statements, but another may demand a detailed and comprehensive audit. The nature of the business and industry involved, the state of the economy and technology, time constraints, and the size of the accounting firm can also influence the scope of the accountant's engagement.
6. See *Statement of Financial Accounting Standards*, Nos. 35 and 36.

# Chapter 11

# Professional Liability Insurance, Continued

The preceding chapter described the types of professional liability insurance designed for physicians, accountants, architects, and others who provide professional services. This chapter examines additional types of professional liability insurance (as defined broadly in the preceding chapter) responding to liability exposures that many types of businesses face, including businesses that do not provide professional services to others. The main types of insurance covered in this chapter are as follows:

- **Directors and officers liability insurance**, which (1) protects the directors and officers of a corporation against liability allegations arising out of their "wrongful acts" and (2) reimburses the corporation when it is legally required or permitted to indemnify its directors and officers for their wrongful acts (in other words, replacing corporate treasury funds after the corporation has reimbursed its directors and officers).
- **Employee benefits liability insurance**, which protects the insured organization and certain employees against claims alleging administrative errors and omissions in connection with the organization's employee benefits plans.
- **Fiduciary liability insurance**, designed to cover the insured organization and certain employees against claims alleging breaches of their fiduciary duties in connection with the organization's employee benefit plans. In addition, fiduciary liability policies often include coverage for the same errors or omissions covered under employee benefits liability policies.

- **Employment practices liability insurance**, which covers the insured organization, its directors and officers, and, often, all employees for liability arising out of various employment-related offenses alleged to have been committed against its employees, such as wrongful termination, discrimination, and sexual harassment.

There are no standard forms for any of the coverages listed above. Each insurer develops its own form. Thus, this chapter describes the coverages in a general manner after reviewing the liability exposures to which the insurance responds.

# Directors and Officers Liability Insurance

The directors and officers of a corporation are insured persons with respect to their duties as such under most of the liability policies that a corporation ordinarily carries, such as the commercial general liability policy and the business auto policy. Those policies, however, only protect the directors and officers of the named insured against covered claims for bodily injury, property damage, personal injury, and advertising injury as those terms are commonly defined in liability insurance policies.

The directors and officers of a corporation can also be held personally liable for a wide range of wrongful acts or omissions that cause other persons or organizations to suffer harm that does not qualify as bodily injury, property damage, personal injury, or advertising injury. For example, the shareholders of a corporation might suffer financial harm because one or more directors have made bad investments with corporate funds. Directors and officers (D&O) liability insurance can be obtained to protect the directors and officers against claims or suits alleging such acts or omissions. Thus, D&O liability insurance could be viewed as "managerial professional liability" insurance, designed primarily as personal liability coverage for the directors and officers of the corporation.

## Loss Exposure

Organizations can take various forms, some of the most common being sole proprietorships, partnerships, joint ventures, and corporations. Each type of entity has a distinctive organizational structure with liability exposure implications. For example, a sole proprietor retains profits and responsibility for legal liabilities. Partners usually share duties, profits, losses, and liabilities.

Corporations are owned by stockholders and operated by boards of directors. The board of directors appoints personnel to oversee daily operations. Power to conduct business affairs, such as the purchase of insurance or the institution of risk control procedures, is delegated to the management team. Stockholders share profits in direct proportion to their stock ownership. Their liability for injuries arising out of the corporation's activities is generally limited to the value of their shares of stock in the corporation.

The management of a corporation includes the board of directors, executive officers, and higher-ranking employees. The board of directors may include stockholders as well as outside business or social leaders who have no financial interest in the corporation. These individuals bring a variety of backgrounds, political viewpoints, and skills to guide the corporation's activities. A very basic aspect of D&O loss prevention and control involves choosing diverse and highly qualified individuals to function in management capacities.

## Major Responsibilities and Duties

In general, directors and officers must manage the business in compliance with the law and the corporate structure. Some major responsibilities of corporate directors include the following:

1. To establish the basic objectives and broad policies of the corporation
2. To elect or appoint the corporate officers, advise them, approve their actions, and audit their performance
3. To safeguard and approve changes in the corporation's assets
4. To approve important financial matters and see that proper annual and interim reports are given to stockholders
5. To delegate special powers to others to sign contracts, open bank accounts, sign checks, issue stock, make loans, and conduct any activities that may require board approval
6. To maintain, revise, and enforce the corporate charter and by-laws
7. To perpetuate a competent board through regular elections and the filling of interim vacancies with highly qualified persons

In addition to performing these functions, directors and officers occupy a position of trust for shareholders, the board of directors, and the general public. Thus, directors and officers are said to have "fiduciary duties"; that is, they have legal obligations to others by virtue of the positions they hold. (This terminology should not be confused with the concept of "fiduciary liability" exposures and insurance coverage, which will be discussed later in this chapter.) These duties include, but are not limited to, those described below. When directors and officers fail to observe the appropriate degree of care in performing these duties, they can be held liable for resulting damages.

### Duty of Care

Directors and officers have the general duty to exercise reasonable care in the performance of their corporate functions. "Reasonable care," in this case, is the degree of care that a prudent director or officer would ordinarily exercise in similar circumstances.

In applying the concept of the general duty to exercise reasonable care, courts have held that directors and officers are not guarantors of the profitability of the enterprise. Nor are directors required to have special business skills. Nevertheless, according to the so-called "business judgment rule," the decisions of both directors and officers must be within the range of disagreement normally to be expected among prudent directors and officers.

Directors and officers also have a duty to keep themselves informed of the facts and other matters required to make prudent decisions of the type each must make. At a minimum, directors have a duty to attend board meetings and meetings of the committees on which they serve. (Many larger, for-profit corporations pay their directors to attend board and committee meetings.)

### Duty of Loyalty to the Corporation

Directors and officers have the general duty of undivided loyalty to the corporation they serve. Accordingly, a director or an officer cannot secretly seize for himself or herself a business opportunity that properly belongs to the corporation. For the same reason, a director or an officer cannot own or operate a business that competes with the corporation.

### Duty of Loyalty to the Stockholders

Since directors (and sometimes officers) obtain their positions by the vote or consent of the stockholders, they also owe a duty of loyalty to the stockholders. Under the common law and the Securities and Exchange Act of 1934, no person—including a director or an officer—may use "insider information" to buy or sell stock of the corporation, whether the information was obtained directly or from others. Under that act, if a director or an officer or an owner of at least 10 percent of the outstanding stock makes a profit (within a six-month period) by dealing in shares of the corporation, the profit may be taken by the corporation—whether or not such a person actually had "insider information." If the person used material inside information that was not disclosed, the party who bought or sold the stock to the insider may also have an actionable cause for damages.

The duty of reasonable care and the business judgment rule are also applied to situations involving abuse of minority stockholders (stockholders having an insufficient number of shares to control the management of the corporation). Under certain circumstances, a minority stockholder may have a valid cause of action against the directors and officers of the corporation in which it holds a minority interest.

### Duty of Disclosure

Directors and officers have the general duty to disclose material facts to all persons who have a right to know such facts and would not otherwise be able to obtain them. Examples include the following:

- The duty of officers to disclose facts that are material to directors
- The duty of officers to disclose facts material to various regulatory bodies
- The duty of directors to disclose facts material to creditors or potential creditors
- The duty of directors and officers to make public disclosures of facts that are material to stockholders, bondholders, and potential investors in the securities of the corporation

Many such disclosure requirements are contained in the Securities and Exchange Act of 1934 and in regulations of the Securities and Exchange Commission (the federal agency that administers the Securities and Exchange Act of 1934 and related statutes). Similar or identical requirements may also be found in court decisions and in state statutes and regulations.

### Duties Under ERISA

The **Employee Retirement Income Security Act of 1974 (ERISA)** is applicable to most employee benefits plans. It imposes federally legislated duties on all persons who may be deemed "fiduciaries" within a very broad definition of the concept. Generally, an officer or a director (or anyone else) who exercises discretionary control in the management of a benefit plan or its assets, or who gives investment advice, is a fiduciary with rather strictly prescribed duties and liabilities. These duties include, but are not limited to, the duty to act solely in the interest of plan participants, the duty to exercise the care and skill that a prudent person would exercise in like circumstances, and the duty to observe sound and safe investment practices.

Any fiduciary who breaches such a duty may be held personally liable for any resulting loss to the plan. The violator may also be subject to other penalties stipulated in ERISA. (Although D&O liability insurance typically excludes liabilities evolving from ERISA, directors and officers can cover their fiduciary exposures under fiduciary liability insurance, which will be discussed later in this chapter.)

## Derivative and Nonderivative Suits

Corporate directors and officers can be held personally liable if they breach their corporate duties. The legal actions taken against corporate directors or officers as remedies for their breaches of duty are generally classified as either (1) derivative suits or (2) nonderivative suits.

### Derivative Suits

A **derivative suit** is a suit brought by one or more stockholders on behalf of the corporation. Any damages recovered in a derivative suit go directly to the corporation, not to the plaintiff-stockholder(s). However, successful plaintiffs are often awarded the expenses incurred in bringing the suit, including a reasonable amount for attorney fees.

To be successful in a negligence action against directors and officers, the plaintiff-stockholders normally must establish that the defendants' conduct was outside the permissible boundaries of sound management practice, including the **business judgment rule** mentioned earlier. Essentially, this rule prevails in the absence of fraud, breach of trust, or the commission of an *ultra vires* act. (*Ultra vires* means beyond the scope of the powers of the corporation, as defined by its charter or act of incorporation.) The business judgment rule dictates that the conduct of directors is not negligence when the alleged acts or omissions were discretionary, performed in good faith, and within the boundaries of prudent business conduct.

### Nonderivative Suits

**Nonderivative suits** against corporate officers and directors may be initiated by competitors, creditors, governmental units, or other persons outside the corporation. The outside party must show that an injury or injustice resulted from tortious acts or omissions of directors and/or officers. Examples are claims for violations of legislative statutes; failure to fulfill legal duties; and intentional, unfair, or harmful conduct.

Stockholders who suffer harm may also bring nonderivative suits.[1] These claims name specific directors or officers and the corporate entity as codefendants. If the stockholder wins the case, other stockholders may bring derivative suits to recover judgments from the directors or officers individually.

According to information gathered by Watson Wyatt & Company between 1993-1995, approximately 45 percent of claims made against corporate directors and officers were made by the corporation's own shareholders; 25 percent by employees; 20 percent by clients and consumer groups, and the remaining 10 percent by competitors, government entities, or other third parties.

The most frequent allegations in shareholder claims were inadequate or inaccurate disclosure, merger/divestiture/acquisition and related activities, and breach of fiduciary duties. The most frequent allegations in employee-related claims were wrongful termination and discrimination (both of which are more likely to be covered under an employment practices liability policy rather than a D&O policy). The most frequent allegations in client and consumer group claims were dishonesty and fraud, and the most frequent allegations in competitor claims were contract disputes, business interference, and deceptive trade practices.[2]

## Indemnification of Directors and Officers

There has been considerable debate over a director's or an officer's right to be indemnified by the corporation for costs incurred by the director or officer in a suit against the director or officer. At common law, a corporate director or officer who had been *unsuccessful* in defending against a derivative suit had no right to indemnification from the corporation. It was reasoned that a wrongdoing insider cannot justifiably be reimbursed by the same party that his or her misconduct had harmed. Although this rationale would seem inappropriate when the insider was *successful* in defending against a derivative suit, early cases denied indemnification in such situations, because the expenditure of corporate funds would not produce a benefit to the corporation and would thus be *ultra vires*.

As a result of the confusion surrounding the right to corporate indemnification—especially in the context of a stockholders' derivative suit—the legislative bodies of various states have enacted statutes granting the right to indemnification in certain situations. Some of the statutes permit indemnification, others require it, and still others make court approval or a court order a necessary prerequisite. Some of the indemnification statutes are "exclusive" in that they authorize indemnification only to the extent provided by the statute. Other statutes declare that statutory indemnification will not be considered exclusive of any of the rights to which the director or officer may be entitled under any bylaw, agreement, vote of stockholders or disinterested directors, or otherwise.

In most states, as a prerequisite to indemnification, the corporation must have adopted some form of contractual provision that sets guidelines for reimbursement, since the statutes are merely permissive. This provision—whether incorporated in the bylaws, a corporate resolution, or other written agreement, such as an employment contract—can obligate the corporation to indemnify the corporate official as long as the standard of conduct that must be followed is in harmony with the statute. Some states offer more liberal statutory indemnification than others. This helps to explain why a company's corporate office may be far removed from its state of charter.

The basic difference among corporate indemnification agreements is the standard of conduct that must be maintained by the director or officer in order to obtain indemnification. Some agreements deny indemnification to the director or officer who has been adjudged liable for negligence or misconduct, while others deny indemnification only when the director's or officer's action constitutes gross negligence or willful misconduct.

## Policy Provisions

To protect its directors and officers against D&O liability suits and to finance its own indemnification agreements with its directors and officers, a corporation typically buys a D&O liability policy. Because there is no standard form of D&O policy, the discussion that follows is general in nature. However, specific policy provisions are quoted in some cases to provide examples of provisions that might appear in a D&O liability policy. Another important general characteristic of D&O liability insurance is that it is very rapidly evolving. Some areas of exposure that were excluded just a few years ago may now be covered for an additional premium, or they may even be covered for no additional premium.

### Insuring Agreements

D&O liability policies ordinarily contain two inseparable insuring agreements, frequently designated Coverage A and Coverage B.

- Coverage A insures the individual directors and officers. This coverage might be captioned "**Individual Coverage**," "Direct Coverage," or simply "Directors and Officers Coverage."

- Coverage B insures the corporation for the amounts that it is lawfully permitted or required to pay to defend or settle claims against the directors or officers. Coverage B is commonly captioned "**Corporate Reimbursement Coverage**" or "Indemnification Coverage."

In order to prevent these two coverages from overlapping, Coverage A typically states that it covers losses only for which the corporation has not provided indemnification to the directors or officers. Thus, if a director is held liable for a loss caused by a covered wrongful act and the corporation is lawfully able to indemnify the director, the loss will be paid under Coverage B. If, for any reason, the corporation could not indemnify the director, the director's loss would be payable to the director under Coverage A.

Most D&O liability policies sold to for-profit organizations do not cover the corporation for claims made against the corporation itself. (However, this is a rapidly evolving issue with coverage becoming more widely available for the corporation.) As explained above, Coverage A covers the corporation's directors and officers as individuals, and Coverage B reimburses the corporation for payments it makes to indemnify its directors and officers. Coverage for suits against the corporation (called "entity coverage") will be discussed in more detail in a later section of this chapter dealing with allocation of claims.

### "Loss"

D&O liability policies typically agree to pay the individual directors and officers for the amount of "loss" they sustain because of claim (Coverage A) or to reimburse the corporation for the amount of "loss" for which the corporation has indemnified the directors and officers (Coverage B). When analyzing a D&O liability policy, one should carefully review the definition of "loss," because it usually *excludes* certain types of damages.

The term "loss" is typically defined to include all damages that the directors and officers become legally obligated to pay, as well as defense costs. However, the definition typically excludes certain items such as taxes, criminal or civil fines or penalties imposed by law, punitive or exemplary damages, or the multiplied portion of any damages (such as treble damages awarded under the Sherman Antitrust Act or Racketeer Influenced and Corrupt Organizations [RICO] laws).

Because D&O policies normally define "loss" to *include* defense costs, the "each loss" limit of liability (as well as the annual aggregate limit) in the policy applies to both damages and defense costs combined, in contrast with the CGL policy and other liability policies that cover defense costs in addition to the limits of liability. Since defense expense is included within the policy limit of most D&O policies, this aspect can motivate insureds to purchase higher limits of D&O insurance.

### "Wrongful Act"

Typically, the insuring agreements of D&O policies are worded so that the claim against the individual director or officer must be for a "wrongful act." This term is defined in different ways that can have a strong effect on coverage.

In one sense, "wrongful act" is defined broadly, because it ordinarily includes a wide range of acts or omissions, such as "any error, misstatement, misleading statement, act, omission, neglect, or breach of duty committed, attempted, or allegedly committed or attempted, by an Insured Person. . . ." However, the definition is typically restricted to such acts or omissions *in the insured's capacity as a director or officer for the corporation.* This restriction might cause coverage problems for some directors or officers who perform additional duties (such as serving as general counsel) for the corporation besides their duties as directors or officers, or for service on outside, related boards.

The definition of "wrongful act" sometimes includes a provision stating that all claims arising out of the same wrongful act or any related wrongful acts will be treated as a single claim. That is, all such claims will be subject to the limit of insurance, and the limit will not apply separately to each claim. In some policies, this provision is contained in some provision other than the definition of "wrongful act."

### Claims-Made Trigger

The Coverage A and B insuring agreements typically contain provisions requiring that, in order to be covered, a claim for a wrongful act must be first made against the insured during the policy period or during an extended reporting period (if applicable). The insured's options for extended reporting periods can vary considerably from policy to policy. Generally, extended reporting periods for D&O policies are likely to run for up to one year after policy expiration, in contrast with the longer extended reporting periods available under the ISO claims-made commercial general liability policy. Some D&O policies provide a brief extended reporting period (such as sixty or ninety days), an extension of which can often be negotiated for no additional premium.

Some D&O policies require that the wrongful act for which the insured is seeking coverage must have occurred after the beginning of the policy period or after a retroactive date indicated in the policy. However, many D&O policies do not contain either of those requirements. Instead, such policies cover claims made during the policy period for wrongful acts that occurred either during the policy period at any time before the policy period, subject to a warranty made in the application for insurance that none of the directors or officers knew of any circumstances likely to give rise to a claim. The coverage for wrongful acts that occurred before policy inception is often called **prior acts coverage**.

Many D&O policies contain a discovery provision stating that if the insured becomes aware of a wrongful act that is reasonably expected to result in a covered claim, the insured may provide written information on the wrongful act to the insurer. If the insurer receives the required information before the policy terminates, and before the permitted discovery period expires, then any subsequent claim for the wrongful act will be considered to have been made during the policy period.

### Persons Insured

The persons insured for Coverage A of a D&O policy are the directors and officers of the corporation. Usually, this coverage grant extends not only to those who currently are serving as directors and officers but also to past and future directors and officers. In addition, most D&O policies cover the estate, heirs, legal representatives, or assigns of any past, present, or future director or officer.

The entities insured for Coverage B (with respect to coverage for reimbursement in accordance with corporate bylaws) are the company or companies named in the declarations. Depending on the policy, coverage may be automatically extended to unnamed subsidiaries of the named company. When mergers or acquisitions occur, the insured company should always check the policy to ascertain whether the insurer needs to be notified in order to extend coverage to the acquired entities. As discussed earlier, the named corporation is covered only for payments the corporation makes to indemnify its directors or officers; it does not cover the corporation for liability claims made against the corporation.

### Defense Coverage

Defense costs are a significant element of D&O claims. According to the 1995 Watson Wyatt D&O liability survey, average defense and legal costs were $1.4 million for each D&O claim paid in the approximately nine-year period of 1986 through early 1995.[3]

As mentioned above, many D&O policies include the reasonable cost of defense in the definition of "loss," and so defense costs are covered (subject to the deductible and the limits of liability). However, unlike many other types of commercial liability policies in which the insurer assumes the duty to defend against claims, most D&O policies state that the insured, and not the insurer, has the duty to defend. In addition, D&O policies often require the insured to obtain the insurer's consent before incurring any claim expenses. Thus, the insurer must approve the insured's choice of defense counsel, as well as proposed settlements, despite the insured's obligation to initiate these actions.

Some policies state that the insurer will make advance payments of defense costs or will forward payments to the insured as defense expenses arise; other policies state that the insurer has no obligation to pay defense costs until final disposition of the claim; and still other policies are silent on this matter. Because legal costs can be very high in a directors and officers liability claim, the matter of *when* the insurer will make payment is extremely important to many insureds. Any prospective D&O liability policy should therefore be carefully analyzed to determine that the insurer's obligation to pay defense costs is consistent with the insured's ability to bear such costs until the insurer is obligated to pay them.

## Exclusions

The exclusions can vary considerably from one D&O policy to another, and thus the exclusions of any prospective D&O policy should be carefully reviewed.

### Other Insurance

Many exclusions in D&O liability policies are aimed at eliminating coverage for exposures that can be insured under other insurance policies. Thus, D&O policies commonly exclude claims for bodily injury, property damage, personal injury, advertising injury, pollution, employment practices, fiduciary liability under ERISA and similar laws, and claims covered or reported under prior policies.

### Difficult-To-Insure Exposures

Another category of D&O policy exclusions eliminates coverage for wrongful acts that are considered to be difficult to insure or uninsurable. Common examples of such exclusions are as follows:

- Fraudulent acts of directors and officers
- Acts resulting in personal profit or advantage to which a director or officer is not legally entitled
- Violations of the Securities Act of 1933, the Securities Exchange Act of 1934, and amendments thereto, or any similar state or federal statutes or regulations

The securities laws referenced above prohibit certain practices involving insider trading of corporate securities and "short swing" profits made on the purchase and sale of corporate securities within a period of less than six months.

### Insured Versus Insured

D&O policies also typically exclude claims brought by or on behalf of any other insured, such as one director's suit against another. However, the exclusion is often subject to exceptions that allow coverage for claims such as the following:

- A derivative action brought on behalf of the insured corporation by one or more persons who are not insured directors or officers

- A claim brought by an insured director or officer for wrongful termination of the director or officer
- An action in which an insured director or officer seeks indemnity or contribution from another director or officer for a claim covered under the policy

### Maintenance of Insurance

Another exclusion sometimes found in D&O policies eliminates coverage for liability resulting from the failure to effect or maintain adequate insurance for the corporation. If, for example, the directors negligently decide that the corporation should retain (and not insure) its products liability losses, and unusually high products liability losses cause the corporation to experience severe financial problems, the D&O policy would not protect the directors against a shareholder suit alleging that they negligently failed to authorize the purchase of products liability insurance. Insurers will often delete this exclusion after examining the corporation's insurance program, and in recent years, this exclusion has begun to disappear from D&O policies.

### Outside Directorships

D&O policies typically exclude liability arising out of the insured directors' or officers' performance of duties for organizations that are not affiliated with the insured corporation. (The same effect can also be accomplished through policy provisions other than exclusions.)

Sometimes a corporation will encourage its directors or officers to take on "outside directorships" for an unaffiliated organization. In such cases, the sponsoring corporation may want to provide D&O coverage for its directors while serving the unaffiliated organization, which may either have no D&O coverage or have D&O coverage with limits that are deemed insufficient.

Two approaches to covering outside directorships are available. One approach is to add an endorsement to the sponsoring corporation's D&O policy that eliminates the applicable exclusion in return for an additional premium. The other approach is to obtain a separate policy, called an **outside directors liability policy**. The advantage of the second approach is that claims payable under that separate policy will not reduce the aggregate limit of liability under the sponsoring corporation's regular D&O policy, as would be the case with the endorsement approach. In either case, the coverage for outside directors is usually excess over other insurance.

Often, D&O insurers will provide coverage for outside, nonprofit directorships at no additional premium charge, but there are usually restrictions to this extension. The outside service must be with the knowledge and/or direction of the sponsoring organization, and such an extension is almost always excess coverage over (1) any D&O coverage available to the outside entity or (2) any indemnification available from the outside entity itself.

### Severability of Interests

Most D&O policies contain a severability clause stating that a wrongful act of any director or officer will not be imputed to any other director or officer for the purpose of determining the applicability of the exclusions. This provision ensures that if all of the directors are sued jointly for an excluded wrongful act committed by one director, the exclusion will apply only to the one director who committed the wrongful act. Some D&O policies provide full severability (extending the severability provision to all exclusions), and other D&O policies provide only limited severability (extending the provision to only specified exclusions).

## Limits of Liability

A D&O liability policy is ordinarily subject to an *each loss* limit of liability and an *aggregate* limit of liability. The each loss limit is the most that the insurer will pay for any one loss under Coverage A or Coverage B or both. The aggregate limit is the most the insurer will pay for all claims first made during the policy period or the extended reporting period (if applicable). The policy usually contains a statement to the effect that all loss arising out of the same wrongful act and any related wrongful acts of an insured director or officer will be deemed to be one loss—and thus payable only for the each loss limit.

## Deductibles

D&O policies ordinarily have significant deductibles. The deductibles can be structured in various ways. The policy deductible might apply only to corporate reimbursement claims. Alternatively, different and separate deductible amounts might apply to Coverage A and Coverage B.

When a deductible applies to Coverage A (individual directors and officers), the deductible may apply separately to each individual against whom claim is made. When that is the case, an aggregate deductible typically applies as well. An example of this option is a $10,000 deductible for each involved director or officer, up to an aggregate deductible of $50,000 for the total loss, regardless of how many directors or officers might be involved.

As discussed earlier, D&O policies typically define "loss" to include defense costs. Thus, D&O policy deductibles ordinarily apply to both defense costs and damages payable because of judgments or settlements.

Originally, D&O policies commonly included a "coinsurance" or participation provision that obligated the insurer to pay only a percentage (typically 95 percent) of loss above the deductible and up to the applicable limit of liability. The insured was required to bear its percentage of loss without the benefit of other insurance. In recent years, participation provisions have virtually disappeared from D&O liability policies.

## Allocation

As discussed earlier, D&O liability insurance ordinarily covers the insured *corporation* only for Coverage B (corporate reimbursement). Historically, the corporation has not been covered against third-party claims made directly against the corporation. Consequently, when a claim is made against the directors or officers *and* the corporation jointly, the part of the claim pertaining to the directors and officers may be covered under the D&O liability policy, whereas the part of the claim pertaining to the corporation will not. Depending on the circumstances of the case, courts have allowed D&O insurers to allocate a certain percentage of defense costs and any resulting settlement or judgment to the corporation. The amount so allocated is payable by the corporation rather than by the insurer and has historically been uninsured, due to the lack of liability coverage for the corporation.

In allocating defense costs, many courts have followed a "reasonably related" test, which holds that as long as defense costs are reasonably related to the defense of a covered claim, they may be entirely allocated to that covered claim, even though the defense might have responded to some allegations that were not covered by the policy. In allocating settlements and judgments, courts have developed various rules that are still evolving.[4] Consequently, it is difficult for corporations to know how D&O liability losses might be allocated between the covered claim and the corporation.

To eliminate uncertainty as to how a claim might be allocated, D&O policies increasingly contain provisions that address the problem of allocations between the insurer and the insured corporation. Different types of provisions used for this purpose are summarized below.[5]

### "Best Efforts" Allocation

The first type of allocation provision to be used simply states that the insured and the insurer will use their best efforts to reach an acceptable allocation between covered loss and uncovered amounts.

### Arbitration/Alternative Dispute Resolution Allocation

The provision calls for arbitration or other alternative dispute resolution mechanisms to resolve allocation disputes. Until arbitration is concluded, the insurer is obligated to advance defense costs under an allocation that the insurer believes is appropriate. After the allocation has been determined through arbitration or other means, that allocation will be applied retroactively.

### Predetermined Allocation

Under this approach, the insurer and the insured corporation agree on a predetermined allocation, such as 80 percent to the insurer and 20 percent to the corporation. Initially, this approach was limited to allocation of defense expenses. More recently, it has been applied to both defense expenses and all other loss resulting from securities claims. A securities claim is a claim alleging violation of securities laws (as discussed earlier) in connection with the purchase or sale of, or an offer to purchase or sell, securities issued by the insured corporation. The insurer generally, but not always, requires an additional premium for predetermination of allocation.

### Entity Coverage

Another approach—called **entity coverage**—being used by some insurers to address the allocation problem is the inclusion of provisions that make the corporation (the "entity") an insured with regard to claims made against the corporation. Initially, entity coverage was restricted to securities claims and subject to a predetermined allocation. More recently, some insurers have broadened entity coverage to cover claims in addition to securities claims, generally subject to a percentage participation by the corporation. Entity coverage is rapidly evolving and is expected to undergo significant change over the next few years.

## Loss Control

Corporations can prevent or reduce wrongful acts by obtaining and following the advice of competent legal and accounting advisors. Full disclosures to the board of directors' and officers' personal finances are a must. Strict voluntary adherence to a meaningful code of ethics will reduce loss probability. Open, clear, and concise communication among directors and officers is an important factor in reducing losses. Clear understanding relevant laws, including securities laws and antitrust acts, and knowledge of the corporation's charter and bylaws, by all directors and officers, can also reduce the likelihood of loss.

## Additional Types of D&O Insurance

The foregoing discussion has concentrated on D&O liability insurance of for-profit corporations. Specially designed versions of the D&O policy are also available for directors (or trustees) and officers of nonprofit organizations, for directors and officers of condominium and homeowners associations, for school boards, and for public officials. In all cases, the basic purpose of the policy is the same: to cover a variety of wrongful acts that would not be covered under the organization's other liability policies. However, nonprofit organizations can usually find broader coverage, lower deductibles, and lower premiums for D&O liability insurance than for-profit organizations.

# Employee Benefits and Fiduciary Liability Insurance

Most employers provide some noncash employee benefits (such as retirement plans and medical insurance) as part of the total compensation of their full-time employees. Providing employee benefits exposes the employer to liability under the common law and under state and federal statutes. Two types of insurance—employee benefits liability insurance and fiduciary liability insurance—are available for covering those liabilities. The sections that follow describe (1) the liabilities arising out of employee benefit plans and (2) insurance covering those liabilities.

## Loss Exposures

The liability exposures associated with employee benefit plans are faced by literally thousands of individuals and businesses, including the following:

- Almost all private employers
- Employees of commercial entities who are directly involved in employee benefit management, such as benefit managers, human resource directors, personnel managers, labor relations specialists, in-house legal advisors, tax specialists, and financial managers
- Various legal agents and subcontractors of employers, such as insurance agents, benefit consultants, outside legal advisors, public accountants, consulting actuaries, investment advisors, benefit plan administrators, trust officers, labor union leaders, insurers, and others who are involved in the design, installation, financing, and administration of specific employee benefit plans or overall employee benefit programs

Before this chapter examines the specific liability exposures that can arise out of employee benefit plans, it provides a necessary overview of the general nature and scope of employee benefits.

## Nature and Scope of Employee Benefits

Privately sponsored retirement and medical expense insurance plans are the most costly and perhaps best known employee benefits. The overall benefit programs of many employers also include the following:

- Group life insurance
- Group nonoccupational disability income insurance
- Group dental expense insurance
- Paid time off for vacation, national holidays, funerals, family leave, and military reserve duty
- Educational assistance plans
- Moving and travel expense allowances

Many employers provide additional employee benefits, including, but not limited to, stock ownership plans, personal financial counseling, child-care assistance, wellness programs, club memberships, alcohol and drug abuse assistance, and employer-owned or leased autos.

Some employee benefit plans are provided on a "noncontributory" basis under which (1) no employee contributions are required and (2) the costs of the plans are paid entirely by employer contributions and the investment earnings thereon. Other private benefit plans are provided on a "contributory" basis, especially the benefits available to family members of employees. Under a contributory financing arrangement, the employee may either reject the benefit or voluntarily elect to accept the benefit and authorize the necessary payroll deductions.

Employees always have some choices to make with regard to employee benefit plans. Under contributory plans, they must decide whether to participate in the plans and, if so, whether to cover their spouses and dependent children. Under both contributory and noncontributory plans, employees must make decisions concerning such matters as naming of beneficiaries and the selection of settlement options under life insurance plans, the selection of annuity options under retirement plans, and the selection of investment options under tax-deferred annuity plans.

The range of employee choices has expanded significantly, in recent years, for the employees of companies that have adopted so-called flexible benefit programs. The specific features of such programs vary from one program to another, but they all have one noteworthy thing in common: they increase the number of choices that must be made by eligible employees.

## Liability for Negligent Advice and Other Administrative Errors

Some of the decisions that employees must make about their benefit plans are inherently complex. Incorrect decisions can have enormous consequences for employees or their survivors. Understandably, employees who are faced with such decisions will turn to others for advice, and therein lies one important source of employee benefit liability exposures. Providing employees with incorrect information or negligently counseling them on employee benefits can be the basis of a liability action against the individual who gave the advice. Moreover, the employer of the individual providing negligent advice can be held vicariously liable.

### Landmark Employee Benefits Liability Case

The landmark case of Gediman v. Anheuser Busch* was one of the first to put employers on notice of their benefit-related duties to employees. In this case, an employer was held liable to an employee's estate for providing incorrect pension information.

For health reasons, Gediman took early retirement from Anheuser Busch in 1956. At that time, Gediman had a vested interest in Anheuser Busch's pension plan with a present value of $78,356. Gediman's written request was to take his pension benefits in cash or in the form of an annuity. An Anheuser Busch employee advised Gediman to defer his retirement benefits until 1958, two years later, so they would increase to $84,482. Gediman selected this option.

Gediman died in 1957. Anheuser Busch offered a $32,000 death benefit in place of the retirement funds. Gediman's executor refused the offer and sued for the $78,356 retirement benefits. The executor claimed Anheuser Busch was vicariously liable for the incorrect advice given to Gediman, which caused Gediman to lose his vested monies in the Anheuser Busch plan. Gediman's health problems were known by Anheuser Busch, and the advice to defer the retirement benefits was to Anheuser Busch's advantage, not Gediman's. The court ordered Anheuser Busch to pay Gediman's estate $78,358, plus interest from 1956.

*193 Fed. Supp. 72, 1961.

Counseling employees with respect to employee benefit programs is not the only source of employee benefit liability. An employer can be held liable for various negligent errors or omissions in administering employee benefits. For example, the employer might fail to enroll an employee in its group health insurance program, with the result that the employee has no health insurance for a serious illness. Or the employer might have calculated a retiree's pension benefits improperly, resulting in wrongful reduction of the retiree's retirement income.

Generally speaking, employee benefits liability (EBL) insurance protects an employer against claims alleging improper counseling or negligent errors or omissions in the administration of employee benefit plans. As discussed below, the maintenance of employee benefit plans also creates a liability exposure that arises out of the fiduciary duties of plan officials as defined under the Employee Retirement Income Security Act of 1974 (ERISA). The so-called fiduciary liability exposure is not covered under EBL insurance. Separate fiduciary liability policies are available to cover the fiduciary liability exposure. In many cases, fiduciary liability policies cover both the fiduciary liability exposure and the administrative exposures covered under EBL coverage. EBL and fiduciary liability insurance will be described in more detail later in this chapter. They are noted here only to show how they correspond to the different liability exposures arising out of employee benefit plans.

## Fiduciary Liability Under ERISA

ERISA, including related regulations and court cases interpreting ERISA, applies to almost everyone involved in the employee benefit plans of employers that are engaged in interstate commerce or otherwise subject to federal minimum wage law. Federal, state, and local governmental bodies are specifically exempted from ERISA. Religious organizations are exempt from some of the provisions of the law. Despite the word "retirement" in the official title of the act, many important provisions of ERISA apply to almost every imaginable kind of employee benefit plan.

The specific rules prescribed under ERISA pertain to a wide range of matters, such as disclosure of plan information, minimum funding requirements, the pension rights of terminating employees, restrictions on the investment of plan funds, who must be covered under the plans, and a host of other matters related to the design and financial security of plans and the legal rights of plan participants and beneficiaries.

Violators of ERISA law are subject to such penalties as fines and loss of favorable tax status. However, of particular importance to this discussion are the duties and liabilities imposed on plan fiduciaries.

In general, a **fiduciary** is a person in a position of trust who has the duty to act primarily for another's benefit with regard to an agreed-upon matter. As defined in ERISA, the term "fiduciary" includes practically anyone whose role in employee benefits involves discretionary control or judgment in the design, administration, funding, or management of a benefit plan (or in the management of its assets). Each fiduciary of an employee benefit plan has the specific duties that are prescribed with respect to the particular function the fiduciary is performing. All fiduciaries are under a general duty to act solely in the interest of plan participants, to abide by the relevant dictates of plan documents, and to avoid doing things that are expressly prohibited by ERISA.

In the observance of specific or general duties under ERISA, fiduciaries are held to a standard of care that has been called a "federal prudent person rule." Like others, a fiduciary is expected to exercise reasonable care under the circumstances; however, "reasonable" care for a fiduciary is that degree of care and skill that would have been exercised by a prudent person to discharge the stipulated fiduciary duties. That is a relatively high standard of care.

If a fiduciary breaches a statutory duty and the breach causes loss to a benefit plan, the fiduciary is personally liable to the plan for the full amount of the loss. Additionally, the guilty fiduciary might also be subject to a fine and an action for money damages brought by an aggrieved plan participant. A fiduciary may even be liable for the breach of a duty by a second fiduciary if the first fiduciary knowingly participates in the breach, conceals it, or makes no attempt to correct it.

Any employer—including the employer of a fiduciary—may be held vicariously liable for (1) torts committed by its employees in the scope of their employment and (2) torts committed by other agents in the scope of the agency relationship. This liability is described as being joint and several, meaning that the plaintiff may recover damages from either or both of the defendants. Theoretically, the vicariously liable employer might be able to recover its share of the damages awarded in a negligence action against the agent. As a practical matter, the better alternative is for the employer to purchase fiduciary liability insurance that covers the employer, as an entity, and all employees who may be involved in employee benefit functions, especially those who may be deemed fiduciaries under ERISA.

### ERISA Bonds

ERISA requires each fiduciary and each person who handles qualifying employee benefit plan assets to be bonded. The type of bond required is a *fidelity* bond, which is now better known as employee dishonesty insurance. This is the only type of insurance actually required by ERISA. (Several types of organizations, including financial institutions and governmental entities, are granted regulatory exemption from the fidelity bond requirement.)

*Continued on next page.*

> Unfortunately, ERISA bonds are sometimes confused with EBL or fiduciary liability insurance. The basic differences between (1) ERISA bonds and (2) EBL and fiduciary liability insurance are as follows:
> 
> - An ERISA bond is essentially employee dishonesty coverage, a type of property insurance. It protects the assets of the employee benefit plan against loss resulting from a dishonest act of a fiduciary or other person handling those assets. To be covered, the dishonest act must be committed with manifest intent to cause a loss to the plan and to obtain financial benefit for the fiduciary or another party. The bond does not cover losses resulting simply from mismanagement (such as making bad investments with plan assets).
> 
> - In contrast, EBL insurance and fiduciary liability insurance protect the employer, the plan fiduciaries, and perhaps other parties against third-party claims resulting from their negligence in managing the plan assets. A fiduciary liability policy will, for example, pay claims made against a plan fiduciary for losses resulting from the fiduciary's making of bad investments with fund monies.
> 
> ERISA bonds can be provided using the standard employee dishonesty coverage form (Form A), with the particular plan or plans named as insureds and an ERISA compliance endorsement attached to the policy. When outside agents (nonemployees of the plan sponsor) are used as plan administrators or investment advisors, they can, if the insurer is willing, be defined as "employees" by endorsement, thus covering the plan against loss resulting from their dishonest acts. ERISA requires the bond amount to be at least 10 percent of the amount of each plan's assets handled, not to exceed $500,000 for each covered plan (unless the Secretary of Labor prescribes a higher amount).

### Employee Benefits Liability Insurance

EBL insurance, as noted earlier, is limited to covering errors or omissions in administering employee benefit plans. Unlike fiduciary liability insurance, EBL insurance does not cover discretionary acts of plan fiduciaries, such as negligent decisions involving the selection of outside fund administrators or the investment of plan assets. Thus, EBL insurance alone is an incomplete treatment of the loss exposures arising out of employee benefit plans. In many cases, fiduciary liability policies include coverage for both administrative and discretionary exposures, thus eliminating the need for obtaining separate EBL coverage.

Nevertheless, many insureds choose not to buy fiduciary liability insurance but still purchase EBL coverage, which is usually much less expensive than fiduciary liability coverage. EBL coverage is usually provided as an endorsement to the sponsoring company's commercial general liability policy rather than through a separate policy. Some insurers automatically include EBL coverage in their package policies, and thus insureds receive the coverage without specifically requesting it.

## *Insuring Agreement and Limits*

EBL endorsements, like the CGL policies to which they are attached, typically express the insurer's right and duty to defend claims in addition to paying, on the insured's behalf, damages that the insured becomes legally obligated to pay. Defense costs are usually payable in addition to the applicable limits of liability.

The limits of liability in an EBL endorsement normally consist of the following:

- An each employee limit (the most the insurer will pay for all damages to any one employee) or an each claim limit (the most the insurer will pay for all damages in any one claim)

- An aggregate limit (the most the insurer will pay under the EBL endorsement during the policy period)

The EBL limits are usually independent of the CGL limits. When that is the case, an EBL claim payment will not reduce the aggregate limits that apply to CGL coverage. Most EBL endorsements carry a deductible, which is frequently $1,000. The deductible applies to each employee or to each claim.

Some EBL endorsements have an occurrence coverage trigger, and others have a claims-made trigger even though they are attached to occurrence CGL forms. The provisions regarding extended reporting periods under an EBL endorsement are often more liberal than those found in D&O liability and other professional liability policies, in some cases resembling those of the claims-made CGL form. Some EBL endorsements refer to the policy inception date as the retroactive date. Thus, whenever the policy is renewed, the retroactive date is advanced, creating a possible gap in coverage.

## *Persons and Organizations Covered*

An EBL endorsement covers the sponsoring organization named in the policy, as well as various additional parties. These additional parties typically include the directors and stockholders of the named insured in their capacities as such and also the officers and employees of the named insured who are authorized to administer the plan.

The requirement that an officer or employee must be authorized to administer the plan is important. For example, assume that an employee unauthorized to administer the plan (perhaps a file clerk) gives faulty benefit information to another employee. If that employee suffers damages as a result of the faulty information and brings suit against (1) the employee who provided the faulty information and (2) the named insured, the EBL coverage will cover the named insured but not the employee.

## Plans and Functions Covered

An EBL endorsement either defines or schedules the specific types of employee benefit plans covered. The insured should make sure that the definition or schedule encompasses all of the insured's plans, including not only the usual kinds of group insurance and retirement plans but also public programs requiring employer financing, such as workers compensation insurance, unemployment compensation insurance, and Social Security benefits.

In connection with the covered employee benefit plans, EBL insurance usually covers the exposures involved in the performance of four basic administrative functions:

1. Counseling employees on existing or future benefits
2. Interpreting employee benefits
3. Processing employees' personal records
4. Enrolling, terminating, adding, and removing employees for benefits

## Exclusions

Exclusions vary among EBL endorsements. Many of the exclusions encountered in EBL endorsements are designed to eliminate coverage for exposures that are covered under other policies.

For example, most EBL forms exclude dishonest acts of any insured. Loss of plan assets because of the dishonest acts of the insured's *employees* can be covered under employee dishonesty insurance. Similarly, liability for bodily injury and property damage is covered under various liability forms such as the CGL and business auto coverage forms. Several other exclusions eliminate coverage for claims, such as the following, that are often insured under fiduciary liability policies:

- Claims based on the failure of stock to perform as represented by an insured
- Claims based on advice given by an insured to an employee to participate or not to participate in stock subscription plans

- Claims based on faulty investment or noninvestment of funds
- Claims based on the insufficiency of funds to meet plan obligations
- Claims based on liability under ERISA

Other EBL exclusions eliminate coverage for the following, which are not usually covered under any policy:

- Claims for failure to provide benefits because the insurer fails to honor its policy
- Claims based on the insured's failure to comply with any law concerning workers compensation, unemployment insurance, Social Security, or nonoccupational disability benefits

## Fiduciary Liability Insurance

Fiduciary liability insurance is known by several names, such as the following:

- Pension and welfare fund fiduciary responsibility insurance
- Employee benefit plan fiduciary insurance
- Employee pension welfare benefit plan fiduciary liability insurance

In contrast with EBL insurance, which is usually provided as an endorsement to the sponsoring company's CGL policy, fiduciary liability insurance is ordinarily provided in a self-contained policy. In some instances, it is provided in conjunction with a D&O liability insurance policy, subject either to the same limits as D&O coverage or with separate limits.

### Insuring Agreement and Limits

The insuring agreement of a fiduciary liability insurance policy covers damages that the insured becomes legally obligated to pay because of a breach of fiduciary duty with respect to covered employee benefit plans. This coverage encompasses the types of discretionary acts (such as faulty selection of a benefit plan manager or improper investments of plan assets) that are not covered by EBL insurance.

Some fiduciary liability policies cover breaches of fiduciary duties only if the duties breached are those imposed by ERISA; other policies cover fiduciary duties beyond those imposed by ERISA. If employee benefit plans established by an employer are not subject to ERISA, the fiduciary liability insurance should be broadened correspondingly. In addition, fiduciary liability policies frequently include coverage for the EBL exposure, thus covering claims based on negligence in the administration of covered employee benefit plans.

When obtaining fiduciary liability insurance, the named insured should ascertain that all of its employee benefit plans are covered, either by being scheduled in the policy or through an all-encompassing definition of covered plans in the policy.

Fiduciary liability policies differ with respect to coverage of defense costs and supplementary payments. In some policies, these expenses are payable in addition to limits, and in others they are payable within limits. Some policies give the insurer the right and duty to defend, and other policies permit the insured to control the defense.

The major insurers in the fiduciary liability insurance market can usually provide high limits of insurance, such as $25 million or even $50 million. Frequently, the limit selected for a policy applies to each claim and the annual aggregate. Some fiduciary liability policies have no deductible. When a deductible does apply, it normally applies on an each claim basis.

### *Persons and Organizations Insured*

Typically, a fiduciary liability policy insures the employer sponsoring the employee benefit plans and the plans themselves. In addition, the policy ordinarily covers all past, present, or future partners, directors, officers, or employees of the sponsoring organization or plan in their capacities as fiduciaries, administrators, or trustees of a covered plan.

In the past, fiduciary liability policies often contained a recourse provision, which permitted the insurer to seek reimbursement from any insured individual on whose behalf the insurer made a claim payment. ERISA requires this provision when coverage is purchased by the plan but allows the recourse provision to be waived when the sponsoring organization or a fiduciary buys the coverage.[6] Fiduciary liability policies in the current market typically either omit the recourse provision or have an acceptable modification of the provision.

As was mentioned earlier in this chapter, various parties, in addition to employers and employees charged with fiduciary responsibilities, have EBL/fiduciary liability exposures. These outside parties include various legal agents, subcontractors, consultants, and third-party administrators. Generally, the professional liability policies of these parties cover their EBL/fiduciary liability exposures, but each insurance policy must be reviewed to determine whether this specific coverage feature is included. For the organization that hires third-party administrators and others, it is important to verify (generally, through the use of a certificate of insurance) that the outside party has appropriate liability insurance in an amount sufficient to satisfy the needs of the employer organization.

## Claims-Made Provisions

Fiduciary liability insurance is usually provided on a claims-made basis. Some policies have a retroactive date. Other policies cover prior acts without any limitation except that the insured at policy inception must not have had any knowledge of past circumstances that would result in a claim.

Policies differ in their provision of extended reporting options. Some policies cover a claim made any time after policy expiration if the full particulars of circumstances that could lead to a claim are reported to the insurer before the policy expires. Other policies cover claims made after policy expiration only if they are made during an applicable extended reporting period.

A fairly common approach is for the insurer to allow the insured to obtain, for an additional premium, a one-year extended reporting period when the insurer cancels or nonrenews the policy. Less commonly, the extended reporting period is made available when either the insurer or the insured terminates the coverage. In some cases, optional extended reporting periods of a duration longer than one year are available.

## Exclusions

The exclusions contained in fiduciary liability policies can vary considerably among insurers, and so each prospective policy must be analyzed carefully. One can expect to find exclusions of exposures that are normally covered under other policies, such as liability for bodily injury, property damage, libel, slander, and pollution. Other exclusions target exposures that are difficult or against public policy to insure, such as illegal discrimination, criminal acts, or personal profit to which the wrongdoer/insured is not legally entitled.

Many policies exclude fines, penalties, and punitive or exemplary damages. However, some policies allow coverage for penalties under Sections 502(i) and 502(l) of ERISA. Section 502(i) imposes a civil penalty of 5 percent of the amount involved in certain prohibited transactions, and Section 502(l) imposes a civil penalty of 20 percent of the amount recovered because of a settlement agreement or judicial proceeding involving a breach of fiduciary duty.

## Loss Control

A key point in preventing EBL and fiduciary liability losses is the selection of appropriate individuals to serve as employee benefit plan fiduciaries. ERISA itself has some general prohibitions relating to persons serving in a fiduciary capacity. For example, persons convicted of various criminal offenses are ineligible.

Apart from the basic requirements of ERISA, a person serving in a fiduciary capacity should not only be willing and able to do so but should also possess the qualities of honesty, strength of character, and sound judgment. Moreover, a fiduciary should have the ability to function independently from the plan sponsor, thus avoiding the possibility of a "no questioning" approach to the desires of the sponsoring organization.

Fiduciaries should be familiar with plan documents and specifically the stated requirements and responsibilities of the various plans. Familiarity with legal guidelines and procedures in connection with the plan documents is also desirable. As ERISA regulations evolve and undergo change, fiduciaries must fully understand the changes in order to make the best possible decisions affecting the financial futures of the plan participants.

Given the intricacies of ERISA and its amendments, fiduciaries must often obtain competent legal, accounting, and actuarial counsel from outside firms. The ability to select appropriate firms and individuals in this regard is crucial.

Decisions concerning employee benefits and the investment of plan assets are very important to plan participants. Thus, an important loss control aspect involves the maintenance of minutes of meetings of investment committees and plan fiduciaries. Timely and accurate communication of committee decisions is also important.

Because of the complexities of properly administering their own employee benefit plans, many employers find it necessary, desirable, or economically efficient to hire third parties to administer their employee benefit plans. Proper care in selecting these third parties is essential to loss prevention and control of the overall exposure.

# Employment Practices Liability Insurance

Lawsuits by employees against their employers for various employment-related wrongful acts have increased greatly over the past twenty years. These so-called employment practices liability (EPL) claims generally allege wrongful acts in three major categories: (1) wrongful termination, (2) discrimination, and (3) sexual harassment. In some cases, these categories can overlap, as, for example, in the case of a claim alleging wrongful termination of employment because of age discrimination.

## Wrongful Termination

Wrongful termination of employment accounts for the majority of cases of alleged wrongful employment practices. Employers are under increasing pressure not to fire workers without documented business reasons for doing so. Traditionally, the legal doctrine of "employment at will" has allowed employers or employees to terminate the private employment relationship with or without cause at any time. This legal doctrine has been slowly eroding in a number of states, thus permitting terminated employees to sue for termination of their employment without proper cause.

## Discrimination

Suits alleging discrimination of employers against their employees have been a natural consequence of various federal statutes passed during or after the civil rights movement of the 1960s. Two important examples of these statutes are as follows:

- The Civil Rights Act of 1964 (and as amended in 1967 and 1991), which prohibits discrimination on the basis of race, color, national origin, sex, religion, or age.
- The Americans with Disabilities Act (ADA) of 1990, which mandates that an employer must give equal opportunities to disabled workers or job applicants as long as they can perform the essential functions of the job with or without some reasonable accommodation, depending on specific circumstances. Generally, the ADA applies to employers with fifteen or more employees.

These statutes help to define the standards of acceptable employment practices. An employer who breaches these standards is exposed to the possibility of being sued for damages by the affected employees.

## Sexual Harassment

The basis for sexual harassment claims developed mainly over the past two decades. In 1980, the Equal Employment Opportunity Commission (EEOC) issued its "Guidelines on Discrimination Because of Sex," which define sexual harassment as "Unwelcome sexual advances. . .when submission to such conduct is made either explicitly or implicitly a term or condition of an individual's employment."

The EEOC's subsequent 1988 memorandum "Policy Guidance on Current Issues of Sexual Harassment" provided guidance on the meaning of "unwelcome conduct" and on determining if a "hostile environment" exists. Since then, the U.S. Supreme Court has determined, in the 1993 ruling in the Harris v. Fork Lift Systems case, that neither psychological damage nor an intolerable workplace is necessary in order to prove sexual harassment.

## Insurer Response

In some cases, emotional distress, mental anguish, humiliation, and similar psychological effects have been considered to be bodily injury for purposes of insurance coverage. Thus, if a claimant alleged that such injuries resulted from employment practices, a court might hold such allegations to be covered under a CGL, employers liability, or other commercial liability policy. As the frequency of EPL claims increased dramatically in the late 1980s, many insurers added an employment-related practices exclusion to their CGL policies. The current version of this exclusion, quoted in part below, eliminates coverage for bodily injury or personal injury to any person arising out of any of the following:

(a) Refusal to employ that person;

(b) Termination of that person's employment; or

(c) Employment-related practices, policies, acts or omissions, such as coercion, demotion, evaluation, reassignment, discipline, defamation, harassment, humiliation or discrimination directed at that person

A similar exclusion is contained in the employers liability section of the standard workers compensation and employers liability insurance policy. Excess and umbrella liability policies (the subject of Chapter 13) also frequently contain an employment-related practices exclusion. Because of these exclusions, employers usually cannot rely on those policies to cover claims for wrongful employment practices. Accordingly, many employers obtain separate **employment practices liability (EPL) insurance**.

## EPL Policy Provisions

As early as 1982, Lloyd's of London was providing coverage for defense costs (but not damages) because of sexual harassment claims. However, policies covering both defense costs and damages resulting from a variety of wrongful employment practices were not widely bought by employers until the early to mid 1990s.

An EPL policy is written either as a separate, self-contained policy or in connection with a D&O liability policy. If the EPL coverage is written as an endorsement to a D&O policy, the insured corporation should ascertain that the policy includes coverage for EPL claims made against the employer, not just against the individual directors and officers. Free-standing EPL policies cover the employer, its directors and officers, department heads, and, generally, all other employees. In some policies, only supervisory employees are insured. Another potential advantage of free-standing EPL policies is that they provide a separate limit of insurance apart from the employer's D&O limits. Of course, the premium for a separate EPL policy is likely to be higher than the premium for endorsing coverage onto the D&O policy, subject to specific underwriting and market conditions.

The coverage provided by EPL policies varies widely among insurers. One policy, for example, covers only the costs of *defending* against claims alleging wrongful termination, discrimination, or sexual harassment. Most other policies cover both defense costs and judgments or settlements, but the wrongful employment practices covered vary among different insurers' policies. Thus, when acquiring EPL insurance, the insured or its agent or broker should carefully review the particular provisions that enumerate the covered employment practices and compare them with those covered under other available policies. The covered practices can be specified in different ways. In one policy, they may be included in a definition of "claim," and in another policy, they may be enumerated in policy definitions of terms such as "employment termination," "discrimination," and "sexual harassment."

Coverage is usually provided on a claims-made basis. Claims-made provisions—such as retroactive dates, extended reporting periods, and reporting requirements—can differ from policy to policy.

Exclusions can vary considerably among different insurers' policies. Some of the many exposures that might be excluded consist of the following:

- Circumstances reported under prior EPL policies
- Deliberate fraud or purposeful violation of statutes, rules, or regulations
- Liabilities of others assumed under contract, other than employment contracts
- Bodily injury or property damage other than emotional distress, mental anguish, or humiliation
- Actual or alleged violations of various state and federal statutes, such as ERISA, the National Labor Relations Act, and workers compensation acts
- Wrongful termination practices committed with dishonest, fraudulent, criminal, or malicious intent
- Mass layoffs of employees

As for retention provisions, an EPL policy typically imposes a deductible between $2,500 and $100,000 for each insured event. Moreover, the insured might also be required to participate in losses above the deductible. The percentage of participation is commonly 5 to 10 percent.

The capacity of the relatively few insurers who offer EPL coverage varies considerably for this line. Some insurers offer relatively low maximum EPL limits, such as $1 million, and others have far greater capacity for the EPL line, providing limits between $5 million and $100 million.

## Loss Control

The following procedures have been cited as ways of reducing the frequency or severity of claims alleging wrongful termination, discrimination, and sexual harassment.[7]

With regard to wrongful termination claims, an employer can do the following:

1. Perform thorough pre-employment interviews and background checks
2. Avoid promises of permanent employment
3. Review with legal counsel all employer-produced material, such as employee handbooks and benefits descriptions, for misleading statements
4. Conduct periodic performance evaluations
5. Record in the employee's personnel file any warnings to the employee concerning tardiness, unacceptable work, or misconduct
6. Establish written termination procedures and distribute to supervisors

With regard to discrimination claims, an employer can do the following:

1. Adopt a written anti-discrimination policy
2. Use job application forms and interview procedures complying with federal and state discrimination laws
3. Prepare written job descriptions
4. Set up leave of absence policies complying with the Pregnancy Disability Act and the Family Leave Act

With regard to sexual harassment claims, an employer can do the following:

1. Establish a written policy against sexual harassment
2. Provide appropriate training to managers and supervisors
3. Investigate complaints promptly and thoroughly
4. Take appropriate actions following investigations of complaints
5. Implement procedures to prevent future incidents

# Summary

The directors and officers of a corporation have various duties, including the duty to exercise reasonable care, to be loyal to the corporation and its stockholders, and to disclose material facts to various parties. If the directors and officers do not perform these duties or if they perform them negligently, thereby causing financial harm to another party, they can be held personally liable to the wronged party. The wronged party might be the corporation's stockholders, its customers, its creditors, or others.

Directors and officers (D&O) liability insurance, which might be thought of as a type of managerial professional liability policy, covers the liability exposure described above. In addition, D&O liability insurance covers the corporation itself for those sums that the corporation is lawfully permitted or required to pay to indemnify its directors or officers for defense or settlement costs arising out of claims made against the directors or officers. Traditionally, D&O policies have not covered the corporation for claims made directly against the corporation. However, D&O policies are increasingly providing "entity coverage" that protects the corporation for covered claims made directly against the corporation.

Most employers provide some noncash employee benefits to their full-time employees. Providing these benefits exposes the employer and some employees to liability for errors or omissions in the management of these plans. Two types of insurance are available to cover these exposures. Employee benefits liability (EBL) insurance is limited to covering *administrative* errors or omissions, such as failing to enroll an eligible employee in a health insurance plan. Fiduciary liability insurance covers *discretionary* errors or omissions, such as negligent investment of employee benefit plan funds. Fiduciary liability policies frequently also cover the EBL exposure, eliminating the need for a separate EBL policy.

In recent years, the incidence of claims against employers alleging various employment-related offenses has increased dramatically. These claims most commonly allege that the employer has wrongfully terminated the claimant's employment, illegally discriminated against the claimant, or sexually harassed the claimant. A growing body of state and federal statutes, regulations, and court cases has more clearly defined unlawful employment practices and thus increased employers' exposure to such claims.

In response to the increased exposure, insurers added an exclusion of employment-related practices to their commercial liability policies beginning in the late 1980s. Accordingly, employers then had a need for insurance specifically covering the excluded offenses. A number of insurers have responded to this need, developing a new type of coverage known as employment practices liability (EPL) insurance. An EPL policy typically covers the employer and its employees against specified types of employment-related offenses.

## Chapter Notes

1. R.A. Hersbarger and M.L. Cross, "Nature and Major Provisions of Directors and Officers Liability Insurance," *CPCU Journal* 32(1), (1979), pp. 37-43.
2. *Watson Wyatt D&O Liability Surveys*, 1993, 1994, 1995 (Chicago, IL: Watson Wyatt & Co.).
3. *Watson Wyatt D&O Liability Survey*, 1995.
4. For a summary of the various rules, see Joseph P. Monteleone, "D&O Allocation: Problems and Solutions," *The Risk Report*, vol. XVIII, no. 8 (April 1996), pp. 1-12.
5. This classification of allocation provisions is based on Monteleone, "D&O Allocation."
6. "Insuring Your Fiduciary Liability Exposure," *John Liner Letter*, June 1993.
7. Wallace L. Clapp, Jr., "Employment Practices Liability—Employers Respond to a Growing Need," *Rough Notes*, November 1993, p. 20.

## Chapter 12

# Environmental Insurance

Pollution exclusions in general liability, automobile liability, and property insurance policies have created a coverage void for many industrial and commercial insureds that can, in part, be filled with various forms of environmental insurance. Although environmental impairment liability insurance has existed as a separate insurance coverage since 1977, the market for environmental insurance remained relatively restricted until the late 1980s. Since that time, the marketplace for environmental insurance has expanded rapidly.

In this chapter, the term "environmental insurance" is used in a general sense to denote any of various types of insurance—both first-party (property) coverages and third-party (liability) coverages—whose primary purpose is to manage pollution-related loss exposures. Environmental impairment *liability* insurance (also called pollution liability insurance) is thus *one type* of environmental insurance.

It is not possible in the space of this chapter to review all of the different environmental insurance policies offered by insurers today. However, the broad intent of the most popular insurance forms will be presented along with an analysis of the more common exclusions contained within the various policy forms. The legal basis for environmental liability, as it has evolved under American law, will also be examined.

# Legal Basis for Environmental Liability

Sources of environmental legal liability follow the sources of legal liability set forth in Chapter 1 of this text. Environmental liability losses can be incurred through torts, contractual obligations, or violations of statutes. The source of the liability in the case of an environmental loss will most frequently be the actual or alleged release of pollutants or the violation of a law designed to protect human health and the environment from those pollutants.

## Torts

In the realm of torts, liability for pollution can be based on negligence, intentional torts, or strict liability.

### Negligence

To summarize, negligence is the failure to do what is reasonable under the circumstances to protect third parties from injury or damage. The following are examples of negligent acts that have resulted in environmental liability claims:

1. An oil spill from a petroleum refinery contaminated a municipal water supply, which resulted in bodily injury and property damage claims.
2. A contractor working at a manufacturing facility left a valve open on a process line overnight. The next day it was discovered that the contents of a storage tank connected to the line had been released into an adjacent stream, causing property damage, bodily injury, and natural resource damage.
3. A hazardous waste hauler transporting toxic waste to a disposal facility had an auto accident in the downtown section of a major city. The hazardous liquid being transported was released into the street. Passersby inhaled the fumes, and the business district of the city was evacuated for two days as cleanup contractors responded to the spill. Claims were filed against the transporter alleging bodily injury, property damage, and business interruption.

Other sources of potential liability in cases involving negligence include the following:

1. Hazardous or toxic products
2. Improper disposal of hazardous wastes
3. Product failures that cause releases of pollutants
4. Careless actions that cause pollution

5. Inadequate emergency response procedures
6. Selection of incompetent contractors for the following activities:
   - Waste transportation
   - Waste disposal
   - Environmental consulting

## Intentional Torts

The intentional torts most commonly alleged in environmental claims are nuisance and trespass.

### Nuisance

A property owner is entitled to the peaceful enjoyment of his or her property. If a neighbor or another third party engages in an activity that interferes with the owner's right of enjoyment of the property, the owner may bring an action alleging nuisance against the party causing the interference. There are two types of nuisance actions:

1. Public nuisance, which involves interference with a right of public enjoyment. The remedy must be sought by a public authority.
2. Private nuisance, which involves interference with one or more individuals' right to use private property. The remedy is sought by the party or parties alleging injury, damage, or interference.

Sources of potential liability in tort cases involving nuisance could include the following:

1. Loud noises
2. Noxious odors
3. Bright lights
4. Generation of fog
5. Electrical waves
6. Electromagnetic fields

### Trespass

Unlike nuisance, which requires no transmission of materials from one property to another, trespass involves the physical deposition of pollutants on the property of the claimant alleging injury. The material that is deposited may be a toxic substance, but it does not have to be. Claims have resulted from releases or deposits of water, sand, and clean soil. As long as the deposits are objectionable to the property owner, a trespass claim can be brought against the party responsible for the release.

Sources of potential liability in tort cases involving trespass could include the following:

1. Dust
2. Discharge of chemicals into a stream
3. Release of particulate from a stack
4. Runoff of pesticides onto a neighbor's property
5. Stack emissions of harmful gases
6. Thermal emissions into water
7. Silting of waterways

## Strict Liability

When manufacturing operations use inherently hazardous materials or processes, courts may impose strict liability, which eliminates the common-law defenses normally available to the defendant in a negligence suit. No degree of care is considered to be adequate for ultrahazardous activities or materials. For example, a remediation contractor working on a job to incinerate nerve gas could face strict liability for ultrahazardous activity if a release of the nerve gas injures a third party—even though the contractor might exercise a very high degree of care in performing the work.

Sources of potential liability in tort cases involving strict liability include the following:

1. Nuclear materials
2. Explosives
3. Polychlorinated biphenyl (PCB) materials
4. Pesticides and fungicides
5. Highly toxic chemicals
6. Hazardous waste disposal
7. Transportation of oil

## Contractual Obligations

A general contractor that agrees to hold harmless and indemnify a project owner for all claims that arise during the course of the project may incur an environmental loss under the contract if the proximate cause of the loss is a release of pollutants. For example, a worker who is employed by a subcontractor at the project and is injured as a result of breathing ammonia might sue the project owner, thus activating the general contractor's contractual obligation to hold harmless and indemnify the owner.

## Environmental Statutes

Environmental statutes contain provisions that can lead to injunctions, fines, and penalties for noncompliance. They also contain provisions for criminal prosecution of individuals, including corporate officers, and cost recovery schemes to offset expenses that the government may incur in enforcing the regulations. Environmental laws and regulations are the most complicating factors in the management of environmental risks.

The "modern era" of environmental legislation began with the passage of the National Environmental Policy Act (NEPA) of 1969. NEPA resulted from the efforts of conservationists to compel the federal government to consider the environmental ramifications of proposals for new highways, dams, and other public projects capable of affecting wildlife or scenic areas. NEPA is important because it reflected an initial public interest and determination sufficient to push environmental legislation through Congress. However, the focus of the public's interest in environmental protection quickly moved beyond aesthetic considerations and public works projects.

The public interest soon changed from protecting conservationist values to protecting specific environmental media, primarily surface waters (the Clean Water Act) and the air (the Clean Air Act). As the "environmental movement" caught on, the more ambitious and complex Resource Conservation and Recovery Act (RCRA) of 1976 and the Comprehensive Environmental Response, Compensation, and Liability Act (CERCLA) of 1980 soon followed. By this time, the linkage between "environmental" concerns and "health" concerns, which now characterizes much environmental regulation, had already been established. Those federal environmental laws have since been supplemented by a profusion of state and local environmental initiatives. Periodic revisions, furthermore, have materially transformed each of the principal federal statutes. Typically, federal statutes have provided the baseline standards for state and local environmental laws, which have also evolved to keep pace as the federal laws have been changed.

These environmental laws have extended common-law theories of liability, but they typically do not require fault on the part of the party charged with responsibility—that is, they are strict liability statutes. The most influential federal environmental laws are summarized in the sections that follow.

# CLEAN WATER ACT

### Purpose

The **Clean Water Act (CWA)** seeks to improve the quality of surface waters by prohibiting or regulating the discharge of pollutants into navigable waters and restoring them to "fishable" and "swimmable" quality.

### Requirements and Features

a. The discharge of any pollutant into a navigable waterway from a point source without a permit is prohibited.

b. "Pollutant" is broadly defined and includes all solid waste; chemical waste; heat; and industrial, municipal, and agricultural waste.

c. National Pollution Discharge Elimination System (NPDES) permits also require elaborate water quality monitoring and self-reporting of violations.

d. The CWA also regulates industrial discharges that do not go directly into a receiving surface water body but instead discharge into publicly owned treatment works.

e. The 1987 CWA amendments added a new program for regulating stormwater runoff discharges. A permit is now required for stormwater discharges. Standards are still evolving for this group of CWA regulations.

f. Section 404 of the CWA prohibits dredge or fill activities in any navigable waterway—including wetlands (very broadly defined)—without a permit from the Army Corps of Engineers.

g. Section 311 of the CWA prohibits most discharges of oil and hazardous substances, including any quantity sufficient to cause a sheen on the water. Discharges must be reported. Oil-handling facilities must develop Spill Prevention, Control, and Countermeasure (SPCC) plans, and the U.S. Environmental Protection Agency (EPA) will soon establish SPCC plan requirements for hazardous substances as well.

h. The Clean Water Act contains a full range of civil and criminal penalties. Penalties were increased substantially in the 1987 amendments and in the 1990 Oil Pollution Act.
   1. Negligent Violations
      a. Maximum $25,000/day
      b. One year in jail

2. Knowing Violations
    a. Maximum $50,000/day
    b. Three years in jail
3. Knowing Endangerment
    a. Maximum fines $250,000 for individuals/$1,000,000 for organizations
    b. Fifteen years in jail
4. False Information
    a. $10,000 fine
    b. Two years in jail

Note: All fines and penalties are for first violations; for subsequent offenses, the penalties are automatically doubled.

## CLEAN AIR ACT

### Purpose

The **Clean Air Act (CAA)** seeks to improve the quality of ambient air by regulating emissions from both mobile and stationary sources of air pollution. Permits are required to construct or operate sources of air emissions. The terms of the permit vary from one emission source to another and from one pollutant to another. Similarly, restrictions are tighter in areas of poor air quality (such as urban areas) than elsewhere. These zones around cities are classified as "Nonattainment Areas" where ambient air quality fails to meet CAA requirements.

### Requirements and Features

a. The CAA (§ 109) establishes "National Ambient Air Quality Standards" (NAAQS) for six specific common air pollutants, known as the "criteria pollutants": sulfur dioxide, nitrogen oxides, particulate matter, carbon monoxide, ozone, and lead.

b. The CAA requires the EPA to establish "New Source Performance Standards" (NSPS) for new stationary sources of the six criteria pollutants. These standards impose different levels of control technology upon new sources depending on their location. In addition, merely to locate a new source in a Nonattainment Area, one must also guarantee emission reductions from existing sources in the area that will more than offset new emissions from the proposed source.

c. Existing sources must meet different technology-based emissions standards. Major stationary sources in Nonattainment Areas must install

# 118 Commercial Liability Insurance and Risk Management

pollution control equipment to reduce emissions from existing sources over a prescribed period of time.

d. Hazardous air pollutants (air toxins) are also strictly regulated as a result of 1990 amendments to the CAA.

e. Application of the various standards for new and existing sources is achieved through a comprehensive permit program, mandated by the new Title V of the CAA. Permit applications must contain a wealth of information, including a detailed compliance plan, actual emissions data, identification of emissions sources and their rates of discharge into the environment, a description of control equipment, and a summary of how the equipment achieves the applicable control requirements.

## RESOURCE CONSERVATION AND RECOVERY ACT

### Purpose

The **Resource Conservation and Recovery Act (RCRA)** provides "cradle-to-grave" regulation of hazardous waste. It imposes strict waste management requirements upon generators and transporters of hazardous wastes and upon hazardous waste treatment, storage, and disposal (TSD) facilities, including, in some instances, cleanup requirements. It also regulates underground storage tanks, medical wastes, and nonhazardous solid wastes, although the requirements for some of these waste categories are considerably less stringent than those for hazardous wastes.

### Requirements and Features

a. RCRA includes a wide variety of wastes within the scope of its regulatory program. The most notable exceptions are waste oil and certain high-volume, low-toxicity wastes (such as various mine wastes and incinerator ash).

b. Waste generators must manage hazardous wastes in accordance with detailed regulations governing containers, labels, record keeping, storage, spill prevention and control, and employee training. On-site storage is limited both with respect to amounts and time, and shipments off-site require completion of a manifest that ensures disposal only at proper facilities.

c. RCRA regulates facilities that treat, store, or dispose of hazardous wastes. TSD facilities must meet specific technological standards and conduct regular groundwater monitoring. They must also perform waste analyses on incoming wastes, provide security, take precautions to prevent accidents, and maintain contingency plans to deal with spills or releases.

d. RCRA is the first federal environmental law to require proof of financial responsibility. Owners of TSD facilities are required to demonstrate their financial ability to pay for third-party claims resulting from a release of contaminants and for closure/post-closure care costs. Owners of underground storage tanks are also required to demonstrate their ability to pay for third-party claims and cleanup costs associated with a release of contaminants.

## OIL POLLUTION ACT OF 1990

### Purpose

The **Oil Pollution Act (OPA) of 1990** seeks to reduce the risk of spills of petroleum or hazardous materials into United States coastal or navigable waters by mandating technical standards for facilities and vessels operating in or near such waters and by imposing requirements upon owners of facilities and vessels to prevent releases and/or pay for the costs of releases that are not prevented.

### Requirements and Features

a. OPA mandates that each party responsible for a vessel or facility from which oil is discharged (or is threatening to be discharged) into or upon navigable waters, adjoining shorelines, or the exclusive economic zone is liable for removal costs and damages. Liability is limited as follows:

1. For a tank vessel of more than 3,000 gross tons, the greater of $1,200 per gross ton or $10,000,000

2. For a tank vessel of 3,000 gross tons or less, the greater of $1,200 per gross ton or $2,000,000

3. For any other (non-tank) vessel, the greater of $600 per gross ton or $500,000

4. For an offshore facility except a deep water port, the total of all removal costs plus $75 million

5. For any onshore facility and deep water ports, $350 million

b. The responsible party for any vessel over 300 gross tons subject to jurisdiction of the United States or any vessel using the waters of the exclusive economic zone shall establish and maintain, in accordance with the regulations, evidence of financial responsibility sufficient to meet the maximum level of liability described above. If the responsible party owns or operates more than one vessel, evidence of financial responsibility need be established only to meet the amount of maximum liability applicable to the vessel having the greatest maximum liability.

c. Methods of financial responsibility that may be used to meet these requirements include any one or a combination of the following:
- Insurance
- Surety bond
- Guarantee
- Letter of credit
- Qualification as self-insurer

d. As part of the OPA implementation process, the Minerals Management Service Agency of the Department of the Interior has proposed regulations governing the establishment of financial responsibility requirements as established in the Oil Pollution Act of 1990. The proposed regulations will require that offshore oil facilities in, on, or under the navigable waters of the United States establish a level of financial responsibility at $150 million per facility, superseding Title III of the Offshore Coastal Shelf Lands Act (OCSLA). Other vessels and facilities affected by OPA are currently being regulated under the amended Federal Water Pollution Control Act, the Deep Water Port Act of 1974, and the Trans Alaska Pipeline Authorization Act of 1973.

## MOTOR CARRIER ACT OF 1980

### Purpose

The purpose of the **Motor Carrier Act of 1980** is to protect the environment from releases of harmful materials during transportation of such materials by motor carriers in interstate or intrastate commerce.

### Requirements and Features

a. The Motor Carrier Act of 1980 established minimum levels of financial responsibility sufficient to cover third-party liability including property damage and environmental restoration for both private and for-hire carriers of hazardous materials. The requirements set forth by that law are outlined in Exhibit 12-1.

b. Intrastate for-hire and private carriers transporting hazardous materials in situations not covered in Exhibit 12-1 would have to comply with any state requirements. Currently, eighty different Hazmat transportation

**Exhibit 12-1**
Financial Responsibility for Hazardous Transportation

| Type of Carriage | Vehicle Size | Commodity | Insurance Amount |
|---|---|---|---|
| For-hire and private for intrastate, interstate, or international commerce. | Gross vehicle weight (GVW) of 10,000 lbs. or greater. | Reportable quantity of an EPA CERCLA-listed hazardous substance in cargo tanks, portable tanks, or hopper-type vehicles with rated capacity in excess of 3,500 water gallons; bulk shipments of Class 1.1, 1.2, & 1.3 explosives; any quantity of class 2 gas; all shipments of highway route controlled quantities of radioactive materials as defined in 49 CFR 173.403. | $5,000,000 |
| For-hire and private in interstate and international commerce. | Gross vehicle weight (GVW) of less than 10,000 lbs. | Any quantity of Class 1.1, 1.2, 1.3 explosives; any quantity of Class 2.3 poison gas; all shipments of highway route controlled quantities of radioactive materials. | $5,000,000 |
| For-hire and private in interstate or international commerce in any quantity, or in intrastate commerce in bulk only. | Gross vehicle weight (GVW) of 10,000 lbs. or greater. | Oil listed in 49 CFR 172.101; any hazardous waste, hazardous materials, or hazardous substances defined in 49 CFR 171.8 and 49 CFR 172.101 but not mentioned above. | $1,000,000 |
| For-hire in interstate or international commerce. | Any | Nonhazardous property | $750,000 |

programs exist in forty-two states, making compliance very difficult for operators of multi-state transportation companies. A soon-to-be-established uniform Hazmat transportation permitting program will result in uniform financial responsibility requirements across all states.

One insurance mechanism that meets the requirements set forth in Exhibit 12-1 is the MCS 90 endorsement. This endorsement must be attached to a commercial vehicle liability insurance policy and, when attached thereto, becomes a promise from the insurer that the insurer will pay any claims or judgments made against the transporter for public liability (bodily injury, property damage, or environmental restoration costs) resulting from operation of the vehicle.

The MCS 90 endorsement is essentially a surety instrument in that it requires the insured to reimburse the insurer for any payments made under the provisions of the MCS 90 that would not have been paid under the insurance policy in the absence of the endorsement. Because commercial auto insurance policies typically exclude most claims for loss caused by the release of pollutants, it is probable that the insured will have to reimburse the insurer for many losses that might be paid by the insurer under the MCS 90 for release of contaminants. To provide true insurance coverage, an additional endorsement (ISO endorsement CA 99 48 being the most common) must be used to modify the pollution exclusion on the standard business auto, truckers, or motor carrier coverage form.

## TOXIC SUBSTANCE CONTROL ACT

### Purpose

The primary purpose of the **Toxic Substance Control Act (TSCA)**, enacted in 1976, is to regulate the chemical manufacturing industry and to prevent the importation or manufacture of dangerous chemical substances without adequate safeguards to ensure that their use does not harm human health or the environment. Its statutory framework, however, also facilitates extensive regulation of individual hazardous substances on a case-by-case basis. Consequently, TSCA has been used to regulate PCBs and, to a more limited extent, asbestos and radon. The EPA has also contemplated using TSCA to impose extensive regulations on the use of lead.

### Requirements and Features

a. Manufacturers of chemical substances must provide extensive information to the EPA regarding the formulation, use, and risks of each such substance they manufacture or import, including any information with respect to known or suspected adverse health or environmental effects.

b. EPA can limit or prohibit manufacture or use of a chemical substance.

c. TSCA includes extensive record-keeping requirements that apply to manufacturers and importers of chemical substances regulated under the act.

d. TSCA prohibits most uses of PCBs and regulates the labeling, maintenance, and cleanup of PCB equipment.

## COMPREHENSIVE ENVIRONMENTAL RESPONSE, COMPENSATION, AND LIABILITY ACT

### Purpose

Because RCRA regulations cover active but not abandoned waste disposal sites, the **Comprehensive Environmental Response, Compensation, and Liability Act** (**CERCLA** or "**Superfund**") was passed in 1980 to facilitate the cleanup of any abandoned or uncontrolled sites containing hazardous substances, including numerous old dump sites. CERCLA was amended in 1986 (as the Superfund Amendment and Reauthorization Act, or SARA) to enlarge the fund itself and further strengthen the already substantial powers of the EPA to regulate the technical aspects of cleanups. Superfund is harsh and expensive. The average cost of a Superfund cleanup of a site on the National Priority List is approximately $30 million, exclusive of transaction costs, which are usually substantial. Approximately 1,300 Superfund National Priority List sites and more than 3,500 sites are targeted for cleanup under state programs similar to CERCLA. The EPA has investigated over 40,000 potential Superfund sites between 1980 and 1995.

### Requirements and Features

a. CERCLA allows the EPA to clean up sites where there is a release or threat of release of a hazardous substance into the environment.

b. The EPA can recover its cleanup costs from liable parties.

c. The EPA can force liable parties to conduct the cleanup.

d. Private parties may conduct a cleanup voluntarily and, under appropriate circumstances, recover their costs from other liable parties.

e. Potentially Responsible Parties (PRPs) include current owners and operators of contaminated property, prior owners and operators who were involved at the time of the disposal of hazardous materials at the site, the generators of waste materials disposed of at the site, transporters who selected a site and hauled waste to it, and anyone who "arranged for disposal" of hazardous substances at the site. Intervening owners/operators theoretically are not liable, although failure to identify a contamination problem and/or failure to take steps to prevent a release or to control it may constitute a basis for liability. Owners/operators immediately preceding state or local government ownership or control acquired "involuntarily through bankruptcy, tax delinquency, abandonment," etc., are also liable.

Parties involved with a Superfund site are referred to as Potentially Responsible Parties (PRPs) until liability under the act is established. At that point they become Responsible Parties (RPs). They are responsible for all costs associated with cleaning up the site, including the costs of identifying and evaluating contaminants and developing a plan for remediation.

f. Lessees may be liable as "operators."

g. Individuals, such as corporate officers or shareholders, can be liable as "operators."

h. Parent corporations may be liable for subsidiaries that are PRPs, depending on the extent of control over their subsidiaries and/or their involvement in waste disposal practices or decisions. Traditional notions of "piercing the corporate veil" (invalidating the legal protections of the corporate entity and suing the owners individually) will generally be applied. However, it appears that, as in other cases involving environmental issues, courts are more willing to pierce the corporate veil to impose environmental liability upon a corporation than to impose liability for other corporate debts and obligations. Nonetheless, there are important instances in which the courts have not pierced the corporate veil and liability was not imposed upon a parent corporation, primarily because the parent strictly observed corporate formalities and specifically did not become engaged in waste management or disposal functions of its subsidiary. Similarly, corporate successors may also be liable, depending on their involvement and/or the application of traditional principles of successor liability (e.g., "continuing enterprise," "de facto merger," or "fraudulent conveyance" theories of liability).

i. Lenders can incur Superfund liability—as "owners" or "operators."

j. Even bankrupt parties may incur liability under CERCLA.

k. Superfund liability is strict, i.e., without regard to "fault," and it is retroactive.

l. Superfund liability is also joint and several (i.e., any liable party may be responsible for the entire amount, regardless of its "fair share") if, as is usually the case, the harm is indivisible.

m. CERCLA provides an express right of contribution. A private CERCLA recovery action may be brought against any liable party regardless of whether the federal government has initiated either cleanup or a cost recovery action of its own. Parties that settle with the government, however, are not liable for contribution.

n. The time, expense, and frustration of litigating CERCLA issues are usually substantial. EPA routinely sues some, but not all, Potentially Responsible Parties. Effort is not always made to single out the largest or most appropriate defendants.

o. There are only three defenses to CERCLA: (1) acts of God, (2) acts of war, and (3) acts of an unrelated third party. The third-party defense is narrowly defined as "an act or omission of a third party other than an employee or agent of the defendant, or than one whose act or omission occurs in connection with a contractual relationship, existing directly or indirectly, with the defendant." The third-party defense rarely applies and is largely intended to be limited to such occurrences as the unanticipated acts of vandals.

p. Included in the "third-party defense" is a provision known as the "innocent landowner defense," an important provision for lenders and those who lease or acquire real property. Section 101(35) excludes from CERCLA liability persons who acquire contaminated property and did not know, and had no reason to know, it was contaminated and who did not contribute to the contamination. The purchaser must, at the time of acquisition (which may have occurred many years ago), have undertaken "all appropriate inquiry into previous ownership and uses of the property consistent with good commercial and customary practices in an effort to minimize liability."

## APPLICATIONS

### Potential Loss Exposure Under CERCLA

ACE Manufacturing Company disposed of its off-specification chemical materials in Joe's Dump between 1960 and 1970. Joe's Dump was licensed for this entire period by the state in which it is located under a law applicable to municipal solid waste disposal facilities. ACE had hired Sam's Sanitary Service to transport the hazardous waste material from ACE to Joe's Dump. In 1972, Joe sold his land to Wonder Products Incorporated. Wonder still owns the land but discontinued use of the landfill in 1980.

In 1984, the drinking water supply of a nearby municipality was found to be contaminated. Groundwater investigations determined that Joe's Dump site was the source of the contamination. The cost to clean up, remediate, and reconstruct Joe's Dump is expected to be $30,000,000. Under CERCLA, the following parties are Potentially Responsible Parties, subject to strict liability for the cleanup and third-party bodily injury and property damage expenses:

- Joe's Dump as an owner/operator
- ACE Manufacturing Company as a waste generator
- Sam's Sanitary Service as a transporter to the site
- Wonder Products Incorporated as the current owner and a past operator of the site

All responsible parties face joint and several liability for the cleanup expenses. In this case, if Joe's Dump, ACE Manufacturing, Sam's Sanitary Service, and other PRPs were out of business at the time of the EPA Superfund cleanup action, Wonder Products could be assessed the entire cleanup expense.

## Enforcement of Environmental Laws

For many years, the focus of environmental regulatory activities was compliance in a very technical sense. Under the Clean Air Act, the Clean Water Act, and a host of earlier environmental laws, compliance involved monitoring the outflow from pipes into streams and from smokestacks into the air. The EPA set standards, counted contaminants in parts per million, and lowered the enforcement boom on people who could not measure up to the standards. The process was highly empirical. Technically trained inspectors met with the corporate mechanics who controlled the tools of compliance. Those subjected to enforcement actions were often the compliance personnel and technically trained employees who operated pollution control systems or the equipment that failed to meet the EPA standards. Risk managers were rarely involved in this process.

This enforcement model has changed dramatically in recent years. Now, an evaluation of compliance not only includes a review of the physical facilities, but it also considers management systems and control of the processes that pose a threat to the environment. Such an evaluation reviews the accountability of the board of directors for environmental matters, the assignment of environmental responsibility within senior management ranks, the effective dispersion of responsibility through all levels of the organization, and the day-to-day operation of the system in controlling activities that involve hazardous materials.

Also of concern to the EPA in its compliance evaluation is the appropriate assignment of personnel and other corporate resources to environmental affairs. This includes a realistic budget for all environmental activities, including compliance with the laws.

## Executive Accountability for Environmental Management Decisions

A trend has developed in recent years to hold a corporation's management accountable for its strategic decision-making process as it relates to environmental matters. This means that the EPA and the corporation's shareholders and employees expect that certain components of a corporate environmental risk management program will be in place.

Such a program begins with a written corporate environmental policy, which is implemented by written procedures. This formal plan is carried out by executives with responsibility for management of day-to-day activities, and it is adequately funded to ensure that it will be successful. A reporting system provides management and the board of directors with enough information to assure that all is working as intended. When extraordinary events take place within a corporation, such as a major environmental incident or the merger with or acquisition of an organization having environmental exposures that are different from those of the acquiring company, additional expectations must be addressed.

## APPLICATIONS

### Management's Responsibility for Environmental Compliance

One company's experience illustrates the current trend to focus on the responsibility of management in assessing environmental compliance. The corporation was involved in metal fabrication processes at thirteen plants geographically dispersed in seven states with a total workforce of more than 8,000.

At one facility, the regulators were called in when neighbors discovered hydrocarbon solvents in drinking water supplies. An inspection of the facility found that the normal practice for cleaning up trichloroethylene spills from the shop floor was to hose the material out the door and let it run into stormwater drains. Further inquiry revealed that the company had only one employee assigned to environmental compliance for all thirteen manufacturing facilities.

Fines were assessed against the corporate executives and the corporation for failure to adequately provide for environmental management within the company when the hazards associated with the materials in use were widely known. The chief executive officer of the firm was given a suspended sentence and three years' probation as a first offender—a result that would not occur today under the Federal Sentencing Guidelines.

The environmental enforcement litigation was followed by a shareholder suit against the officers and directors for failing to properly manage environmental matters, a failure that led to the unnecessary depletion of corporate reserves to resolve the ensuing enforcement actions. The company's directors and officers liability insurance policy had a pollution exclusion that prompted a denial of coverage for the shareholder claims.

The risk manager quickly learned how important his environment risk management program was when he was asked to provide a detailed analysis of the incident and an explanation of what protection the company had against future events of a similar nature. Of course, the insurance available to help pay for this costly claim was also of great importance to the company.

# Environmental Risk Management

As the effort to clean up contaminated sites in America gains momentum, risk managers are increasingly faced with the daunting task of effectively managing their firms' environmental impairment liability exposures. In 1983, predictions that cleanups under CERCLA's Superfund program would ultimately cost up to $100 billion seemed radical. By 1989, the estimated cost for just Superfund sites had increased to $300 billion. Estimates for the cost of the environmental cleanup effort at all contaminated sites in the United States range between 700 billion to well in excess of one trillion dollars.

Sharing the costs of cleanup efforts of this magnitude will obviously have a significant financial impact on thousands of companies, public institutions, and individuals. Unfortunately, environmental loss costs are not currently incorporated into the financial planning schemes of the majority of affected businesses. It is still common, for example, to see financial statements in annual reports and elsewhere that fail to reflect these expected future costs, in spite of recent changes in accounting rules that require corporations to disclose these liabilities. The relatively small size of the environmental insurance market is another good indicator of the lack of risk finance planning for environmental costs among businesses in the United States and around the world.

Thus, a common misconception is that environmental liability losses affect relatively few industries and a limited number of organizations within a given industry group. However, with the far-reaching cost recovery provisions of Superfund and similar state cleanup laws, the ultimate cost of environmental remediation and of liability claims will be shouldered by a relatively large number of organizations within the U.S. economy. Banks, insurance companies, property managers, and many other segments of the economy have become entangled in this web of environmental liability. When the costs of environmental liability are reflected in the increased costs of products and higher insurance premiums, the ultimate price of the cleanup will be paid by society as a whole. From a risk management standpoint, however, organizations must plan if they are to survive long enough to pass these increased costs of doing business on to their customers. To implement such a plan, managers must develop effective environmental risk management programs that include adequate funding and support from corporate management.

A risk management process can be used to manage any type of loss exposure effectively. The process includes the following steps:

1. Identify and analyze loss exposures.
2. Examine the feasibility of alternative risk management techniques.
3. Select the best risk management techniques.
4. Implement the techniques.
5. Monitor the risk management program.

Risk management techniques can be categorized as either risk control or risk financing. Risk control, also known as loss control, includes any measures taken to reduce the frequency or severity of accidental losses. Measures taken to operate in compliance with environmental laws are examples of risk control. Risk financing, in contrast, is concerned with raising funds to pay for losses that actually occur. Buying environmental impairment liability insurance is an example of risk financing.

When the risk management process described above was first developed, risk managers did not recognize all of the environmental exposures that are known today. Not only were many of the problems associated with exposures to toxic substances unknown, but most of the environmental laws that have created a large part of the environmental exposures faced by most organizations have been enacted since 1970. The normal steps that are applied in managing other exposures can also be used to manage environmental exposures, but some differences in environmental exposures must be taken into account.

## *Characteristics of Environmental Loss Exposures*

Environmental loss exposures have some unique characteristics that must be considered when developing a plan to manage them. Some of the more prevalent of these characteristics are as follows:

1. Environmental exposures can be difficult to identify because they may arise from activities that were conducted many years in the past or may be created by extremely small quantities of hazardous substances.
2. Environmental loss exposures tend to elude traditional exposure identification tools. Summaries of past losses may not contain any indication of environmental claims. Physical inspections of facilities do not always reveal possible causes of environmental damage. Business records may contain little or no information on prior waste disposal activities of the organization.
3. Often, no apparent "cause-and-effect" relationship is apparent between exposure to a substance and measurable injury because of the long latency period of some injuries or diseases associated with toxic exposures.
4. A claim may arise as a result of a perceived, rather than real, exposure to a toxic material or a fear of future injury due to an actual exposure.
5. The amount of the loss may be difficult to measure at a particular point in time.
6. There is often no direct cause-and-effect relationship between a release of pollutants and actual damages, which can make establishing the time, place, and amount of the loss difficult.
7. Some environmental laws are funded in accordance with a "let the polluter pay" concept. Under these laws, organizations and individuals can be retroactively liable, without fault, to pay for bodily injury, property damage, cleanup expenses, and natural resource damages. There is also a danger that courts will award multiplied damages, fines, and criminal prosecution under these laws.
8. Environmental losses tend to be expensive. The average cost to clean up a Superfund National Priority List site is $30 million. The average cost to clean up a leaking underground storage tank is $150,000. The *Exxon Valdez* oil spill in Alaska is reported to have cost the Exxon Corporation in excess of $3 billion in cleanup costs and $1 billion in third-party claims.
9. Advances in technology can change the exposure to loss. As detection equipment that can measure smaller quantities of contaminants is developed, the loss exposure increases. For example, if current state-of-the-art equipment can measure concentrations of contaminants only to ten parts

per *million*, a new machine with detection capabilities of ten parts per *billion* would change the detection threshold a thousandfold. In a cleanup project in which the goal is to achieve "non-detect" levels, a change in technology could dramatically change the costs of the cleanup.

10. Environmental damages can increase substantially over time as the contamination migrates farther from its source.

## Overcoming the Difficulties in Managing Environmental Exposures

Because most managers are not scientists or lawyers, environmental exposure identification is challenging for them. After the passage of more than twenty years of dealing with environmental laws and the hazards of working around toxic materials, many environmental exposures still have not been adequately identified or evaluated. Exposures that have not been identified and inventoried cannot be effectively managed. The difficulty of identifying environmental exposures can sometimes be overcome by the use of internal and external resources. Environmental compliance personnel are often familiar with the laws that apply to the operations of the firm. Legal counsel is another source of expertise with respect to the regulatory risks that the company must address. Operational personnel who work with hazardous materials on a daily basis are usually familiar with those that are toxic and the risks associated with their use. Environmental consultants can also be used to assist in the identification of environmental exposures, through independent audits or as part of an internal/external environmental audit team.

To effectively manage environmental loss exposures, the risk manager must distinguish between exposures stemming from prior activities and those from ongoing and future operations. Obviously, a lesser number of risk management options are available if the activity that created the exposure has already been conducted. For example, a firm that has been designated a responsible party in a Superfund cleanup action cannot prevent that loss from occurring, nor is it possible for the firm to purchase insurance coverage for the loss that has already occurred.

Risk managers can, however, formulate effective strategies for dealing with the environmental liability exposures associated with past activities of the entity. Here is where exposure identification continues to be important in the overall risk management program. Risk managers should attempt to identify the "skeletons in the closet" and address as many of the environmental exposures as possible before having to answer to a regulatory body, citizens' action committee, class action suit, or third-party claim.

If an environmental problem can be identified and corrected, the risk manager may have the opportunity to prevent all or part of a liability loss from occurring. For example, leaking barrels of toxic waste material may have already caused contamination that requires a cleanup, but perhaps their prompt removal will prevent contamination of groundwater and possible third-party bodily injury claims. Such action can be considered a risk control measure—that is, preventing a small loss from turning into a larger one.

# Pollution Exclusions

Most organizations have one or more liability insurance coverages to protect themselves against various types of liability claims. However, general liability policies, auto policies, and most other types of liability policies exclude some or all claims for injury or damage resulting from pollution, including the cost of cleaning up released pollutants. Commercial property policies provide coverage for cleanup of pollutants, but such coverage is often subject to low limits that would provide little relief for a substantial pollution incident. Those who wish to insure environmental loss exposures must therefore understand to what extent, if any, their various policies cover pollution claims. Pollution liability exposures that are not covered by an organization's traditional liability policies can be covered either with pollution coverage extensions to the traditional policies or through an appropriate form of environmental liability insurance.

## 1970 Exclusion in CGL Policy

Environmental awareness in the late 1960s prompted insurers in 1970 to introduce a pollution exclusion endorsement for use with the comprehensive general liability policy and other commercial liability policies. The exclusion, which was later incorporated in the 1973 CGL policy form, was expressed in the following language:

> This insurance does not apply to bodily injury or property damage arising out of the discharge, dispersal, release or escape of smoke, vapor, soot, fumes, acids, alkalis, toxic chemicals, liquids or gases, waste materials or other irritants, contaminants or pollutants into or upon the land, the atmosphere or any water course or body of water; but this exclusion does not apply if such discharge, dispersal, release or escape is sudden and accidental.

Because the exclusion reinstated coverage for "sudden and accidental" releases of pollutants (thus implying that only gradual releases were excluded), it was often referred to as the "gradual pollution exclusion" even though it did not use the word "gradual." This exclusion remained in the standard CGL policy form until ISO introduced the commercial general liability coverage forms in 1986.

The gradual pollution exclusion in occurrence-based comprehensive general liability policies became a problem for the insurance industry in the early 1980s. The passage of the Superfund legislation with its "polluter pays" funding mechanism created retroactive, strict liability for large groups of PRPs at most of the sites that were targeted for Superfund cleanup actions. As the PRPs received their cost recovery letters from the government beginning in 1982, some of them submitted claims to their general liability insurers, asserting that the letters were a demand for money or damages as a result of property damage.

By the mid-1980s, courts had accepted legal theories that enabled a claimant who had been exposed to a hazardous substance to recover damages under any liability policies that were in effect during the time the claimant was exposed to the hazardous substance, while the hazardous substance was residing in the claimant's body, and when a resulting disease was manifested. The courts' decisions to cumulate policy limits over many policy years greatly expanded insurers' exposures to environmental claims because (1) comprehensive general liability policies did not have pollution exclusions before 1970, (2) the policy aggregate limits typically did not apply to premises and operations claims before 1986, and (3) the phrase "sudden and accidental" in the 1970 pollution exclusion was not defined in the policy.

## APPLICATIONS

### Environmental Claim Under Pre-1986 CGL Policy

To understand the possible effects of CGL policy provisions on the liability insurers for environmental damage claims, assume that ACE Corporation used the Alpha and Beta waste disposal sites from 1960 to 1982, when both sites were closed by the EPA under Superfund. ACE Corporation had purchased a comprehensive general liability policy from the Ultimate Insurance Company from 1960 to 1982 with limits of liability of $1,000,000 per occurrence and a $1,000,000 annual aggregate for products and completed operations.

In 1982, ACE received a cost recovery letter from the EPA seeking to be reimbursed for the cleanup costs of $22,000,000 at each disposal site for a total cost of $44,000,000. Theoretically, Ultimate Insurance Company could be exposed to all $44,000,000 in claims under the expired $1,000,000 per occurrence comprehensive general liability policies.

Ultimate Insurance Company would argue in court (1) that only one policy should apply (the 1982 policy year), (2) that a leaking disposal site claim should be excluded because the pollution was not sudden and accidental, and (3) that damage to the insured site should be excluded. However, ACE Corporation would argue (1) that prior to 1970 the policy had no pollution exclusion, (2) that the words "sudden" and "accidental" are ambiguous in the policies and should therefore be interpreted to mean "unexpected" and "unintended," and (3) that since the unexpected and unintended pollution took place over twenty-two years (from 1960 to 1982), each policy year should provide a per occurrence limit to address the government's $44,000,000 demand.

Variations of the facts detailed in this case have been litigated in the U.S. courts for more than a decade, with the insureds and insurers prevailing in a roughly equal number of cases.

## Pollution Exclusion in 1986 and Subsequent CGL Policies

The insurance industry's exposure to environmental damage claims and long-tail products liability claims was largely responsible for the redrafting of the comprehensive general liability policy into the commercial general liability policy, which was introduced in many states in 1986. The two most significant changes in the policy regarding environmental damage claims were the addition of a general aggregate limit and the rewriting of the pollution exclusion to make it more effective at barring coverage for claims arising from the release of contaminants.

Despite ISO's effort to clarify the intent of the exclusion with several revisions since 1986, the pollution exclusion still creates confusion for practitioners. One problem is that the exclusion is widely referred to as the "absolute pollution exclusion" even though it does not contain the word "absolute" and does not absolutely exclude all pollution claims. Theoretically, the pollution exclusion in the commercial general liability policy does not eliminate coverage for pollution-related bodily injury and property damage claims arising from the products and completed operations hazard. It may, however, exclude coverage for cleanup costs arising from a product failure, even if bodily injury and property damage caused by a release of pollutants in the same incident are not excluded. This unexpected outcome is the result of cleanup costs being excluded separately from bodily injury and property damage in the pollution exclusion.

The current CGL pollution exclusion effectively eliminates all coverage for pollution claims arising from the insured's premises, waste streams, or disposal sites. It also excludes bodily injury, property damage, and cleanup costs when the insured is a contractor and either brings the pollutant onto the site or is involved in operations that are testing for, monitoring, removing, or remediating contamination.

To give underwriters an additional tool to eliminate pollution claims under CGL policies, a "total pollution exclusion" endorsement was introduced in 1986. Unlike the regular pollution exclusion in the policy form, which does not exclude all pollution liability claims, the total pollution exclusion attempts to eliminate any potential coverage for pollution liability claims from the CGL policy, including those arising from the insured's products or completed operations.

The widespread use of the regular CGL pollution exclusion and the total pollution exclusion in CGL policies has protected insurers from many of the claims that arose under earlier forms. Although the regular pollution exclusion does provide limited coverage for bodily injury or property damage claims arising under the products-completed operations hazard, this coverage has not led to frequent claims against underwriters by insureds attempting to broaden the pollution coverage available under the CGL policy. There are even fewer challenges to the exclusion of pollution claims under the total pollution exclusion. The majority of cases seeking to find pollution coverage under the 1986 and later editions of the CGL policy have been unsuccessful.

## APPLICATIONS

### Environmental Claim Under Post-1986 CGL Policy

A company that manufactured and installed fuel tanks for emergency generators was insured under a standard ISO commercial general liability policy that included the 1993/96 wording of the pollution exclusion. Products and completed operations of the insured were covered by this policy. A tank that the company manufactured and installed last year leaked, resulting in a release of diesel fuel inside the customer's warehouse building. Stock was damaged by contamination, and two employees of the customer were injured by inhaling fumes. The diesel fuel seeped through a floor drain into soil where it had to be cleaned up in accordance with an order by state environmental officials. The insured received a claim for the following amounts:

| | | |
|---|---|---:|
| a. | Tank replacement | $ 6,500 |
| b. | Lost fuel | 150 |
| c. | Stock damage | 15,000 |

| | | |
|---|---|---|
| d. | Employee injuries | $25,000 |
| e. | Cleanup of spill | 75,000 |

**Question:** Which parts of this claim will be allowed under the CGL policy described above?

**Answer:**

a. The damage to the insured product itself is excluded by exclusion k (damage to your product).

b. The policy will pay for the lost fuel.

c. The pollution exclusion does not exclude coverage for the property damage claim for damage to or destruction of the warehouse stock arising from a release of pollutants (read carefully the four subparts of part (1) of the exclusion).

d. Similarly, the pollution exclusion does not exclude bodily injury resulting from exposure to pollutants released because of failure of the insured's products.

e. The cost of cleanup is excluded by part (2) of the absolute pollution exclusion, even though these costs are the result of a release of contaminants caused by a failure of the insured's products.

## Pollution Exclusions in Other Liability Policies

The loss experience of the pre-1986 CGL insurers was mirrored by a similar flood of pollution claims under other liability policies. This was particularly true for automobile liability policies, since the release of hazardous materials from vehicles was a relatively common occurrence. With new environmental laws, releases of hazardous materials that were being transported as cargo or even of fuels that the vehicle carried for its own power became much more expensive to clean up. Emergency response requirements meant that special teams equipped to manage spills of toxic materials were required for a release of any hazardous substance. Treatment and disposal of the materials that were picked up also became much more expensive. Third parties, aware of the potential for toxic injuries, were also more likely to bring claims for bodily injury or property damage or both when hazardous materials had been released as a result of a vehicle accident. When the new absolute pollution exclusion was added to the commercial general liability policy in 1986, a similar exclusion was added to commercial auto policies.

In the mid-1980s, pollution exclusions were also added to professional errors and omissions liability policies for architects, engineers, consultants, and other professionals, as well as directors and officers liability policies. The worsening loss experience in CGL and auto liability policies often resulted in a secondary claim against a design professional, manufacturer, or other party that was alleged to have been responsible for or shared the blame with the owner of a site or vehicle from which contaminants were released.

Similarly, corporate executives found that they were being held responsible for poor management of hazardous materials on the part of their corporations, and suits alleging their fault were filed by shareholders and other parties seeking to recover the loss of value of their investments following a major environmental incident or the discovery of the organization's involvement in historical activities that made it a PRP under Superfund or similar state strict liability statutes. Unlike the pollution exclusions found in the CGL and commercial auto policies, the exclusions incorporated into E&O and D&O policies were intended to exclude all pollution-related claims. With some exceptions, courts have upheld the exclusion of pollution claims under E&O and D&O policies written since the mid-1980s in the majority of cases.

## Common Pollution Coverage Extensions in Standard Liability Forms

With the introduction of strict or total pollution exclusions in commercial general liability and other policies, it is now necessary to add pollution coverage endorsements to these forms or to purchase environmental liability insurance if pollution liability claims are to be insured. The fact that underwriters must specifically add these coverage provisions to the policies gives them an opportunity to review the exposures of the insured and charge an appropriate additional premium if they choose to provide pollution coverage. Even with the opportunity to underwrite these exposures, many insurers in the standard commercial property and liability insurance market do not routinely add pollution coverage to general liability policies or other liability forms. If pollution coverage is provided by the CGL underwriter, it is often time element or sudden release coverage that does not include claims for damage to soil or groundwater resources. Time element coverage typically limits coverage to pollution incidents discovered within seven days of their commencement and reported to the insurer within thirty to forty-five days of their discovery.

Most general liability insurers have been reluctant to offer any significant pollution coverage in the CGL form, often because of restrictions against such coverage in their own reinsurance programs. In contrast, auto liability insurers more commonly provide pollution coverage for insureds that require the protection. The business auto policy is commonly modified by either the MCS 90 endorsement and the ISO endorsement CA 99 48 when some form of pollution coverage is required.

U.S. Department of Transportation regulations require that vehicles carrying Class A or B explosives, poisonous gases, or bulk quantities (defined as a load weighing more than 3,500 gallons of water) of hazardous materials demonstrate financial responsibility with limits of $5 million per occurrence. Consequently, that limit is most often selected for pollution liability coverage by firms that transport hazardous materials or wastes. Transporters moving smaller quantities of hazardous materials, including oil, may have lower limits than those required for bulk transporters. These transporters usually select a limit of $1 million per occurrence.

Professional errors and omissions liability policies for engineers, architects, consultants, and others are modified for firms that need coverage for environmental exposures by deleting the pollution exclusion in its entirety. Unlike general liability or auto policies, there is no standard form used by the insurance industry to write professional E&O coverage. Many of the policies offered in the marketplace are similar, but no two are exactly alike. This makes the analysis of coverage extremely difficult for both the insured professional organization and for the entity that is employing the professional. Hiring professional services, therefore, is best done with a carefully prepared set of insurance specifications that must be met by the engineer or consultant.

The pollution exclusion that is typically incorporated in the D&O liability policies removes all coverage for pollution-related claims brought against executives of the firm or against the entity itself. When underwriters are willing to modify this broad pollution exclusion, they most often allow coverage only for shareholder derivative actions filed against individual officers or directors. With this modification, the policy will provide not only indemnity payments for such claims, but also defense, which is often as important in the D&O field as coverage for indemnity.

## Cleanup Coverage in Commercial Property Policies

Contemporary commercial property forms usually provide a nominal amount of coverage for the cost of cleaning up pollutants from land or water at the insured premises. This type of coverage was added to commercial property forms after insurers began to be confronted with claims for cleanup of pollutants at the insured's premises. Such claims were often covered because the pollutants were debris of covered property and thus covered under the debris removal provision.

By excluding cleanup of pollutants from debris removal coverage and covering them under a separate coverage agreement for a small amount, insurers reduced their exposure to such losses. For example, the ISO building and personal property coverage form limits pollutant cleanup and removal coverage to $10,000. Some insurers are willing to increase the amount of insurance provided for pollutant cleanup in return for an additional premium. However, many underwriters are reluctant to provide higher limits, and limits in excess of $100,000 are rarely available in commercial property policies.

# Types of Environmental Insurance Available

Today, more than two dozen types of environmental insurance are available, and many different insurance forms are used to provide coverage for different types of environmental loss exposures. The business is characterized by manuscript policy forms and a limited number of underwriters capable of writing a full range of environmental coverages.

It is not possible in this chapter to explore all of the forms of environmental insurance available today. However, the following major types of environmental insurance will be reviewed:

1. Site-specific environmental impairment liability insurance
2. Contractors environmental impairment liability insurance
3. Environmental professional errors and omissions liability insurance
4. Asbestos and lead abatement contractors general liability insurance
5. Environmental remediation insurance
6. Remediation stop-loss insurance
7. Underground and above-ground storage tank insurance
8. Combined CGL/EIL insurance

## Site-Specific Environmental Impairment Liability Insurance

**Site-specific environmental impairment liability (EIL) insurance** evolved directly from the early EIL policies written in the 1980s. The new forms cover claims arising from sudden as well as gradual releases. Coverage enhancements allow policyholders to purchase protection against the costs of on-site cleanup, to protect themselves against claims arising from releases from third-party disposal sites, and to insure against claims arising from pre-existing pollution at insured sites that has not been discovered.

## Insuring Agreement

The typical insuring agreement in an EIL policy obligates the insurer to pay on behalf of the insured a *loss*, in excess of any deductible, for *bodily injury*, *property damage*, or *cleanup costs*. The loss must result from *pollution conditions that exist beyond the boundaries of the site*(s) listed within the policy declarations. All of the italicized terms shown above have specific policy definitions. The policy definitions of "bodily injury" and "property damage" are the same as those in other liability insurance policies, with two notable qualifications. The first is that the bodily injury or property damage must result from pollutants emanating from an insured site. The second qualification is that some of the policy forms require physical injury or actual (as opposed to suspected) exposure to pollutants in order to trigger coverage for bodily injury claims. These requirements could substantially restrict coverage under the EIL policy for claims alleging "cancer phobia" or a similar fear of future disease or injury. Because some EIL policies do not contain these restrictions, each policy must be analyzed to determine the extent of coverage provided.

The definition of the term "loss" includes both cleanup costs and the cost to defend pollution claims in the scope of the policy. The term "cleanup costs" may appear as a separate coverage term, or it may be included within the definition of "property damage." The policies sold by different insurers may contain differences in their definitions of "cleanup costs." Most of the definitions include, as a minimum, the expenses the insured incurs in the removal or remediation of soil, surface water, groundwater, or other contamination in responding to a covered pollution liability loss.

EIL policies respond to loss arising from "pollution conditions." The definition of "pollution conditions" follows the definition of "pollutants" in the ISO pollution exclusions found in general liability, auto liability, and other liability insurance policies. Accordingly, EIL policies are often viewed as filling the coverage gap created by the introduction of the strict pollution exclusion in the 1986 CGL policy. Since the EIL policy is replacing coverage that has been removed from the CGL policy, it is important to compare the language of the CGL pollution exclusion with the definition of "pollution conditions" in the EIL policy to make certain that all coverage gaps are filled.

A typical definition of "pollution conditions" reads as follows: *"Pollution conditions* means the discharge, dispersal, release or escape of smoke, vapors, soot, fumes, acids, alkalis, toxic chemicals, liquids or gases, waste materials or other irritants, contaminants or pollutants into or upon land, the atmosphere or any watercourse or body of water."

The definition of "pollution conditions," like the definition of "pollutants" in the CGL and other policies, does not include the words "hazardous waste" or "hazardous material." The definition is much broader than hazardous waste, which is an important point to remember when analyzing potential coverage gaps between EIL policies and the insured's other liability policies.

## Claims-Made Coverage

EIL policies apply on a claims-made basis. In most respects, the policies operate like other forms of claims-made insurance, except that EIL forms have three noteworthy characteristics not shared by all other liability policies: (1) no retroactive date, (2) a relatively short extended reporting period, and (3) treatment of all claims arising from a pollution incident (release) as a single loss.

In order for a claim to be covered in a typical claims-made policy, the injury or damage must occur on or after the retroactive date contained in the policy, and the claim must be reported to the insurer during the policy period or during the extended discovery period. EIL policies, in contrast, often do not contain a retroactive date. In effect, a claims-made policy without a retroactive date provides unlimited prior acts coverage—a valuable feature for covering environmental impairment exposures that are often unknown to the insured. However, when the prior use or the current conditions at the site might make the risk unacceptable, the underwriter can impose a retroactive date in an EIL policy to limit the time period for coverage of prior acts. Adding a retroactive date allows the underwriter to provide EIL coverage prospectively without being overly concerned about the prior use of the site. Once the insured and the underwriter have developed more information about the site, the underwriter might be willing to remove the retroactive date from the policy.

Like other claims-made policies, EIL polices contain extended reporting period provisions that obligate the insurer to provide an extended reporting period for a specified additional premium upon the termination of the insurance. Coverage is provided only for claims that result from pollution releases that occurred (in total or in part) before the termination of the EIL policy. The typical time allowed for the reporting of such claims under the extended reporting period is only one year, in contrast with the option for an unlimited extended reporting period under the ISO claims-made CGL coverage form. One year is a short period of time for an environmental damage claim to manifest itself.

The third difference between an EIL policy and other claims-made forms is the way that multiple claims are treated. Several separate claims can arise from a single pollution incident. There may also be a delay in the discovery of damages after the incident that could result in a delay in the reporting of claims. To address these issues, EIL policies commonly treat all claims arising out of the same pollution incident as a single loss, subject to one limit of liability and one deductible. This approach prevents the stacking of policy limits from successive claims-made policies over multiple years. The insured benefits by avoiding the application of multiple deductibles to the same loss.

## APPLICATIONS

### Application of EIL Limit and Deductible

ACE Manufacturing Company discovered through an inventory reconciliation that approximately 1,000 gallons of plating bath solution from its chrome plating operations could not be accounted for. Further investigation revealed that over a three-year period the materials in the plating bath had seeped from a drain pipe into an adjacent stream. ACE immediately reported the situation to the appropriate governmental agency and completed a cleanup of the stream. ACE had a claims-made EIL policy at the time of the loss. The EIL policy paid for the cost of cleaning up the stream, subject to the policy deductible.

Two years after the cleanup had been completed, a group of fishermen brought a class action suit against ACE alleging that they had been exposed, through the consumption of fish, to harmful levels of heavy metals released by ACE into the stream. The EIL policy that paid for the cleanup will also respond to the fishermen's class action. However, any damages for which ACE becomes liable because of the class action will be considered part of the same loss as the earlier cleanup. Thus, the amount of insurance available for the class action will be the limit of liability less the cleanup costs paid earlier. However, ACE would not have to pay another deductible amount for the second claim. In this situation, it would also be common for all subsequent EIL policies issued by the same or different underwriters to contain an endorsement that would exclude all losses arising from the previous release of plating materials into the stream.

## Exclusions

Site-specific EIL policies typically exclude all or most of the following:

1. Known pre-existing conditions

2. Deliberate noncompliance with environmental laws
3. Punitive damages
4. Workers compensation and employers liability
5. Contractual liability
6. Damage to the insured site
7. Alienated premises
8. Nuclear liability
9. Products and completed operations
10. Acid rain
11. Transportation exposures
12. War

### Known Pre-Existing Conditions Exclusion

To provide a reasonable degree of protection for the insurer without eliminating all pre-existing conditions, EIL policies commonly exclude only those pre-existing conditions that are known to an individual or a group of designated persons. The exclusion usually limits the list of employees who must have knowledge of pre-existing pollution conditions to (1) those directly responsible for environmental affairs or (2) senior managers. To trigger the exclusion, the specified employees must have known or reasonably foreseen that the pre-existing condition would give rise to a claim under the policy.

### Exclusion of Deliberate Noncompliance With Environmental Laws

Environmental losses that are caused by the insured's intentional, willful, or deliberate noncompliance with any current environmental statute or regulation are excluded from coverage under the EIL policy.

### Punitive Damages Exclusion

EIL policies usually have broad exclusions for punitive, multiplied, and exemplary damages and for environmental fines and penalties. Insuring such costs is considered to be contrary to public policy in many jurisdictions because it would relieve guilty parties of a portion of the burden imposed by law for their culpable acts. In those states where the law allows insuring punitive or exemplary damages, the exclusion can be modified to cover such damages.

### Workers Compensation and Employers Liability Exclusions

EIL policies contain workers compensation and employers liability exclusions that are, in most cases, nearly identical to those found in the CGL coverage form.

### Contractual Liability Exclusion

Unlike CGL policies, EIL policies do not cover liability assumed under an "insured contract." The contractual liability exclusion in an EIL policy eliminates coverage for all liability assumed under contracts, other than liability that the insured would have incurred in the absence of the contract.

### Exclusion of Damage to the Insured Site

The purpose of an EIL policy is to insure third-party claims for bodily injury and property damage arising from the release of pollutants and to provide for the cleanup of the pollutants. In order to reinforce the third-party nature of the contract, EIL policies have traditionally contained exclusions that eliminate all coverage for releases of contaminants that did not migrate beyond the boundaries of the insured site. It is also common for the policies to specifically exclude on-site cleanup expenses. However, this is changing, and EIL policies that cover first-party exposures are now available. On-site cleanup coverage is particularly important where groundwater beneath the insured's property is contaminated by a release emanating from the site. Some, but not all, courts have determined that such water resources are owned by the people or the state (third parties). If groundwater is considered to be a part of the insured site, an EIL policy would not cover cleanup costs to remove contamination from an aquifer beneath the site without a specific endorsement that includes on-site cleanup.

### Alienated Premises Exclusion

This exclusion eliminates coverage under the EIL policy for an insured location that the insured has sold or leased to others, or of which the insured has otherwise relinquished operational control. Underwriters have felt this exclusion to be necessary because they expect the insured to exercise operational control over the site.

### Nuclear Liability Exclusion

EIL policies have nuclear exclusions comparable to the broad form nuclear liability exclusion that is attached to the CGL policy. The exclusion refers to the Atomic Energy Act of 1954 and defines certain terms within the exclusion as they are referred to in the act. In general, the nuclear exclusion eliminates coverage for high-level nuclear materials. Low-level nuclear materials can be covered under the EIL policy, with the exception of materials that are covered under liability policies underwritten by the nuclear pools.

### Products and Completed Operations Exclusion

Products and completed operations loss exposures are not contemplated within the insuring agreement or in the underwriting process that leads to the issuance of an EIL policy. Under the terms of the current CGL pollution exclusion, pollution claims for products and completed operations are not excluded unless the insured's products are used at a waste disposal site or the completed operations involve remediation of contamination at any owned or nonowned site. Products pollution liability coverage is available in a stand-alone policy that is often issued without a pollution exclusion. Contractors can purchase environmental liability coverage for completed operations, including remediation of contaminated sites. This type of insurance is discussed later in this chapter.

### Acid Rain Exclusion

Claims arising from acid rain are excluded in most EIL policies. Acid rain is a phenomenon caused by sulfur dioxide emissions from large industrial and commercial boilers that are fired by fossil fuels. Because the damage caused by acid rain can be widespread and occur at considerable distances from the source of emissions, underwriters have been unwilling to delete this exclusion from EIL policies unless the insured does not operate the type of equipment that can cause acid rain.

### Transportation Exposures Exclusion

Site-specific EIL policies exclude liability based upon or arising out of the maintenance, operation, use, loading, or unloading of any automobile, aircraft, watercraft, or railcar. Exposures to environmental impairment liability arising out of the transportation of pollutants are insurable under separate policies.

### War Exclusion

EIL policies typically exclude liability resulting from war in any form.

## Limits of Liability and Deductibles

As discussed earlier, EIL policies are typically subject to a per loss limit of liability, which is the most that the insurer will pay for bodily injury, property damage, cleanup costs, and defense expenses resulting from each release of pollutants. Some, but not all, EIL policies also contain an aggregate limit of liability.

The inclusion of defense expenses within EIL policy limits is an important difference from the CGL policy, which pays defense costs in addition to the applicable limit of liability until such time as the limit is used up by the payment of damages. Defense expenses in an environmental damage claim can be substantial due to the normal requirement for technical experts and testing of materials. Provisions should be made for these costs when selecting limits of liability. For example, installing one groundwater monitoring well can cost $10,000. If a claim is made against an insured for contamination of an aquifer, the groundwater investigation used to determine the condition of the resource can easily cost in excess of $100,000. These costs, along with attorney fees and other defense costs, reduce the amount of recoverable insurance for other claim expenses under the EIL policy.

Selecting appropriate limits for the EIL policy is comparable to selecting limits for any other type of insurance. The process begins with an identification of exposures. This is followed by an effort to quantify the loss potential associated with the exposures identified. Quantification of the loss potential requires a systematic approach but is not beyond the capability of many risk managers. If assistance is required, plant environmental personnel, outside consultants, or insurance producers may be able to offer additional expertise in assigning numerical ranges to the identified environmental exposures.

When considering how much pollution insurance is enough, the insured should remember that two elements of claim costs are included in the limit of liability in EIL policies that are not commonly found in other liability policies—cleanup costs and defense expenses. As was mentioned earlier, both cleanup costs and defense expenses in environmental damage claims can be substantial, and the policy limits, which encompass all loss costs, should be established to allow for these costs along with damages for bodily injury and property damage.

Substantial limits of liability are available today from the markets that write environmental insurance. Limits of $40 million per loss are available from a single insurer, and the total market capacity is in excess of $100 million per loss. The high limits available also allow for the integration of EIL policies into overall risk management programs that incorporate offshore programs for excess liability with attachment points above $25 million per loss. Most of these programs contain a form of pollution coverage called "time element" insurance that is the equivalent of sudden-release pollution coverage. By purchasing EIL policies from the environmental insurance markets with limits of $25 million per loss, an insured can obtain substantial sudden-release pollution limits by combining the underlying EIL limit with the limit available in the offshore excess insurance programs.

## Contractors Environmental Impairment Liability Insurance

The **contractors environmental impairment liability insurance policy** (hereinafter "contractors policy") was introduced to the U.S. market in 1987. The policy form was developed to address the environmental insurance needs of contractors that were performing environmental remediation services on contaminated sites. The contractors policy has its roots in the site-specific EIL policy discussed above. In fact, the original contractors policies actually used a lengthy endorsement to a site-specific EIL policy to create the contractors' version of EIL coverage.

Many of the policy terms and conditions in the contractors policy are similar to those found in the EIL policy. Both provide coverage for bodily injury, property damage, cleanup, and defense costs. However, many of the features of the EIL policy had to be modified substantially to address the contractors' insurance needs. The EIL policy is written on a designated premises basis, whereas the contractors policy is designed to cover a contractor's operations and activities at a number of construction sites and to cover the completed operations exposures of the contractor. To accomplish those goals, the EIL policy is modified as described below.

## Insuring Agreement

Unlike site-specific EIL policies, contractors policies provide coverage for loss arising from the described *operations* of the named insured. The obligation of the insurer to indemnify or pay a "loss" on behalf of the insured has the same meaning in the contractors policy as in the EIL policy, which is to cover claims for bodily injury, property damage, cleanup costs, and defense expenses.

There is a significant difference between the way an EIL policy addresses prior acts and the way they are handled in the contractors policy. Although most site-specific EIL policy forms do not contain a provision for a retroactive date and, therefore, provide full prior acts coverage, contractors policies provide coverage for claims that arise only from operations performed subsequent to the retroactive date on the policy.

## Exclusions

The principal differences between contractors EIL policies and site-specific EIL policies are in their exclusions. Contractors policies typically have exclusions similar to those in an EIL policy in the following areas:

1. Known pre-existing conditions
2. Deliberate noncompliance with environmental laws
3. Punitive damages
4. Products liability
5. Workers compensation and employers liability

6. Contractual liability
7. Nuclear liability
8. Transportation risks
9. War

Some exclusions that are commonly found in EIL policies, but are generally omitted from the contractors policy, include the following:

- Completed operations
- Damage to the insured site
- The cost of remediating the job site for loss created by the contractor's operations

The following additional exclusions are commonly found in contractors policies:

- Asbestos abatement operations
- Radioactive matter
- Underground storage tanks

The three additionally excluded exposures can be insured by endorsement to the contractors policy. With regard to nuclear materials, the contractors policy can provide coverage for low-level radioactive exposures but not for risks associated with high-level materials used for weapons or fuel rods in nuclear power reactors.

The exposure of an asbestos contractor is better addressed under an asbestos or a lead abatement liability insurance policy, which will be discussed later in this chapter.

## Environmental Professional Errors and Omissions Liability Insurance

The "Cleanup America" effort of the 1980s has created a rapidly growing environmental consulting industry in the 1990s. Environmental engineers and consultants face many of the same environmental exposures as site owners, with the exception of legislated liabilities for prior acts involving the disposal of hazardous wastes (the major risk of PRPs under Superfund). Environmental service vendors may also incur PRP liability for prospective work at a Superfund site either as an "arranger" for deposit of materials at a designated facility or as an "operator" of a site as those terms are defined in the act. Cleanup contractors have lobbied for a change in Superfund on this issue, arguing that they are there to help solve the problem and should not be considered to be a "polluter" under liability provisions of CERCLA. To date, these changes have not been incorporated into the legislation.

In addition to Superfund liability, environmental service vendors can face potential liability from negligent professional errors, acts, or omissions. Claims against such vendors may include allegations that they have failed to identify contaminants, that their characterization of the site contains errors, that their design for remediation of contamination is faulty, that they have made mistakes in analysis of samples, or that they have otherwise failed to perform in accordance with the standards of their profession.

At the same time that environmental consultants were experiencing rapid growth in their business sector during the 1980s, the insurance industry was adding pollution exclusions to all commercial liability insurance policies, including those for professional liability. Consequently, many environmental consultants had to operate without pollution insurance coverage until environmental consultants professional errors and omissions policies were introduced in 1989.

Unlike contractors EIL insurance, which was introduced and gained market acceptance as a monoline, gap-filling coverage for the pollution exclusion in the contractor's CGL policy, an environmental E&O policy that responded only to pollution claims was quickly eclipsed by a policy that covered all of the traditional E&O exposures of the engineer or consultant, including claims for environmental damages.

## *Insuring Agreement*

The early environmental E&O policy forms amended the insuring agreement of the contractors coverage form to cover "negligent professional errors, acts or omissions in the performance of the Insured's Professional Services," instead of covering the specifically described operations of the insured. Many of these early policies provided coverage only for personal injury (similar to bodily injury, but including libel and slander in the definition), property damage, cleanup costs, and defense expenses. These were different from the broader insuring agreements in traditional engineers professional liability policies that responded to "claims arising out of professional services." "Claims," in the traditional policies, could encompass considerably more than personal injury, property damage, cleanup costs, and defense expenses. Contemporary environmental professional E&O policies now contain insuring agreements that resemble the coverage grants of traditional engineers professional liability policies.

Environmental professional E&O liability policies are written on a claims-made basis, as are nearly all professional liability insurance contracts. They include substantial deductibles and are available on a "pay on behalf of" or "indemnity" coverage format. Retroactive dates are included in most E&O policies.

## *Exclusions*

None of the insurers offering environmental professional E&O liability insurance use the same forms to write this insurance. A careful review of the policies, including all exclusions and endorsements, is important in evaluating the coverage provided by these forms. One popular policy form contains sixteen exclusions. Another form has forty-five. It is also common to find pollution exclusions in the professional liability policies that are supposedly tailor-made for environmental consultants. With a careful review of the policy wording and some negotiations with underwriters, the insured can develop an adequate protection program for E&O liability exposures, but this is not typically offered in off-the-shelf policies issued by insurers.

The exclusions most commonly found in environmental consultants professional E&O policies are as follows:

1. Dishonest or fraudulent errors or omissions
2. Known pre-existing conditions
3. Deliberate noncompliance with environmental statutes
4. ERISA liability (Employee Retirement Income Security Act of 1974)
5. Contractual liability
6. Costs exceeding estimates
7. Insured-versus-insured claims
8. Workers compensation and employers liability
9. Failure to maintain insurance or surety
10. Nuclear losses
11. War
12. Personal injury and advertising injury

In addition to the common exclusions, some policy forms contain exclusions for one or more of the following types of claims:

1. Any claim from an insured entity that performs contracting operations
2. Laboratory analysis
3. Third-party-over claims

4. Automobile or transportation risks
5. Loss arising from real or personal property
6. Asbestos
7. Radioactive matter
8. Lead
9. Active pollution releases
10. Any project in which the insured is providing design/build services
11. Employment practices
12. Waste disposal liability under Superfund
13. Claims from any job in which project-specific insurance was procured
14. Formaldehyde insulation
15. Products liability
16. Claims from subcontractors' operations
17. Securities law violations
18. Infringement of copyrights
19. Mental injury or emotional distress
20. Pollution losses from products
21. Fines and penalties
22. Sexual harassment
23. Subsidence
24. Electromagnetic force fields
25. Liquor liability

The more common exclusions can be categorized as (1) those that address a moral hazard exposure, (2) exposures that are better covered in other policies, (3) exclusions that help the underwriter define the coverage being provided, or (4) those that eliminate coverage for exposures the underwriter simply does not want to insure.

Fraudulent errors and omissions, known pre-existing conditions, and deliberate noncompliance with environmental laws are all moral hazards that cannot typically be insured. ERISA liability, personal injury, advertising injury, contractual liability, high-level nuclear materials, and workers compensation losses are more appropriately insured under other forms of commercial insurance.

The insured-versus-insured exclusion and contractual liability exclusion are common exclusions in engineers professional liability policies that have found their way into environmental consultants professional liability policies. These exclusions address business risk issues that are not unique to the practice of an environmental consultant. The insured-versus-insured exclusion eliminates coverage for claims in which one insured sues another insured for damages arising out of a professional error, act, or omission. Most professional liability underwriters believe that this is a business risk, assumed by the affiliated entities, that should not be insured. The contractual liability exclusion addresses a similar business risk issue.

Failure to maintain insurance can be considered a professional error, act, or omission, if the insurance is required under the consultant's contract. However, most professional liability underwriters try to avoid having their professional liability policy used as a substitute for coverages that are required in a contract for services but are not purchased, for whatever reason.

It is difficult to explain the persistence of the broad array of other exclusions that appear in environmental consultants professional liability insurance contracts. Some are clearly redundant because the coverage provided by the insuring agreement of the policy is not triggered by a claim of the type contemplated in the exclusion. Particular care must be exercised in evaluating the coverage needs of the insured when dealing with environmental consultants E&O insurance. Most underwriters of this type of insurance have an exceptional amount of latitude in their ability to endorse their policies to address the needs of their insured professionals.

## Asbestos and Lead Abatement Contractors General Liability Insurance

In the mid-1980s, the combined effects of legislation, increased public awareness of asbestos risks, and a strong real estate market created a demand for asbestos abatement services. During the same time period, insurance companies were trying to limit their exposure to asbestos products liability and environmental damage claims by adding stronger pollution and asbestos exclusions to all commercial liability insurance policies. Consequently, a demand for liability insurance covering asbestos abatement arose at a time when the availability of liability insurance, in general, and environmental liability insurance, in particular, was very restricted.

Nonetheless, the law of supply and demand in a free market economy resulted in the introduction of **asbestos abatement contractors general liability insurance**. Early policy forms were written on a claims-made basis and were very restrictive in terms of the coverage provided. They were also extremely expensive, costing up to 18 percent of the contractor's revenue for a six-month claims-made policy that included a very short extended reporting period (often less than thirty days). The market for this coverage became more competitive as additional underwriters sought to take advantage of the high premiums and generous profit margins. By 1990, the market for this coverage had switched to occurrence-based policy forms, which are used almost universally for asbestos abatement liability insurance today. The pricing of coverage has also been adjusted to reflect a good loss history in this class of business. The policies are written for one-year terms or longer periods if required by the project owner.

As concern over lead paint has grown, many asbestos abatement insurance markets have expanded their policy forms to include lead paint exposures as well. Coverage terms and conditions for lead abatement contractors are virtually identical to those found in the asbestos abatement forms.

A contractors EIL policy can be used to address asbestos and lead exposures by deleting the exclusions for these particular pollutants. However, because contractors policies are available only on a claims-made basis, the majority of asbestos and lead paint abatement contractors purchase the occurrence-based policy form.

## Coverage Form

The asbestos abatement contractors general liability insurance policy is essentially a CGL policy that contains an amendment to the pollution exclusion deleting asbestos from the definition of "pollutants." Similarly, if the insured's operations include lead abatement, lead can also be deleted from the definition of "pollutants." Thus, unlike the contractors EIL policy, which is a "gap-filler" for the pollution exclusion in the CGL policy of the contractor, an asbestos abatement contractors general liability form covers a contractor's general liability and asbestos abatement liability insurance needs in a single policy.

An asbestos or lead abatement contractors general liability policy often contains other exclusions in addition to those of the standard CGL policy. For example, many policies exclude liability assumed under any contract for injury to any employee of the insured. The standard CGL policy covers such liability as long as it is assumed under an insured contract as defined in the policy. Because such claims are excluded under the employers liability coverage of the standard workers compensation policy, they may represent a coverage gap for asbestos or lead abatement contractors, who should seek either to have the exclusion eliminated from their general liability policy or to have the contractual assumption eliminated from their contracts with customers.

Other important differences from the standard CGL form include changes in the limits of liability, deductibles, and defense cost provisions. The asbestos contractor policy forms usually include defense costs within the general aggregate limit. Deductibles are typically higher than those found in most contractors' CGL forms.

It is also common to underwrite every project before that work is added to the policy. To ensure compliance with this reporting requirement, some policies exclude all asbestos claims unless the job site is specifically endorsed to the policy. However, many policies are now written on a blanket basis, covering all of the insured's work sites.

Like other forms of environmental insurance, the market for asbestos abatement contractors insurance is changing rapidly, and underwriters compete with each other through the use of manuscript coverage forms as well as on price. There are no standard forms in the market except for the ISO CGL policy, which is the basic building block for the policy. Care must be taken in evaluating the coverage provided by these policies because the asbestos modifications to the policy can delete standard CGL provisions in the process.

## Environmental Remediation Insurance

First-party environmental insurance was developed to address the needs of lenders who were concerned that their borrowers might default on loans because the borrowers were faced with unexpected environmental cleanups on the secured properties. Early versions of the coverage forms were often referred to as property transfer environmental insurance. They are now more commonly called **environmental remediation insurance**. As with all environmental insurance policies, environmental remediation policy forms vary a great deal from insurer to insurer.

### Insuring Agreement

Environmental remediation insurance policy forms are designed to pay on behalf of or indemnify the insured for remediation costs or expenses caused by environmental damage at a covered location. To be insured, the environmental damage must be discovered and reported during the policy period. The coverage is intended to insure cleanup costs incurred at the insured location on a first-party basis. In addition, third-party EIL coverage is routinely included within environmental remediation policy forms to insure the traditional third-party EIL loss exposures.

Insuring environmental cleanup costs presents a problem for the insurer in defining what is a covered loss. Environmental cleanups are usually triggered by the discovery of contamination in excess of baseline levels that are set forth in various environmental protection laws. Contamination levels above that level may need to be remediated. To set the baseline for a cleanup action, environmental remediation insurance policies typically define "remediation expenses" as expenses incurred for the investigation, removal, or treatment of pollution conditions only to the extent required by specified environmental regulations such as CERCLA, RCRA, the Toxic Substances Control Act, the Clean Water Act, and the Clean Air Act. Thus, coverage under the policy is triggered when the insured discovers levels of contamination that the environmental laws or regulations require the insured to remediate.

Environmental remediation insurance policies have broad definitions of insureds to address the insurable interests of the buyer, seller, and lender in a property transfer transaction. The additional insureds must be named in the policy for the coverage to apply to their interests.

## Exclusions

The exclusions of environmental remediation policies vary considerably from policy to policy. The exclusions found in nearly all policies include the following:

- Known pre-existing conditions
- Intentional or illegal acts

Different policy forms may exclude one or more of the following exposures from coverage:

1. Lead paint and asbestos
2. Radioactive matter
3. Electromagnetic fields
4. Contractual liability
5. Products
6. A claim by one insured against another insured
7. Bodily injury and property damage
8. Fines and penalties

As is true in all forms of environmental insurance, some of these exposures are excluded so that the purchaser of the insurance is forced to provide additional underwriting information to the underwriter. Once the underwriter has received this additional information, the exclusions can often be removed or modified, usually for an additional premium charge.

## Other Provisions

Environmental remediation policies are usually on a claims-made basis. Policy periods of up to five years are common in this line of coverage. However, environmental remediation policies usually have no provision for extended reporting periods. The policies are written with substantial deductibles. Regardless of the number of the same or related pollution releases from a covered location, only one deductible and one per-loss limit will apply.

## Remediation Stop-Loss Insurance

**Remediation stop-loss environmental insurance** (also known as cost cap coverage) was designed to insure remediation costs that exceed the projected or anticipated costs in the execution of a remedial action plan at a specific location. Remediation stop-loss policies provide only first-party coverage and do not cover third-party claims.

The coverage is useful in facilitating the sale of contaminated property. Usually there will be a range of estimated cleanup costs associated with the remediation of a property. A wide discrepancy often exists between the low and high estimates of cleanup costs, creating a problem for buyers and sellers of property in establishing the sale price. Potential buyers tend to discount the sale price by the maximum potential remediation cost, and, of course, the seller favors the low cost estimate. Since environmental laws impose joint and several liability for cleanup costs on all parties in the chain of title, potential purchasers are extremely cautious about taking title to contaminated property. For similar reasons, sellers desire to transfer properties to parties that have the resources not only to remediate the property but also to protect the seller from any possible future costs related to environmental liability associated with the property.

Remediation stop-loss policies typically agree to pay on behalf of the named insured the expenses (in excess of the deductible) that the insured incurs in completing an approved remedial action work plan at a specified location.

A claim under the policy is defined as "written notice to the insured that the remediation costs incurred at the project have exceeded the costs contained within the scope of work." The description of the "insured scope of work," which is different in each policy, is usually contained in an endorsement to the policy.

Remediation stop-loss policies typically contain relatively few exclusions because they are written on a first-party coverage basis. As with other types of environmental insurance, these policies are manuscript forms without standard terms or conditions. Some of the more common exclusions found in the remediation stop-loss policies eliminate coverage for the following:

- Intentional acts or misrepresentations
- Bodily injury
- Contractual liability
- Fines or penalties
- War

In underwriting these policies, the insurer reviews the insured's proposed remedial action work plan to establish the reasonableness of the cost estimates. A sizable deductible is used as a pricing tool to eliminate loss amounts that have a very high probability of occurring. The deductible may also be used to eliminate any profit motive the contractor may have in intentionally underbidding the job. Legitimate cost overruns on a project may be created by a design or contractor error, the discovery of new contamination, or the failure of the remediation technology.

## APPLICATIONS

### Using Remediation Stop-Loss Coverage

Midland Grain Growers Cooperative would like to sell a grain elevator to Able Elevator Company. The appraised value of the elevator is $3,000,000, and the buyer and seller agree that this is a fair market value for the transaction. However, the land that the elevator is located on is contaminated with chemicals used in the past to fumigate the grain in storage. The seller's estimate for the expected cost to remediate the land is $1,000,000. The work plan for this remediation approach was submitted to and approved by the environmental regulators.

Able Elevator Company was concerned about purchasing this contaminated property, so Able hired an environmental consultant to evaluate the cost estimates for the approved work plan. Able's consultant concluded that the remedial action could cost as much as $6,000,000 but that there is only a 10 percent chance that the costs will exceed $1,000,000.

Assuming the information on expected costs is correct, how much should Able pay for the grain elevator? According to its expert's estimate, an appropriate selling price for this property might be $1,500,000. This sum is equal to the fair market value of the property if it were clean, less the expected cost of remediation in accordance with the approved work plan, calculated as follows:

| | |
|---|---:|
| Appraised value | $3,000,000 |
| Less remediation expenses | |
|   Original work plan | (1,000,000) |
|   Revised work plan | |
|   ($5,000,000 additional cost × 10% probability) | (500,000) |
| Adjusted sales price | $1,500,000 |

In reality, this transaction might never take place. Estimates of environmental remediation expenses are seldom as precise as those cited in this example, and if the cleanup costs an additional $5,000,000, Able would be responsible for all of the additional expenses, not just 10 percent of them. To encourage Able to purchase this property and not incur any risk for excess cleanup costs, the seller might agree to indemnify Able for costs in excess of the discounted sales price. This option might be unacceptable to Midland Grain Growers because that indemnity would show up on its balance sheet as a contingent liability (perhaps forever). Another alternative would be for the seller to discount the agreed sales price by the worst-case loss scenario—$6,000,000. In other words, Midland Grain Growers would give Able the title to the property and $3,000,000 for the maximum expected remediation expenses. Midland Grain Growers would undoubtedly reject this alternative.

A more viable approach to the transaction would be to use a remediation stop-loss insurance policy with a limit equal to the worst-case loss scenario. In this example, there is only a 10 percent chance that the cost of the remediation would exceed $1,000,000. The pure premium for the policy would therefore be $500,000 (10 percent of the $5,000,000 maximum additional cost). The underwriter would set the deductible at the expected remediation costs of $1,000,000.

## Combined Pollution Coverage Forms

As the variety of environmental insurance policies grew, it became apparent that insureds that had more than one type of pollution exposure would benefit from having a single policy that combined multiple environmental coverages. The demand for combined forms began with environmental consulting firms that were also involved in on-site remediation of contamination. Because these firms had both a professional liability exposure and a contracting exposure, they found it necessary to purchase both a contractors EIL policy and a professional E&O liability policy to adequately cover their environmental liability exposures. Once the pattern of combining coverage forms was established, underwriters developed other combinations of coverage to meet the specific needs of various segments of the market. Now, combined forms are an important part of the environmental insurance market.

## *Advantages of Combined Insurance Forms*

Using combined forms for environmental insurance has several advantages. The first is that it provides the coverage needed by the insured to adequately protect it against pollution claims. As was mentioned above for environmental consultants who also do on-site work, the combination of contractor's insurance with professional E&O insurance provides the pollution insurance needed by the insured in a single policy that takes the place of two forms. A combined policy is typically less expensive than if the two coverage forms were purchased separately. The combined policy has a lower price because it typically provides a single limit of liability for both the contracting and the professional liability exposures.

Another advantage of combined forms is that they can eliminate coverage disputes that might otherwise exist if the coverages were provided by two different insurers. For example, when a release occurs during the remediation of a contaminated site, it may be difficult to determine immediately whether the loss is a result of contracting operations or of an error related to the professional activities of the engineer. For example, if a contractor that is excavating soil to remove heavy metals unexpectedly strikes an underground storage tank, releasing diesel fuel into an area of clean soil, the fault may be that of the contractor that directly caused the release or the engineer who failed to identify the presence of the tank. If the firm that had done the site assessment is also doing the on-site remediation, it may experience a third-party claim that falls in a "gray area" between the contracting and professional aspects of its work. Having both exposures insured by the same insurer eliminates the possibility of two separate insurers both denying coverage for the "gray area" claim.

Besides providing protection against either a contracting or a professional liability exposure, the combined insurance form also provides a uniform defense for such claims that assures the environmental consultant of efficient handling of the problem with the client. There is no dispute over which insurer is responsible and no need for subrogation, which might be necessary to establish the rights of the parties and/or the insurers when the coverages are provided in separate policies (typically with different insurers). Because the claim is handled without a dispute, it is less likely to result in a problem in the relationship between the environmental consultant and the firm that hired it to do the site characterization and remediation.

The combined contractors EIL/engineers professional liability insurance policy is typically less expensive than would be the case if these coverages were purchased separately. As was mentioned above, this is primarily due to the use of a single policy aggregate limit that applies to both coverage parts. Although this makes the policy less costly, it does have the drawback of offering only one limit when the purchase of separate policies would provide two limits. If a claim involves *both* contracting liability and a professional error, the lesser limit may be a factor. However, only one deductible applies in the combined form, whereas the use of separate policies would result in the application of two deductibles.

## Types of Combined Insurance Policies Available

Since the development of the earliest combined environmental insurance forms, underwriters have worked with brokers and clients to provide a variety of insurance products needed to protect against diverse pollution exposures. Consequently, insurers have developed numerous combined forms. Although the variety of combined policies is limited only by the imagination of the broker or the underwriter, certain forms have become popular. Some of the more popular combined forms are described below.

### Underground and Above-Ground Storage Tank Insurance

The Resource Conservation and Recovery Act was modified in 1986 to provide regulations that apply to the owners and operators of underground storage tanks. When such tanks are used for storage of fuels or hazardous materials, the RCRA regulations require the owners or operators to demonstrate their ability to pay claims resulting from the release of such materials from the tank. One method by which financial responsibility can be demonstrated is the purchase of insurance. The variety of coverages required has resulted in the development of a special combined form of pollution insurance, called **underground storage tank (UST) insurance**, which covers third-party liability claims for bodily injury, property damage, and off-site cleanup costs as well as first-party claims for cleanup of the insured site.

RCRA requires that the owners or operators of underground storage tanks provide evidence of financial responsibility for specified limits. For most tank owners, the required limit of insurance is $1 million per claim. Larger retailers of petroleum products may be required to provide evidence of $2 million of financial responsibility per claim. Although the current regulations do not require evidence of financial responsibility of owners or operators of above-ground storage tanks, a number of companies also insure above-ground tanks on the same policies used for underground tanks. Most insureds consider the exposure to be similar for both types of tanks, so the same limits may apply to both.

The UST policies written by environmental insurers are not full EIL policies (as described earlier). Although the policy is site-specific, it does not insure all releases of contaminants from the insured site. It responds only to a "corrective action" as that term is defined in RCRA, and not to other environmental damage claims. This distinction is important for any insured that may face environmental liability claims based on grounds other than RCRA.

## APPLICATIONS

### UST Versus EIL Coverage

The owner of a retail service station that has four underground storage tanks is required to provide proof of financial responsibility for the cleanup of releases from the tanks as well as third-party claims for bodily injury and property damage. A UST policy is used by the owner for this purpose. The policy has a limit of liability of $1 million per claim and a deductible of $50,000 per claim. The policy responds only to corrective actions under RCRA.

While a customer of the station was pumping gas into her car, the hose from one of the pumps ruptured. The gasoline injured the customer and a bystander and also damaged the customer's car, which had to be repainted as a result of the gasoline spill.

Because the UST policy responds only to corrective actions under RCRA, it would not cover the bodily injury or property damage claims of the customer or the bystander. To cover such claims, the owner would need to purchase an EIL policy. This policy could be endorsed to provide coverage for the underground storage tank exposures, including on-site cleanup of released materials. Because of the limited pollution coverage provided in UST policies, it is often recommended that the retail service station owner purchase coverage under an EIL form or on a combined general liability/pollution liability form as discussed below.

### Combined CGL/EIL Insurance Forms

Organizations that have pollution exposures frequently purchase an EIL policy because of the limited pollution insurance provided by the commercial general liability coverage form. The EIL policy may exclude products and completed operations, which are supposed to be covered by the CGL policy. However, the coverage that remains in the CGL for products and completed operations provides insurance for bodily injury and property damage but not for cleanup costs related to a release of hazardous materials from a product manufactured by the insured.

To avoid this potential coverage gap, some manufacturers have sought to insure both general liability and pollution liability in a single policy. Environmental underwriters offer **combined CGL/EIL insurance policies** to provide a more complete insurance package for such insureds. Because nearly all pollution insurance is written on claims-made policies and most general liability policies are written on an occurrence basis, it has been necessary for the underwriters to develop combined forms with the flexibility to accommodate a variety of coverage needs. These CGL/EIL forms are offered with the EIL coverage on a claims-made basis and the CGL portion on either an occurrence or a claims-made basis. Separate limits can be specified if the insured needs higher limits for the pollution or the general liability exposures. Both coverages are subject to a single aggregate limit and typically a single deductible (when both EIL and CGL claims are involved).

Combined CGL/EIL policies may also be specifically endorsed to provide products coverage that includes protection against pollution claims related to a release caused by a failure of the insured's product. The insured can also purchase coverage for pollution risks related to transportation of its products or waste materials when they are carried on vehicles owned by third parties.

## APPLICATIONS

### Potential Coverage Gap Between Separate CGL and EIL Policies

A manufacturer of underground storage tanks has both a CGL policy and an EIL policy. The EIL policy excludes products and completed operations.

An underground tank manufactured by the insured is used by a retail service station for gasoline storage. The tank fails, allowing a release of gasoline, which migrates from the premises of the service station to the property of a third party. When the pollution is discovered, the third party brings a claim for property damage and cleanup costs. The retail service station and the manufacturer of the tank are named as defendants in the suit. The EIL insurer for the tank manufacturer does not respond to the claim because its policy excludes products and completed operations. The CGL insurer provides coverage for the property damage claim but does not pay for the cleanup costs, which are excluded by the CGL pollution exclusion. The manufacturer would have coverage for both the property damage claim and the cleanup costs arising from this claim if it had purchased a combined CGL/EIL policy instead of buying the two policies separately.

### Menu-Style Combined Insurance Policies

The most recently introduced combined pollution insurance policies use a menu of coverage parts that allow the insured to tailor coverage to meet its specific needs. Some of these policies allow the insured to elect from many coverage options, such as the following:

1. Discovery of a pre-existing pollution condition (on-site coverage)
2. Discovery of a new pollution condition (on-site coverage)
3. Third-party claims for on-site cleanup of pre-existing pollution conditions
4. Third-party claims for on-site cleanup of new pollution conditions
5. Third-party claims for on-site property damage
6. Third-party claims for on-site bodily injury
7. Third-party claims for off-site cleanup of pre-existing pollution conditions
8. Third-party claims for off-site cleanup of new pollution conditions
9. Third-party claims for off-site property damage
10. Third-party claims for off-site bodily injury
11. Third-party claims for bodily injury, property damage, or cleanup costs at nonowned locations
12. Third-party claims for on-site cleanup costs at nonowned locations
13. Pollution releases from transported cargo carried by covered autos
14. Third-party claims arising from transportation of the insured's product or waste
15. Business interruption resulting from a release of pollution (third-party claim)

Each coverage option is separately underwritten and rated. All coverage parts selected are subject to a single policy aggregate limit. Deductibles can be varied for the different coverage parts selected. The flexibility of these policies allows the insured to develop a comprehensive program for protection against pollution claims arising from a broad range of exposures. The only drawback to these coverage forms is that they are relatively long and may require careful reading to understand the various coverage options. If properly used, they are a powerful tool to provide a broad range of environmental insurance coverages.

# Application Process for Environmental Insurance

The process of making application for environmental insurance has often been considered tedious because of the emphasis on details concerning the prospective insured's operations and activities. Traditionally, applications often contained more than a dozen pages of detailed questions that could not be answered by the risk manager without outside assistance. As a result, the risk manager would have to seek the help from other persons in various parts of the organization just to get an application completed. Moreover, the underwriters would then require an on-site inspection to verify the information contained in the application and to get a firsthand impression of the environmental condition of the site to be insured. Furthermore, the prospect would be charged an inspection fee for the underwriter's review, which might range from $3,000 to more than $30,000, depending on the complexity and geographic location of the sites. After all of this effort and expense, the underwriter might decide not to offer a quotation for coverage.

Recently, some insurers have made the application process less complicated and less expensive for the insured. In some cases, the applications have been reduced from more than twelve pages to as few as two. Such applications ask for little information but request permission for the underwriter to contact persons at the prospect's plants who are familiar with environmental matters. The underwriter's technical experts then contact the plant personnel and complete the application over the phone. Usually, a coverage binder can be issued without a physical inspection. If an inspection is made, it will be done during the policy period rather than as a prerequisite for offering a coverage proposal. Some insurers even pay the cost of the inspection.

Regardless of the process used to underwrite environmental insurance, the application will also include certain warranties that become a part of the policy. The warranties include a statement that the prospect knows of no existing pollution conditions that are likely to lead to a claim against the organization. The warranties also verify the truthfulness of other information submitted to the underwriter. Additional warranties concern disclosure of past claims against the organization and knowledge of violations of environmental laws and regulations. The application is signed by an officer of the organization and attached to the policy when it is issued. Failure to provide honest or accurate information may result in a loss of coverage in the event of a loss.

One of the difficulties for risk managers in applying for environmental insurance has been that the information required is not common to other forms of insurance. Although gross receipts or some other simple measures may be used as the rating base for the policy, much more information is required to underwrite the policy. The type of information required varies depending on the type of insurance involved.

After the insured has completed an application for environmental insurance and submitted it to the underwriter, the underwriter reviews the application to see whether additional information is required to prepare a quotation for insurance. The underwriters at the companies active in the environmental market typically have technical education and experience in some area of the environmental business. Environmental insurers have found that underwriters with experience only in automobile and general liability insurance are not equipped to underwrite pollution risks. They have, therefore, hired geologists, engineers, environmental consultants, or persons with experience at regulatory agencies and trained them to underwrite pollution risks. Over the years, the quality of underwriting has improved as these people have gained experience with a wide variety of environmental exposures.

A producer commonly seeks competitive proposals from two or more insurers in providing alternatives for the client to consider. Pricing has been competitive, and the policy forms are constantly being refined to add additional competition to the selection process. With the different policy forms available and the numerous exclusions that are included in or attached to the basic coverage form, quotations must be compared carefully. Producers knowledgeable in this area can provide valuable assistance in evaluating the proposals of insurers and in assuring that the policies adequately address identified environmental exposures. Risk managers may also use consultants to supplement their knowledge of environmental exposures and to evaluate the proposals of the insurers. Policies should be reviewed annually because the market continues to change each year and because improvements are being made in the policies on a regular basis.

## *Summary*

Liability for pollution incidents can be based on negligence, intentional torts (such as nuisance or trespass), strict liability, or violation of various environmental statutes. Notable environmental statutes include the Clean Water Act, the Clean Air Act, the Resource Conservation and Recovery Act, the Oil Pollution Act of 1990, the Motor Carrier Act of 1980, the Toxic Substance Control Act, and the Comprehensive Environmental Response, Compensation and Liability Act (CERCLA).

These environmental laws have made environmental risk management and insurance much more important than was previously the case. Estimates for the cost of cleanups mandated by CERCLA are estimated at between $700 billion and $1 trillion. Although the risk management process can be applied to environmental loss exposures, such exposures have several unique characteristics that must be considered when planning to manage them.

A pollution exclusion was added to the standard comprehensive general liability policy in 1970, but this exclusion specifically allowed coverage for sudden and accidental releases of pollutants. When ISO introduced new commercial general liability forms in 1986, a much stricter pollution exclusion replaced the previous exclusion. Similar exclusions were added to most other commercial insurance policies. Consequently, many organizations choose to purchase various environmental insurance policies to cover the pollution exposures excluded under their other policies.

Environmental impairment liability insurance (EIL) was first offered in the 1980s by a few insurers. Now a much larger number of insurers provides a variety of environmental policies to meet specialized needs. The major types of environmental insurance include the following:

1. Site-specific EIL insurance
2. Contractors EIL insurance
3. Environmental professional errors and omissions liability insurance
4. Asbestos and lead abatement contractors general liability insurance
5. Environmental remediation insurance
6. Remediation stop-loss insurance
7. Underground and above-ground storage tank insurance
8. Combined CGL/EIL insurance

## Chapter 13

# *Excess and Umbrella Liability Insurance*

Excess liability insurance and umbrella liability insurance are two similar types of coverage that organizations buy for a variety of reasons, including the need to increase the limits of their commercial general liability, commercial auto, employers liability, and other "primary" liability policies. This chapter examines the need for these types of policies, the differences between excess and umbrella liability policies, and the provisions commonly found in excess and umbrella liability policies.[1]

## Need for Excess or Umbrella Liability Coverage

The need for excess or umbrella liability insurance is closely related to three basic issues involved in the use of liability insurance:

1. Difficulty in estimating maximum possible loss for liability insurance exposures
2. Layering of liability coverages
3. Effect of aggregate limits

### Maximum Possible Loss

Most property loss exposures have a reasonably clear maximum possible loss (MPL). For example, the MPL for a building that would cost $2,000,000 to rebuild is $2,000,000; no loss to the building could exceed the amount of money necessary to rebuild it. There is no comparable way to estimate the MPL for most liability exposures. In addition, awards to injured persons can reach staggering totals. For example, a Coca-Cola distributor paid more than $145,000,000 to settle claims resulting from the collision of one of its delivery trucks with a school bus.

Moreover, for claims settled by a judge or jury, million-dollar verdicts have become increasingly more common. There were no million-dollar verdicts in the United States before 1962, but from January 1990 through July 1993, over 2,000 such verdicts were recorded—an average of more than 550 a year. In that period, every state in the nation reported at least one million-dollar verdict.[2]

Although most organizations are unlikely to experience million-dollar liability losses, the possibility of a large liability loss exists for virtually every business, regardless of the size of the business and the type of product or service that it offers. Additionally, the million-dollar verdicts that some businesses sustain increase the MPL of the liability exposures of other businesses.

## *Layering of Coverage*

Insurers that provide primary liability insurance are often unwilling to provide a limit greater than $1,000,000 per occurrence. In some cases, the primary insurer may provide an even lower limit, such as $500,000. Hence, an insured who wants higher limits than are available from its primary insurers can do so only by obtaining additional policies. To achieve its desired limits, a business might need to purchase several excess or umbrella liability policies.

A primary liability policy and corresponding excess or umbrella policies are referred to as **layers** of insurance. The various layers of insurance applicable to a particular set of liability loss exposures can be depicted as shown in Exhibit 13-1, with the primary layer on the bottom and subsequent layers stacked above. The widely used term "underlying insurance" corresponds to this depiction. With reference to a particular excess or umbrella liability policy, **underlying insurance** is the insurance in a lower layer.

Ordinarily, the coverage provided by the primary insurer must be exhausted before the next layer of insurance makes any payment. For example, assume that an insured has a CGL policy with a $1,000,000 each occurrence limit (first layer) and an umbrella liability policy with a $5,000 000 each occurrence limit (second layer). If the insured became legally obligated to pay $1,800,000 in damages for bodily injury to a third party, the primary insurer would pay up to its $1,000,000 limit, and the umbrella insurer would pay the remaining $800,000.

**Exhibit 13-1**
Layers of Liability Insurance

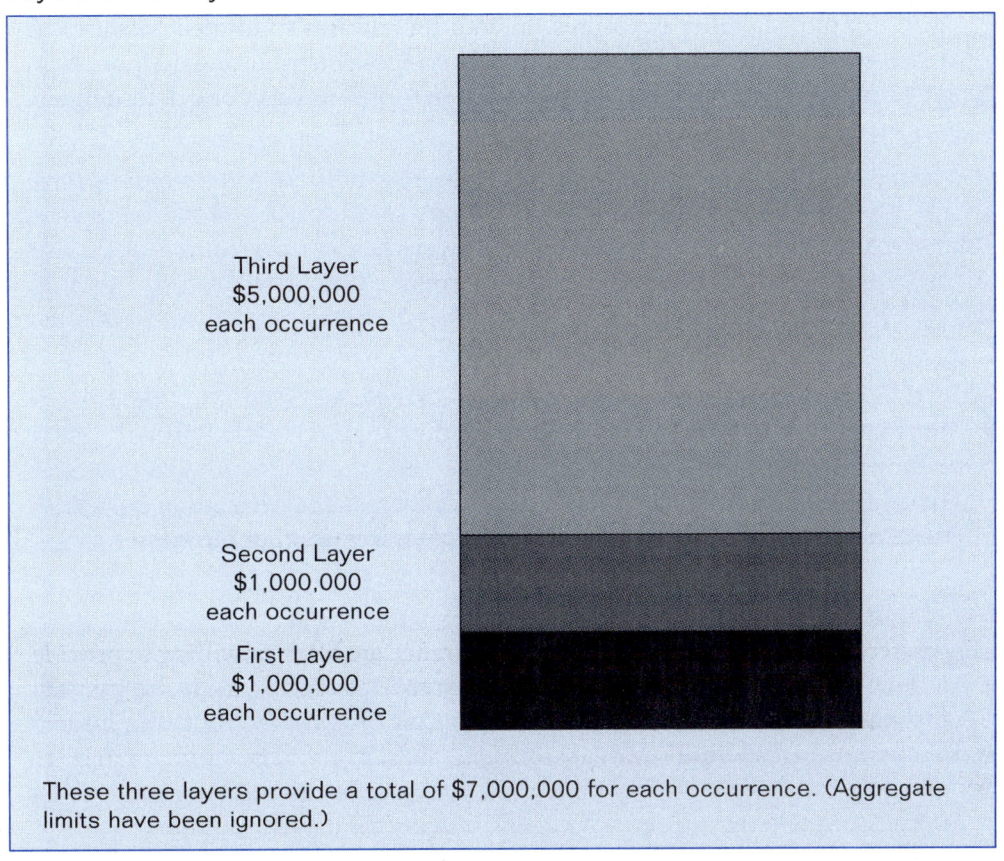

Third Layer
$5,000,000
each occurrence

Second Layer
$1,000,000
each occurrence

First Layer
$1,000,000
each occurrence

These three layers provide a total of $7,000,000 for each occurrence. (Aggregate limits have been ignored.)

The primary layer in an insurance program is not always financed through insurance. Some organizations that are financially able to pay sizable losses out of their own funds prefer to retain ("self-insure") the first layer. For example, a large business might decide to retain the first $500,000 of its liability losses and buy excess or umbrella insurance to pay for losses exceeding $500,000.

The use of two or more layers of liability insurance to build an insurance program will be discussed in more detail later in this chapter.

## *Effect of Aggregate Limits*

In addition to an each occurrence limit, one or more aggregate limits for the policy period often apply to a liability insurance policy. Thus, even if a business never sustains a loss that exceeds the *each occurrence* limit of one of its primary policies, the business could have several liability losses during one policy year that could exhaust an *aggregate* limit, leaving a subsequent claim uninsured or underinsured.

For example, assume that an insured has a CGL policy with a $1,000,000 each occurrence limit, a $2,000,000 general aggregate limit, and a $2,000,000 aggregate limit for products-completed operations. If the insured has four products liability losses for $500,000 each during the policy period, the policy will pay nothing for other products liability losses that occur during the same policy period, even if no subsequent claim exceeds the each occurrence limit (because $500,000 × 4 = $2,000,000, the products-completed operations aggregate limit).

# Basic Characteristics of Excess and Umbrella Liability Policies

Excess and umbrella liability policies can be used to insure the large liability loss exposures described above. The basic distinction between excess liability insurance and umbrella liability insurance is as follows:

- An **excess liability policy** is designed to provide excess limits of coverage above the limits of the underlying coverage. An excess policy therefore offers no broader protection than that provided by the underlying coverage. In fact, the excess coverage may be even more restrictive than the underlying coverage. Many excess policies do not provide defense coverage, for example.

- An **umbrella liability policy** is a type of excess policy that not only provides additional limits (as excess policies do) but that may also offer coverage not available in the underlying coverages, subject to the assumption, by the insured, of a self-insured retention, or "retained limit." Most umbrella liability policies also provide defense coverage.

Exhibit 13-2 illustrates the basic difference between excess and umbrella policies. In the example in the exhibit, both the excess policy and the umbrella policy provide $1,000,000 of additional liability coverage for the same losses covered by the underlying policies. In addition, the umbrella policy covers some losses not covered by the underlying insurance, subject to a self-insured retention of $25,000.

In actual practice, the distinction between excess and umbrella coverage is often blurred, especially because the courts and many in the insurance profession use the terms interchangeably. Moreover, insurers providing excess and umbrella liability insurance do not use standardized policies. Rather, they develop their own policies, which vary considerably in the coverage that they offer and the format in which they are presented. What one insurer calls an excess liability policy may in reality be an umbrella policy (as defined in this text), and what another insurer calls an umbrella policy may actually be an excess liability policy (as defined in this text). The attributes of excess and umbrella liability policies are described in more detail in the sections that follow.

**Exhibit 13-2**
Excess Liability Policy Versus Umbrella Liability Policy

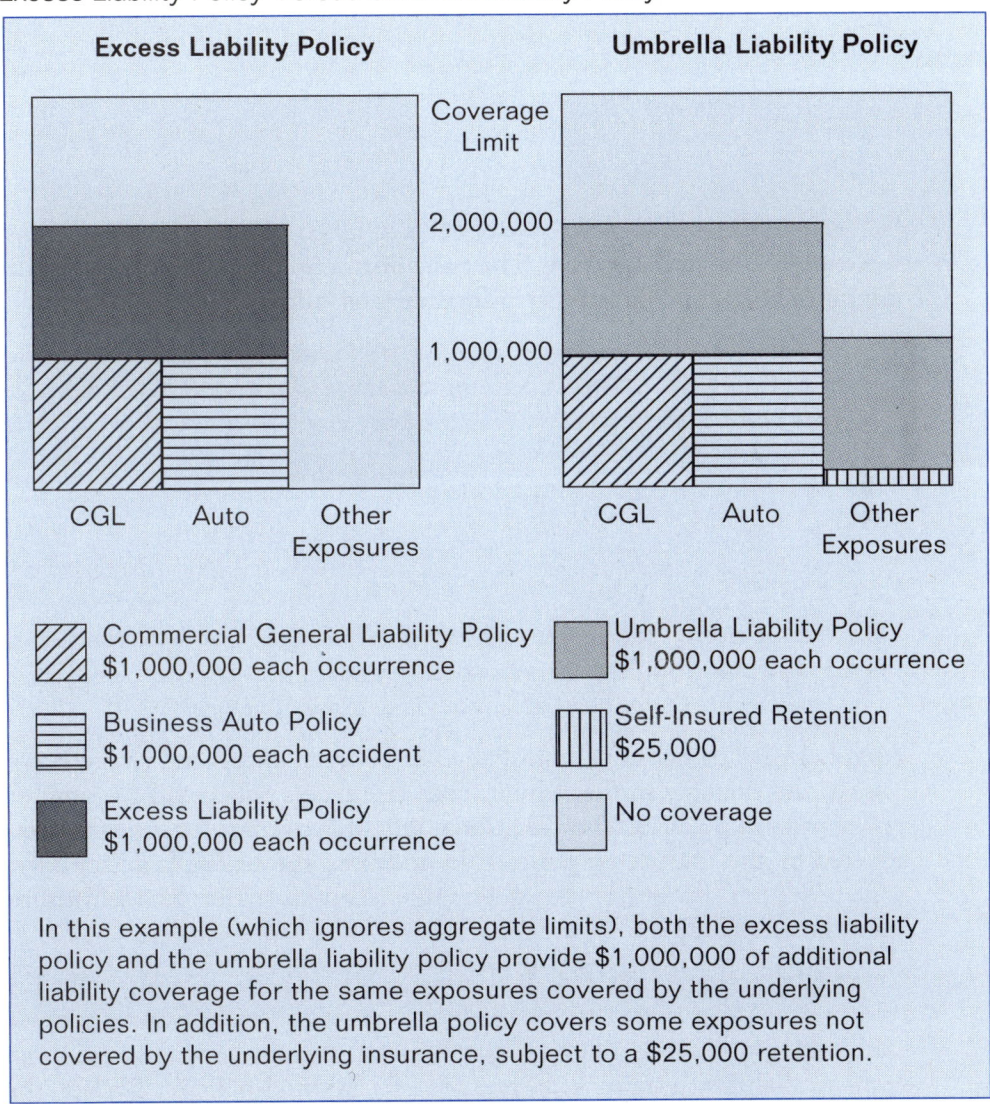

**Excess Liability Policy**

**Umbrella Liability Policy**

Coverage Limit
2,000,000
1,000,000

CGL   Auto   Other Exposures

CGL   Auto   Other Exposures

Commercial General Liability Policy
$1,000,000 each occurrence

Business Auto Policy
$1,000,000 each accident

Excess Liability Policy
$1,000,000 each occurrence

Umbrella Liability Policy
$1,000,000 each occurrence

Self-Insured Retention
$25,000

No coverage

In this example (which ignores aggregate limits), both the excess liability policy and the umbrella liability policy provide $1,000,000 of additional liability coverage for the same exposures covered by the underlying policies. In addition, the umbrella policy covers some exposures not covered by the underlying insurance, subject to a $25,000 retention.

# Excess Liability Insurance

An excess liability policy may take any of three basic forms:

1. A "following form" subject to the same provisions as the underlying policy
2. A self-contained policy subject to its own provisions only
3. A combination of the two types above

In addition, when excess liability insurance applies above a retained primary layer instead of underlying insurance, two additional types of excess insurance are commonly used, particularly in connection with self-insured workers compensation obligations:

1. Specific excess insurance
2. Aggregate excess insurance

## Following-Form Excess Policies

A **following-form excess policy** covers a liability loss that exceeds the underlying limits *only if the loss is covered by the underlying insurance.* To illustrate, assume that an insured has an underlying liability policy with an each occurrence limit of $1,000,000 and a following-form excess policy with an each occurrence limit of $1,000,000. If a claimant obtains a judgment of $1,250,000 against the insured for bodily injury covered by the underlying policy, the underlying policy would pay its each occurrence limit of $1,000,000, and the excess policy would pay the remaining $250,000. The application of primary and excess policies to the claim is illustrated in Exhibit 13-3.

What might be called a "true" following-form excess policy would state that except for the policy limits, all of the provisions and conditions of the designated underlying policy are incorporated into and adopted by the excess policy. A true following-form policy would contain no other provisions. Today, although many excess policies are called following-form policies, most contain endorsements limiting coverage. They follow the provisions of the underlying policy only to the extent that the provisions of the underlying policy do not conflict with those of the excess policy. The result is that the coverage provided by an underlying policy and the coverage provided by a following-form excess policy are likely to differ. If the underlying policy would provide coverage for a loss that the excess policy would not cover, the provisions of the excess policy may take precedence, thus covering a narrower scope of events than the primary policy.

**Exhibit 13-3**
Application of Primary and Excess Liability Policies

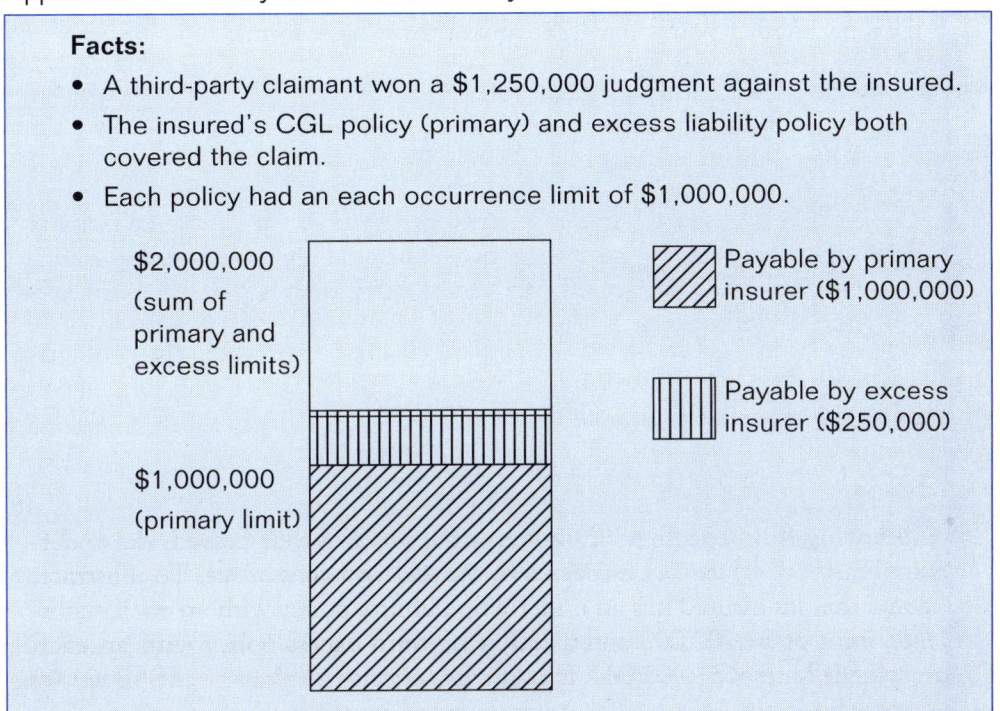

**Facts:**
- A third-party claimant won a $1,250,000 judgment against the insured.
- The insured's CGL policy (primary) and excess liability policy both covered the claim.
- Each policy had an each occurrence limit of $1,000,000.

$2,000,000 (sum of primary and excess limits)

$1,000,000 (primary limit)

Payable by primary insurer ($1,000,000)

Payable by excess insurer ($250,000)

## Self-Contained Excess Policies

A **self-contained excess policy** is subject to its own provisions only, so coverage applies only to the extent described in the policy. The policy does not depend on the provisions of the underlying policies for determining the scope of the coverage (with one exception, noted below). Because self-contained excess policies are independent of the underlying policies, coverage gaps between the excess and underlying layer can occur.

To summarize, a self-contained excess policy applies to a loss that exceeds the underlying limits *only if the loss is also covered under the provisions of the excess policy*. For example, the excess policy may not cover injury within the products-completed operations hazard, even though the underlying policy does. In that case, the excess policy would not pay for a products liability claim, even though the claim was covered by the underlying policy and exceeded the each occurrence limit of the underlying policy.

One exception to the usual approach of a self-contained policy occurs when the excess policy provides coverage in excess of a reduced or an exhausted underlying aggregate limit. Some excess policies provide this coverage on their own provisions, but others specifically state that they will provide this coverage based on the conditions of the underlying coverage that they are replacing. This approach can work to the insured's benefit when the excess policy contains exclusions or other restrictions that are not present in the underlying policy.

## Combination Excess Policies

An excess policy may combine the following-form and self-contained approaches by incorporating the provisions of the underlying policy and then modifying those provisions with additional conditions or exclusions in the excess policy.

One type of combination form is an excess policy that provides the broader coverages typically found in an umbrella liability policy, but without any obligation to "drop down" (provide primary coverage) when a claim is excluded by the primary policy but covered by the excess policy. Because many in the insurance industry do not distinguish between excess and umbrella policies, insureds might not be aware that combination excess policies do not "drop down" (except to replace depleted aggregate limits). One distinguishing feature of an umbrella policy is a provision stating that the policy applies over a self-insured retention if the underlying policy does not cover a loss covered by the umbrella. In the absence of this provision, the policy is probably not an umbrella liability policy.

## Specific and Aggregate Excess Insurance

Specific excess insurance and aggregate excess insurance are commonly used in connection with self-insured workers compensation plans. Because these types of policies are designed to apply over a self-insured layer instead of a primary layer of commercial insurance, they are structured differently from the excess policies described above.

A **specific excess policy** requires the insured to retain a stipulated amount of loss from the first dollar *for all losses resulting from a single occurrence.* The insurer pays losses in excess of the retention, subject to the policy limit. For example, if the policy required a retention of $100,000, the insurer would pay all loss resulting from a single occurrence in excess of $100,000 up to the policy limit of $1,000,000.

An **aggregate excess policy** (also called a stop loss excess policy) requires the insured to retain a specified amount of loss from the first dollar *during a specified* *period of time*, usually one year. The insurer then pays, up to the policy limit, all loss for that period that exceeds the retention. The specific excess and aggregate excess approaches are illustrated in Exhibit 13-4.

Some policies combine the specific and aggregate excess approaches. Such policies provide the insured with the benefits of both approaches. For example, an insured might incur several moderate losses during a policy period, none of which exceeds the each occurrence retention. Under a specific excess policy, the insured would not be able to collect any insurance proceeds. With the combined specific/aggregate excess policy, however, if the total of losses for the policy period exceeded the aggregate retention, the insured could collect insurance proceeds for the amount of loss in excess of the aggregate retention. The combined approach is illustrated in Exhibit 13-5.

**Exhibit 13-4**
Aggregate Excess Versus Specific Excess

| **Aggregate Excess Policy** | |
|---|---|
| $100,000 aggregate retention | $1,000,000 maximum limit |
| Losses from separate occurrences | $ 25,000 |
| | 75,000 |
| | 90,000 |
| | 35,000 |
| Total losses | $225,000 |
| Aggregate retention | 100,000 |
| Excess insurance will pay | $125,000 |
| **Specific Excess Policy** | |
| $100,000 per occurrence retention | $1,000,000 maximum limit |
| Losses from separate occurrences | $ 25,000 |
| | 75,000 |
| | 90,000 |
| | 35,000 |
| | $225,000 |

Since none of the losses exceeds the $100,000 per occurrence retention, the insured must retain all losses.

# Umbrella Liability Insurance

The term "umbrella liability" is generally used to describe a type of excess insurance that is broader than ordinary excess liability policies. Although

**Exhibit 13-5**
Combination Aggregate Excess and Specific Excess Policy

| Aggregate Excess | Specific Excess |
|---|---|
| $200,000 aggregate retention | $100,000 per occurrence retention |
| $1,000,000 maximum limit | $1,000,000 maximum limit |

| Losses from separate occurrences: | |
|---|---:|
| | $ 25,000 |
| | 75,000 |
| | 90,000 |
| | 35,000 |
| | $225,000 |

None of the losses exceeds the per occurrence retention. Therefore, the specific excess part of the policy would pay nothing. However, since total losses exceed the $200,000 aggregate retention, the aggregate excess part of the policy would pay $25,000.

ordinary excess policies may apply in excess of only one underlying policy, an umbrella liability policy provides excess coverage over several primary policies, such as CGL, auto liability, and employers liability. As mentioned earlier, the distinguishing feature of umbrella liability policies is coverage that is broader in some respects than that of the underlying policies, thus providing primary coverage for certain occurrences that would not be covered by any of the underlying policies. In contrast, ordinary excess liability policies tend to be on the same provisions as the underlying coverage or even on narrower provisions than the underlying coverage and thus do not cover claims excluded by the underlying insurance.

## Basic Functions of Umbrella Policies

Although umbrella policy provisions vary among insurers, they generally perform three basic functions. Like an ordinary excess liability policy, they (1) provide additional limits above the each occurrence limits of the insured's underlying policies and (2) take the place of the underlying insurance when underlying aggregate limits are reduced or exhausted. In addition, they (3) cover some claims that are not covered by the insured's underlying policies, subject to a **self-insured retention** (an amount of loss retained by the insured). The latter two functions are frequently referred to as **drop-down coverage**.

## APPLICATIONS

The cases that follow illustrate the application of umbrella liability limits to claims in three situations that correspond to the three basic functions of umbrella liability policies. In each case, the insured is Tri-County Construction Company, whose insurance program includes the following policies and limits:

*CGL Policy*

| | |
|---|---|
| Each occurrence limit | $ 1,000,000 |
| General aggregate limit | $ 2,000,000 |
| Products-completed operations aggregate limit | $ 2,000,000 |

*Umbrella Policy*

| | |
|---|---|
| Each occurrence limit | $ 5,000,000 |
| Aggregate limit | $10,000,000 |
| Self-insured retention | $      25,000 |

### Claim Covered by Underlying and Umbrella

Tri-County was held liable for $1,500,000 in damages resulting from property damage caused by Tri-County's operations in progress at a work site. The claim was covered under both the CGL policy and the umbrella. Since Tri-County's general aggregate limit had not been reduced by prior claims, the CGL policy paid its full $1,000,000 limit for the occurrence. The umbrella policy paid the remaining $500,000 of the claim. The self-insured retention would not apply.

### Claim Involving Depleted Aggregate Limit in Underlying

In a later occurrence, Tri-County was held liable for $1,200,000 in damages resulting from bodily injury caused by Tri-County's operations at an active job site. Because earlier claims had reduced Tri-County's general aggregate limit to $400,000, the CGL policy paid only $400,000 of the $1,200,000 claim. Tri-County's umbrella policy therefore dropped down to pay the additional $600,000 that would have been payable under the CGL policy if the aggregate limit had not been reduced. In addition, the umbrella policy paid the remaining $200,000 of the judgment, since the total damages paid by the umbrella policy ($800,000) were less than the umbrella policy's each occurrence limit and the umbrella's aggregate limit had not been reduced to less than that amount. Again, the self-insured retention would not apply.

### Claim Excluded by Underlying but Covered by Umbrella

Tri-County chartered a forty-foot workboat for use in constructing a floating restaurant beside a river. Through negligent operation of the workboat, Tri-County caused the workboat to collide with a recreational watercraft and injure its occupants. All parties involved, including the insurers, agreed that Tri-County was legally liable to the injured boaters for damages of $200,000. The insurers and Tri-County also agreed that (1) the CGL insurer had no duty to pay any damages because the CGL policy excluded nonowned watercraft that were twenty-six feet or more in length and (2) the loss was covered under Tri-County's umbrella policy. The umbrella insurer therefore paid the damages of $200,000 *minus the $25,000 self-insured retention*, which normally applies only to claims covered by the umbrella but excluded by the underlying.

## Self-Insured Retention

As illustrated above, when a claim covered by the umbrella policy is not covered by any of the underlying policies, the drop-down coverage is subject to a retention known as a self-insured retention. The retention normally does not apply when the umbrella is (1) paying in excess of a claim covered by the primary policy or (2) dropping down to pay a claim because the primary policy's aggregate limit has been exhausted.

Self-insured retentions vary in amount, from as low as $500 for very small businesses to $1,000,000 or more for the largest businesses. In many policies, particularly those issued to small businesses, the retention does not apply to defense costs. Coverage for defense costs is provided in full, often referred to as "first-dollar defense coverage."

Self-insured retentions are similar to deductibles in that both represent loss amounts that the insured must retain and that the insurer will not pay, but they also differ significantly. For example, insureds generally handle all claims and losses falling within the self-insured retention. Insureds need not report those claims and losses to their insurers unless required to do so by the policy provisions. Deductibles work differently. Insureds must report all claims within the deductible for processing, recording, and payment. The insurer charges claim payments to the insured until the deductible amount has been satisfied.

## Required Underlying Limits

Each insurer writing umbrella liability policies has its own requirements for the types and amounts of underlying insurance that the insured must have. For example, an umbrella insurer might require the insured to have the following primary coverages and limits:

*Commercial General Liability*

- $1,000,000 each occurrence
- $2,000,000 general aggregate
- $2,000,000 completed operations aggregate

*Business Auto Liability*

- $1,000,000 combined single limit

*Employers Liability*

- $100,000 bodily injury each accident
- $100,000 bodily injury by disease each employee
- $500,000 disease aggregate

Additional types of underlying insurance might be required depending on the insured's exposures and the anticipated coverage to be provided in the umbrella policy. If, for example, the insured's business involves the sale of alcoholic beverages and the anticipated umbrella policy contains no liquor liability exclusion, the umbrella insurer will likely require underlying liquor liability insurance as well as the coverages listed above. Or, if the insured owns a watercraft or aircraft that would be covered under the umbrella policy, the insurer will likely require underlying watercraft or aircraft liability insurance. Umbrella liability policies seldom apply over directors and officers liability policies, public officials liability policies, and fiduciary liability policies.

The umbrella limits apply in full in excess of each of the underlying coverages. Thus, if an insured with the underlying limits shown above also carried a $10,000,000 umbrella policy, the total coverage available for one occurrence covered by the CGL policy and the umbrella would be $11,000,000 ($1,000,000 primary plus $10,000,000 umbrella), but the total coverage for one employers liability claim would be only $10,100,000 ($100,000 primary plus $10,000,000 umbrella). If the umbrella policy included a $25,000 self-insured retention for coverages it provided on exposures not covered in the primary polices, the $10,000,000 coverage would apply over the $25,000 retention.

## Aggregate Umbrella Limits

The previous example ignored any aggregate limit in the umbrella policy. Almost all umbrella policies now contain aggregate limits that operate like the aggregate limits in the underlying insurance. In some cases, the aggregate limit applies to all claims under the umbrella; in other cases, the aggregate limit applies only to coverages that are subject to an aggregate limit in the underlying policies. For example, the business auto policy does not have an aggregate limit. An umbrella policy with the latter provision described above would not apply its aggregate limit to claims covered by the underlying business auto policy.

If the umbrella policy in the previous example included an aggregate limit, then the total available insurance would be reduced by payments on other claims covered by the umbrella policy. Furthermore, assume that the umbrella policy described in the example had a $10,000,000 each occurrence limit *and a $10,000,000 aggregate limit.* Assuming also that neither policy had paid any other claims, if a $3,000,000 premises liability claim was paid ($1,000,000 by the primary policy and $2,000,000 by the umbrella), only $9,000,000 would be available for the next covered claim: $1,000,000 (the balance of the underlying aggregate) from the primary policy and $8,000,000 (the balance of the umbrella aggregate) from the aggregate.

When an umbrella policy contains an aggregate limit, its limit can actually be exhausted before the primary policy's limit is exhausted. If subject to the same limits as established in the last example, a covered claim settled for $11,000,000 or more would exhaust the umbrella policy. The primary policy would pay $1,000,000, and the umbrella policy would pay its full limit of $10,000,000. The primary policy would still cover subsequent claims, since it has paid only $1,000,000 of its $2,000,000 limit, but the umbrella policy would not cover any additional claims.

## Insuring Agreement

Many umbrella liability policies contain one comprehensive insuring agreement instead of several specific ones. A common approach is for the insurer to promise to pay "ultimate net loss" in excess of the "underlying limit" (both terms will be defined below) that the insured becomes legally obligated to pay as damages for bodily injury, property damage, personal injury, or advertising injury arising out of an occurrence to which the policy applies.

Some umbrella policies have broader or additional insuring agreements to cover exposures such as employee benefits liability or professional liability. However, those coverages are not always available under umbrella liability policies. If an insured wants higher limits for its more unusual types of liability insurance (such as directors and officers or employment practices liability), the coverage must often be arranged under a separate excess liability policy covering only that specific type of liability.

An alternative to the single broad insuring agreement is the Coverage A/B format. Although the use of this format is usually limited to umbrella policies, it actually creates an umbrella/excess hybrid. The Coverage A/B format combines two insuring agreements, usually called Coverage A and Coverage B. Unlike Coverages A and B of the CGL, these coverage agreements do not cover separate types of injury, such as bodily injury or advertising injury. Instead, Coverage A is an excess liability coverage applying over the underlying policies, and Coverage B is umbrella coverage for claims not covered by underlying coverage but covered by the umbrella. The self-insured retention applies only to claims under Coverage B.

Some umbrella insurers using this format make Coverage B (the umbrella coverage) available only on a claims-made basis, which most insureds do not consider a favorable feature. However, when Coverage B is provided on an occurrence/offense, rather than a claims-made, basis, such policies can benefit insureds because they are better at addressing coverage gaps than are the other types of excess and umbrella policies. If Coverage A follows the provisions of the underlying policy, a gap between the underlying insurance and the umbrella insurance is less likely to exist.

## Definitions

The insuring agreements of umbrella liability policies may contain several terms that have specific policy definitions. Common examples of these terms include "ultimate net loss," "underlying limit," "bodily injury," "property damage," "personal injury," and "advertising injury."

### Ultimate Net Loss

The meaning of "ultimate net loss" depends on the umbrella policy in which it appears and other provisions of that same policy. Typically, though, "ultimate net loss" refers to the total amount that the insured is legally obligated to pay as damages for a covered claim. It may or may not include defense costs related to the claim. Often, defense costs are payable in addition to the umbrella limits, in which case defense costs would not be included in "ultimate net loss." Rather than using the phrase "ultimate net loss," some umbrella policies simply state that losses exceeding the underlying limit will be covered, and those policies include other provisions that address how defense costs will be treated.

### Underlying Limit

"Underlying limit" is usually defined to mean either (1) the limit of the applicable coverage listed in the umbrella policy's schedule of underlying insurance or (2) the self-insured retention shown in the umbrella declarations (if the underlying coverage does not apply). For example, if underlying insurance totaling $1,000,000 is used to cover ultimate net loss of $2,500,000, the umbrella insurer will pay (subject to the umbrella policy's limits) the difference between those amounts, which is $1,500,000.

The CGL policy has a personal injury/advertising injury limit that is subject to the general policy aggregate. The CGL policy also contains an each occurrence limit for all bodily injury and property damage sustained in any one occurrence, and that limit is also subject to the general policy aggregate. Determining whether those sublimits have been exhausted can be troublesome because the definitions of personal injury, advertising injury, bodily injury, and property damage in the umbrella policy might differ from the definitions in the CGL or in another underlying policy.

## Bodily Injury, Personal Injury, Advertising Injury, Property Damage

Some umbrella liability policies agree to pay for damages because of bodily injury, personal injury, advertising injury, and property damage, and they define those terms to correspond, in many or most respects, to the definitions of those terms in the CGL policy. Other umbrella policies agree to pay only for "personal injury," "advertising injury," or "property damage" but define "personal injury" to include both bodily injury and personal injury, much as those terms are defined in the CGL policy. Still other umbrella policies phrase the insuring agreement in terms of "injury" and define that single term to include bodily injury, property damage, and various personal injury and advertising injury offenses.

The umbrella policy's definitions of the above terms can be important. If, for example, the umbrella policy has a narrower definition of personal injury or advertising injury than that in the underlying CGL policy, the umbrella policy might not cover a claim that is covered under the CGL policy. More commonly, umbrella policies contain definitions of personal injury that are broader than the CGL definition of that term. For example, the personal injury definitions in some umbrella policies include discrimination based on race, color, religion, sex, and national origin, but not if the discrimination is prohibited by law. If the umbrella policy's definition of personal injury (or another key term) includes some exposure that is not included in the personal injury definition in the underlying policies, the umbrella policy will (assuming no other restrictions apply) provide drop-down coverage for that exposure.

## Occurrence

The insuring agreement of an umbrella policy, like the Coverage A insuring agreement in the CGL policy, often requires that the injury be caused by an "occurrence." Umbrella policies often use a definition for that term that is the same as or similar to that found in the CGL policy: "an accident, including continuous or repeated exposure to substantially the same general harmful conditions."

A problem that exists in some umbrella policies is that the occurrence requirement applies to all claims. That can cause problems for the insured in the case of personal injury and advertising injury offenses (libel, slander, and other intentional torts) that do not qualify as "accidents." A better approach, from the insured's point of view, is to have the "caused by an occurrence" requirement applicable to bodily injury and property damage liability claims, and a "caused by a covered offense" requirement applicable to personal injury and advertising injury liability claims.

## Occurrence and Claims-Made Coverage Triggers

Some umbrella policies contain a coverage trigger that is different from all of the above. These policies trigger coverage for bodily injury or property damage based on when the wrongful act takes place rather than when the injury or damage occurs. With this type of policy, for example, coverage for an injury resulting from a defective product would be provided by the policy in effect when the product was manufactured, not by the policy in effect when a consumer was actually injured by the defective product.

Gaps in coverage can occur when the umbrella or excess policy has a different coverage trigger than the underlying coverage. To avoid this problem, some insurers provide both occurrence and claims-made triggers in their umbrella policies. These policies provide that the trigger for the umbrella coverage will be the same as that used for the underlying coverage. Umbrella coverage provided under the Coverage A/B format (described earlier) is one way to address this issue.

When an underlying policy and the umbrella policy both contain a claims-made trigger, the named insured ordinarily tries to obtain the same retroactive date and extended reporting period options for both policies. This goal may be difficult to achieve, because the extended reporting period provisions of the claims-made CGL coverage form are more generous than most umbrella insurers are willing to provide.

## Defense Coverage

Among the most important coverages provided by umbrella policies is defense coverage. Like the CGL, some umbrella policies provide defense coverage in addition to their limits, and others provide the coverage within their limits. If defense coverage is provided within the policy's limits, those limits may be exhausted much more quickly than if the defense costs were paid in addition to the limits.

In some umbrella policies, defense costs are included in the definition of "ultimate net loss," which in turn is subject to the policy limits. Other umbrella policies, which have a separate defense provision, do not include defense costs in the definition of "ultimate net loss." However, even some of those policies state that payments made under the defense provision will reduce the policy limits, so the effect is similar to having defense costs included in "ultimate net loss."

Another defense coverage issue concerns when the umbrella or excess insurer becomes involved in handling the insured's defense. Generally, an umbrella insurer is not obligated to defend unless (1) the underlying policy limits have been paid, and its defense obligation has ended, or (2) there is an absence of such coverage in the underlying policy, and the umbrella policy is required to drop down to provide coverage.

This issue, however, is not always as uncomplicated as it might appear. For example, assume that the underlying insurer tenders its defense limit and indicates that it wants no more involvement in the insured's defense, effectively making the remainder of the defense the sole responsibility of the umbrella insurer. In such a case, the umbrella insurer should assume responsibility for the defense but also seek judicial clarification on when the obligation of the underlying insurer has been exhausted. An underlying insurer with a defense obligation in addition to its policy limits usually cannot satisfy that obligation simply by tendering its limits and choosing not to be involved any further. If an underlying insurer's defense obligation is payable in addition to the policy limits, that obligation is extensive. Unless the next layer of coverage, whether it is an excess or an umbrella policy, agrees to assume the responsibility for the defense, the underlying insurer will likely be forced to seek judicial approval of its withdrawal from the defense obligation.

## Exclusions

Like a CGL or an auto liability policy, an umbrella liability policy contains exclusions that restrict the broad coverage granted by the insuring agreement. Although the exclusions of umbrella policies resemble those found in underlying policies, they are also likely to vary in several respects. To achieve the coverage that it is willing to provide to meet insureds' needs, an umbrella insurer usually takes a combination of the following actions when drafting its policy form:

1. Using some underlying policy exclusions with little or no change
2. Omitting certain exclusions found in primary policies
3. Using less restrictive versions of some underlying policy exclusions
4. Using more restrictive exclusions than those in the underlying policy

Underwriters also have the option of adding exclusions by endorsement to their policy forms. The number and types of endorsements added to a policy will vary with the underwriter's assessment of the risk.

Because of the many variations among umbrella liability policies, it is not possible in this chapter to describe all of the different exclusions that might be encountered in such policies. Some publishers provide detailed comparisons of the various umbrella liability policies to assist insurance professionals in analyzing and comparing policies.[3] This chapter is confined to discussing common examples of umbrella liability exclusions. These examples are used to illustrate the approaches listed above.

## *Umbrella Exclusions Same as Underlying Policy Exclusions*

Most umbrella liability policies contain some exclusions that are the same as or very similar to exclusions in the underlying policies. The effect is that the umbrella policy will cover like a following-form excess policy with regard to the affected exposures. For example, many umbrella policies contain exclusions that are identical or similar to the following exclusions of the CGL coverage form:

- Expected or intended injury
- Workers compensation and similar laws
- War
- Damage to your product
- Damage to your work
- Damage to impaired property or property not physically injured
- Recall of products, work, or impaired property
- Advertising and personal injury exclusions
- Broad form nuclear energy liability

## *Underlying Policy Exclusions Omitted From Umbrella Policies*

Several exclusions of the CGL, business auto, and employers liability policy are commonly omitted entirely from many umbrella liability policies. These omitted exclusions can be subdivided into two groups:

1. Exclusions that are omitted because they are unneeded in the umbrella
2. Exclusions that are omitted to broaden umbrella liability coverage

### Exclusions Omitted as Unneeded

Because umbrella liability policies ordinarily cover CGL, business auto, and employers liability exposures under one form, many of the exclusions and other provisions found in those primary policies are unnecessary in umbrella policies.

For example, umbrella liability policies usually do not contain any equivalent to the CGL auto liability exclusion, since umbrella liability insurers usually intend to cover auto liability exposures. Similarly, the various exclusions and other provisions that delineate coverage for auto loading and unloading operations under CGL and business auto policies (so that the two policies will not overlap or leave gaps when written by separate insurers) are not needed under an umbrella policy that covers both CGL and business auto exposures. Other examples of exclusions that are usually unnecessary in umbrella liability policies include the following:

- The employers liability exclusion of CGL and business auto policies
- The exclusions of operations and completed operations in the business auto policy
- The CGL exclusion regarding transportation of mobile equipment

### Exclusions Omitted To Broaden Umbrella

Insurers omit some underlying policy exclusions from an umbrella policy in order to broaden the umbrella coverage. For example, an umbrella policy often has no exclusion of liability assumed under contract. If the insured becomes legally obligated to pay damages because of a hold harmless or indemnity agreement under circumstances that are not excluded by other policy provisions, that policy will cover the insured's contractual liability. If the contractual liability is not covered under the insured's primary insurance, the umbrella will provide drop-down coverage subject to the self-insured retention stipulated in the policy.

Other underlying policy exclusions that are frequently omitted from umbrella policies in order to provide umbrella coverage that is broader than any of the underlying policies include the following:

- The CGL liquor liability exclusion
- The employers liability exclusion of accidents occurring outside the United States or Canada

- The employers liability exclusion of injury to persons subject to the Federal Employers' Liability Act, the Jones Act, and similar laws permitting employees to sue their employers
- The employers liability exclusion of injury to persons knowingly employed in violation of law

## Umbrella Exclusions Less Restrictive Than the Underlying

In many cases, an umbrella insurer is willing to broaden coverage for a particular exposure without covering it entirely. Thus, instead of omitting the underlying exclusion from its umbrella policy, the insurer uses an exclusion that is similar to an exclusion in the underlying policy but is less restrictive. When an umbrella exclusion has a narrower scope of application than a comparable exclusion in the underlying insurance, the umbrella policy has the potential for providing drop-down coverage for some claims not insured by the underlying coverage. Two examples of umbrella liability exclusions that commonly allow broader coverage than the underlying insurance are (1) the watercraft and aircraft exclusion and (2) the care, custody, or control exclusion.

### Watercraft and Aircraft

The CGL policy contains an exclusion of liability arising out of the use of autos, watercraft, and aircraft. In most umbrella liability policies, the exclusion is limited to watercraft and aircraft liability, since umbrella policies ordinarily cover auto liability exposures in excess of underlying auto liability coverage. In addition, many umbrella liability policies narrow the scope of the watercraft/aircraft exclusion to provide broader coverage than the underlying insurance.

For example, the watercraft exclusion in an umbrella policy might exclude liability arising out of the use of any watercraft over fifty feet in length, if such watercraft is owned or bareboat chartered (chartered without crew) by the insured. This exclusion would leave coverage intact for the following:

- Watercraft fifty feet or less in length if owned or bareboat chartered by the insured
- Watercraft of any length if not owned and not bareboat chartered by the insured

The CGL coverage form, in contrast, excludes the use of watercraft unless they are (1) not owned by the named insured *and* (2) less than twenty-six feet long. Thus, an umbrella policy with the language shown above would provide considerably broader watercraft coverage than the CGL policy. The umbrella policy would not only provide excess coverage for watercraft covered under the CGL policy but would also provide drop-down coverage for watercraft excluded by the CGL policy but covered by the umbrella.

Normally, if the named insured owns any small watercraft at policy inception that would qualify for coverage under the named insured's umbrella policy, the insurer will require the named insured to carry underlying insurance on such watercraft. Thus, the coverage that the umbrella policy provides on owned watercraft is likely to apply as excess insurance over an underlying policy rather than as drop-down coverage. Moreover, most umbrella liability policies do not cover larger watercraft such as commercial cargo vessels. Larger commercial vessels are insured under marine hull and protection and indemnity policies as described in Chapter 7. If excess liability insurance on such vessels is desired, it is ordinarily provided under a separate marine excess liability form obtained from the marine insurance market.

Typically, a marine excess policy is either a following-form or a so-called bumbershoot policy. A **bumbershoot policy** operates in the same manner as an umbrella policy, providing not only excess limits but also drop-down coverage for some claims not covered by the underlying insurance. The underlying policies for a bumbershoot policy are principally marine coverages but may also include nonmarine coverages, such as the CGL policy of a shipyard or ship repair facility.

Umbrella liability coverage for aircraft is usually more restrictive than the watercraft coverage described above. A typical approach is to exclude liability arising out of any aircraft owned, or hired without pilot or crew, by or on behalf of the insured. This type of exclusion could, for example, allow coverage for a claim against the insured for injury resulting from a charter pilot's operation of an airplane on the named insured's behalf. In actual practice, however, if an organization has aircraft liability exposures, it ordinarily purchases a primary aircraft insurance policy. If excess limits are needed, they are usually provided in an aviation excess policy. However, some umbrella liability insurers will include coverage for small aircraft if acceptable underlying insurance is maintained.

### Care, Custody, or Control

Many umbrella liability policies exclude damage to property in the care, custody, or control of the insured. These exclusions vary considerably from policy to policy. In some umbrella policies, the exclusion applies to any property in the insured's care, custody, or control. In other policies, the exclusion applies only to watercraft or aircraft or both while in the insured's care, custody, or control. In still other policies, the exclusion applies only to the extent that the insured is contractually obligated to pay for damage to the property or to insure it.

An umbrella policy with the last type of exclusion will cover damage to property in the insured's care, custody, or control as long as the insured was not contractually required to insure the property. If, for example, the insured rented or borrowed an electrical generator or some other piece of mobile equipment without any obligation to insure it, the insured's umbrella policy would cover the insured's liability for damaging the equipment while in the insured's care, custody, or control. This type of loss is excluded under the CGL policy because of the flat exclusion of damage to property rented to or borrowed by the insured.

When a *contractor* obtains umbrella liability insurance, the insurer usually adds a contractors limitation endorsement, which eliminates any broadening of the underlying coverage for property in the insured's care, custody, or control. The contractors limitation endorsement will be described in more detail below.

## Umbrella Exclusions More Restrictive Than the Underlying

Because they provide drop-down coverage for claims not covered by the underlying insurance, umbrella liability policies are usually thought of as being broader than the underlying policies in all respects. Nevertheless, most umbrella policies contain some exclusions that are more restrictive than the underlying insurance. To accomplish this effect, the insurer may use modified versions of exclusions found in underlying policies or may add exclusions that have no counterparts in underlying policies. A common example of an underlying policy exclusion that is modified to restrict coverage is the pollution exclusion. Examples of exclusions that are added to umbrella liability policies to restrict coverage are exclusions of punitive damages and cross-liability suits.

### Pollution

The CGL policy, despite its pollution exclusion, does provide some coverage for bodily injury or property damage (but not cleanup costs) resulting from pollution incidents, such as for products-completed operations, smoke and fumes from a hostile fire, and some off-premises incidents. Similarly, the business auto policy covers various pollution incidents other than those involving cargoes of pollutants being transported by the insured's own vehicle.

Umbrella liability policies vary in their treatment of pollution claims. Some umbrellas exclude pollution claims of any kind, subject to exceptions that duplicate, to varying degrees, the pollution coverage found in the CGL and business auto forms. Few of these forms address the cost of relocating businesses or individuals affected by pollution, or the cost of mitigating damages before or during a pollution incident. Other umbrella policies contain total pollution exclusions that are not subject to any exceptions whatsoever. Many umbrella policies also contain an absolute exclusion of liability arising out of exposure to asbestos. Thus, an organization that wants to obtain high limits for its pollution liability exposures might need to obtain those limits under the appropriate form of environmental insurance as described in Chapter 12, or with a following-form excess policy above the environmental policy.

Even if an organization purchases pollution liability insurance, such insurance ordinarily excludes injury to employees of the named insured while in the course of employment. That could leave a significant coverage gap for an employer that might be sued by an employee who has contracted an occupational disease resulting from contact with a "pollutant." If the damages exceeded the limits on the insured's employers liability coverage (which might be as low as $100,000), the insured could face a large uninsured loss if its umbrella policy excludes all claims involving pollutants. To avoid this type of uninsured loss, an insured whose umbrella policy has a total pollution exclusion could consider the following alternative actions:

1. Increasing underlying employers liability limits to the maximum limits available from the primary insurer
2. Requesting a broad-as-primary endorsement (see below) on the umbrella policy
3. Requesting that the umbrella insurer modify the pollution exclusion so that it does not apply to employers liability claims
4. Requesting that the pollution liability insurer delete the employers liability exclusion from that policy

### Punitive Damages

The CGL and commercial auto coverage forms of ISO do not exclude punitive damages, but many umbrella policies do, either with an explicit exclusion of punitive damages or in the language of the policy's insuring agreement. For example, the insuring agreement might state that coverage applies only to compensatory damages, therefore excluding any coverage for punitive damages. When umbrella policies state that they will pay "damages" without defining that term, "damages" is usually, though not always, interpreted to include punitive damages unless the controlling jurisdiction does not permit insurance to cover punitive damages.

### Cross Liability

Like the CGL and business auto policies, umbrella policies frequently exclude suits between fellow employees. In addition, some umbrella policies contain a cross-liability exclusion, which precludes coverage for lawsuits between any insureds, not just fellow employees.

The cross-liability exclusion can cause significant problems, particularly if the same policy that contains this exclusion covers a wide range of additional insureds. For example, the umbrella policy on a swimming club might contain an endorsement stating that all members of the club are additional insureds with respect to their activities as club members. This type of endorsement is generally viewed as being favorable, since it extends insured status to all club members in the event they should be named in a suit for injury arising out of the club's activities. However, if a club member (such as the parent of a child who drowned in the club pool) sues the club, the insurer might have no duty to defend or settle, because of the cross-liability exclusion. In this case, the club would be without coverage for the very exposure that it might have deemed to be its most significant reason for buying umbrella liability insurance.

### Broad-as-Primary Endorsement

To prevent situations in which the umbrella policy provides narrower coverage than the underlying insurance, some insureds request an "at least as broad as primary" endorsement to their umbrella policies. The endorsement states that the umbrella policy will provide coverage at least as broad as that provided by the underlying policy (just as a following-form excess policy provides the same scope of coverage as the primary policy). However, if the umbrella policy provides broader coverage in some area, the insured will still have the benefit of that broadening of coverage. Unfortunately for insureds, "broad as primary" endorsements are often difficult to obtain.

### Contractors Limitation Endorsement

An umbrella policy issued to a contractor is usually amended with a **contractors limitation endorsement**. The provisions of these endorsements vary among insurers, so the actual wording of each endorsement must be analyzed separately. However, the typical purpose of such an endorsement is to restrict umbrella coverage for some of the more hazardous exposures faced by contractors, such as the following:

- Property in the insured's care, custody, or control
- Property being erected, installed, or worked on by the insured
- Liability assumed under contract
- Explosion, collapse, and underground hazards

A contractors limitation endorsement might exclude these exposures entirely, thus making the umbrella policy more restrictive than the underlying insurance. (Most risk managers would reject such an endorsement.) More commonly, a contractors limitation endorsement makes coverage for these exposures contingent on underlying coverage for the same exposures. In other words, the coverage of the umbrella policy will apply to these exposures to the extent that they are covered by the underlying insurance.

### Following-form Endorsements

Sometimes umbrella policies for any type of insured, not just a contractor, are endorsed to limit them to providing following-form coverage for certain distinct exposures, such as auto liability, watercraft liability, and advertising injury liability. That effect can be accomplished with a very brief provision, such as the following:

> This insurance does not apply to "bodily injury," "property damage," or "personal injury" arising out of the ownership, maintenance, use, loading or unloading, or entrustment to others of any "auto." This exclusion does not apply to the extent that coverage is provided for the insured by "underlying insurance."

Although the endorsement contains a broad exclusion of auto liability, the exception to the exclusion makes it clear that the umbrella policy will cover an auto liability claim that is covered by the underlying insurance.

## Other Provisions

Other important provisions that differ between primary liability policies and umbrella policies concern maintenance of underlying insurance and the coverage territory.

### Maintenance of Underlying Insurance

The **maintenance of underlying insurance condition** expresses the insured's agreement to maintain all required underlying coverages in full force and effect during the policy period, except to the extent that their aggregate limits become reduced by the payment of claims. The insured further agrees to notify the insurer promptly if any underlying policy is changed or replaced by a policy issued by another insurer.

If the underlying insurance is not maintained, the umbrella policy will apply only as though the underlying insurance *had* been maintained. That is, a claim that would have been covered by an underlying policy, had it been kept in force, will be covered only for the amount that exceeds the limit of the underlying policy. The umbrella policy will not drop down to pay claims that would have been covered by the required underlying policy.

## APPLICATIONS

### Underlying Insurance Was Not Maintained

CF Oil Service, a distributor of petroleum fuels, stores heating oil, kerosene, and gasoline at its storage facility. CF is insured under an umbrella liability policy that requires CF to maintain CGL insurance and commercial auto insurance with an each occurrence limit of $1,000,000 on each policy. The umbrella policy has an each occurrence limit of $5,000,000 and a $10,000 self-insured retention.

Several months into the policy period, one of CF's primary insurers cancelled CF's CGL policy for nonpayment of premium. CF did not obtain a replacement policy. Later in the policy period, an explosion at the storage facility injured several members of the public, who sued CF for $2,000,000 in damages.

**Question**: How much would CF's umbrella liability insurer be obligated to pay (not including defense costs) if the claimants were awarded the $2,000,000 damages they were seeking?

**Answer**: Because CF did not maintain the underlying insurance as required, the umbrella insurer would only be obligated to pay $1,000,000—the amount that it would have paid if the underlying insurance had been maintained. The self-insured retention would not apply.

## *Concurrency*

The maintenance of underlying insurance condition often includes a clause that, if ignored, can cause great harm to the insured. The effect of this clause is that the inception and expiration dates of an umbrella policy and all underlying policies should be *concurrent*—that is, exactly the same. The clause that requires concurrent policy periods is emphasized by italic type in the specimen maintenance of underlying insurance condition that follows:

> The policies designated in the umbrella schedule or declarations as underlying insurance shall be maintained in full force and effect during the currency of this policy, except for any reduction of the aggregate limit or limits contained therein solely by payment of claims *as a result of occurrences taking place during the period of this policy.*

In other words, the umbrella policy's drop-down coverage for depleted underlying aggregate limits is only for occurrences taking place during the coverage period of the umbrella policy. Thus, if the policy periods are not concurrent, coverage gaps can result, as illustrated below.

## APPLICATIONS

### Consequences of Nonconcurrent Policy Periods

Able Manufacturing Company is insured under a CGL policy with occurrence and aggregate limits of $1,000,000 each. Able also has an umbrella liability policy with an each occurrence limit of $2,000,000. The inception date of the CGL policy is January 1, and the inception date of the umbrella policy is March 1.

Able was sued in February for damages allegedly caused by a products-related occurrence taking place that same month. The CGL insurer settled the claim for $600,000, which reduced the products-completed operations aggregate limit in the CGL policy to $400,000.

In July of the same year, another person was injured by an Able product and made claim against Able for $1,000,000. Able's CGL insurer provided defense coverage and, after the jury awarded the damages being sought, paid $400,000—the remainder of its products-completed operations aggregate limit.

**Question**: Assuming Able's umbrella policy contained the maintenance of underlying insurance provision quoted in the text above, how much would Able's umbrella liability insurer be obligated to pay for this claim?

**Answer**: Able's umbrella insurer would not be obligated to pay any part of the claim. Although the CGL aggregate limit was reduced to $400,000, the claim that reduced the limit was for an injury that did not occur during the coverage period of the umbrella policy. If the policies had had concurrent policy periods, the umbrella policy would have dropped down and paid $600,000.

## Coverage Territory

Most umbrella policies provide worldwide coverage, in contrast with the more limited coverage territories ordinarily found in primary policies. However, some umbrella policies require that suit be brought in the United States or Canada. If the policy's requirement is limited solely to suits, it does not preclude the insurer from investigating and settling claims (unaccompanied by suits) made outside the United States or Canada. In many cases, an insurer might benefit from settling a foreign claim promptly rather than waiting for suit to be made in a U.S. or Canadian court.

# Structuring the Liability Insurance Program

As explained earlier in this chapter, liability insurance is arranged in layers. The primary (first) layer of a layered liability insurance program consists of one or more primary policies (such as the CGL, business auto, employers liability, and so on), with each occurrence limits typically ranging between $500,000 and $2,000,000. In some cases, principally with large organizations, the primary layer is "self-insured" (retained).

Many organizations have only one layer in excess of the primary. Typically, an organization in this category has an umbrella liability policy above its primary CGL, commercial auto, and employers liability policies. It may also have one or more separate excess liability policies providing a second layer of coverage above other primary policies that are not covered by the umbrella policy. The primary and umbrella layers are generally referred to as the **working layers**, because they are the layers most often called on to pay claims.

In some cases, an insured must purchase a **buffer layer** of excess insurance between the primary layer and the umbrella policy. This approach is used when the umbrella insurer will not provide coverage without underlying coverage limits higher than those that the primary insurer is willing to provide. For example, an umbrella liability insurer may require minimum limits of $1,000,000 for all underlying coverages. One of the primary insurers, however, may be willing to provide limits of only $500,000. To qualify for the umbrella policy, the insured will have to obtain additional limits of $500,000. This can be best accomplished by purchasing an excess liability policy with its own limits of $500,000, which, when combined with the primary policy limits of $500,000, would provide $1,000,000 of coverage beneath the umbrella policy. Naturally, insureds who purchase buffer layer coverage should try to obtain a policy that follows the provisions of the underlying policy as closely as possible, and the policy periods should be concurrent.

Insureds who want higher limits of liability above the working layers usually do so through one or more additional layers of excess coverage. The number of layers varies, depending on the limits desired by the insured and the limits available from the prospective insurers. It is unusual to find a true umbrella policy in the higher layers of excess coverage. A multi-layered liability insurance program that includes a buffer layer policy is shown in Exhibit 13-6.

Whenever excess liability layers are to apply over the first umbrella layer, the excess layers should follow as closely as possible the provisions of the umbrella policy. However, as explained earlier in this chapter, excess policies are seldom

**Exhibit 13-6**
Layered Liability Insurance Program

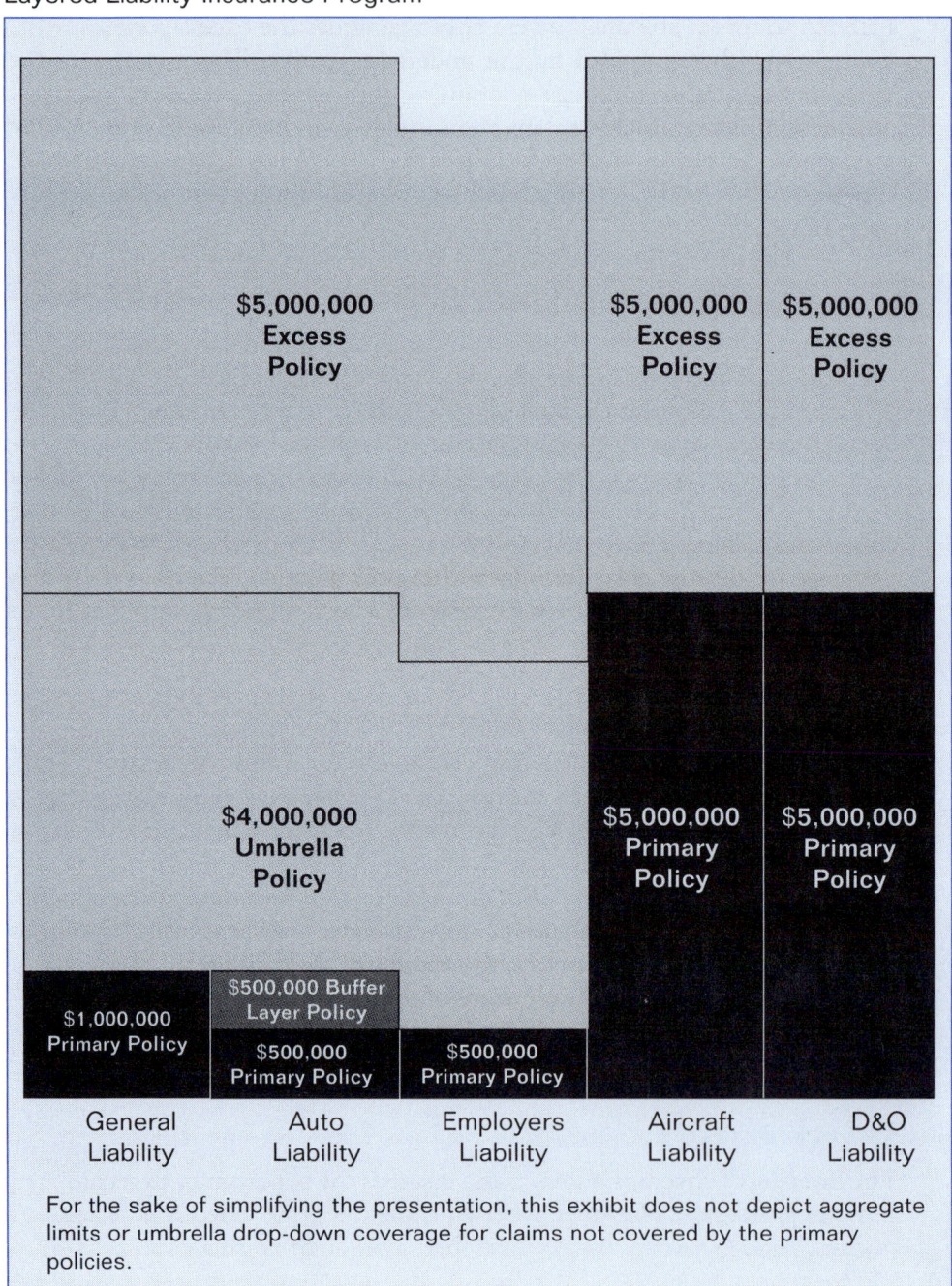

|  |  |  |  |  |
|---|---|---|---|---|
| $5,000,000 Excess Policy | | $5,000,000 Excess Policy | $5,000,000 Excess Policy |
| $4,000,000 Umbrella Policy | | $5,000,000 Primary Policy | $5,000,000 Primary Policy |
| $1,000,000 Primary Policy | $500,000 Buffer Layer Policy | | | |
| | $500,000 Primary Policy | $500,000 Primary Policy | | |
| General Liability | Auto Liability | Employers Liability | Aircraft Liability | D&O Liability |

For the sake of simplifying the presentation, this exhibit does not depict aggregate limits or umbrella drop-down coverage for claims not covered by the primary policies.

truly following form in every aspect of coverage. Even when an excess liability policy states that it is following form, both policies should be compared and analyzed to reveal any areas where coverage under the excess policy is more limited than that provided by the underlying policy. The majority of the excess policies currently in use contain wording to the effect that "except as otherwise provided by this policy, the insurance shall follow all of the terms, conditions, definitions and exclusions of the underlying designated policies." Obviously, it would be important to determine the extent to which any exceptions are made with respect to the excess liability policy.

## Problems in Layering Coverage

Several problems are possible when coverage is layered. For example, the application of aggregate limits may vary with the umbrella and excess layers. The umbrella policy, for example, may be subject to a general aggregate limit and a products-completed operations aggregate limit, whereas some of the excess layers may be subject to a so-called basket aggregate limit, which applies to all coverages. Moreover, the excess policies may differ as to obligations concerning defense. Some excess liability policies, for example, may include coverage for defense costs (usually within policy limits), whereas others may not even recognize such costs in determining whether underlying policy limits have been exhausted.

In addition, whenever excess liability layers are to apply over the first umbrella layer, the excess layers should ideally follow the provisions of the umbrella policy exactly. However, as mentioned previously, excess policies are seldom "true" following-form policies in every area of coverage. Even when an excess policy states that it is a following-form policy, it must be compared with the umbrella (or other underlying) policy to discover areas in which coverage under the excess policy is more restrictive than that provided by the underlying policy. Many excess policies contain wording similar to this: "Except as otherwise provided by this policy, the insurance shall follow all of the terms, conditions, definitions, and exclusions of the underlying designated policies." Obviously, determining the extent to which exceptions are made with respect to the excess policy is extremely important.

## Adequacy of Excess Limits

The layering of coverage allows many insureds the opportunity to secure high levels of protection. However, whether those limits are "adequate" is another matter. Though several writers have shed some light on this issue, answering the question of how much liability insurance is "enough" remains a subjective determination.

Consider a corporation with $1,000,000 in assets, for example. If it carries $1,000,000 in liability insurance, a $2,000,000 court judgment could cause bankruptcy. If it carries $2,000,000 of liability insurance, a $3,000,000 judgment could cause bankruptcy. Moreover, even a smaller uninsured verdict of, say, $500,000 could bankrupt or seriously impair the firm's financial condition, particularly when the possibility of several such losses in a single fiscal period is acknowledged.

How should a risk manager determine the adequacy of liability insurance limits? Unfortunately, that question has no uniformly satisfactory answer. It is no secret that jury awards are getting larger and that, as a practical matter, there is no upper dollar limit on the amount a jury might award.

Accordingly, risk managers of large corporations commonly buy the highest limits they can obtain in the worldwide market and hope that those limits will be adequate. This approach neither guarantees that the available limits will be sufficient, nor does it address the issue of whether the protection obtained was secured at reasonable prices. It does underscore the nature of the current dilemma. Even firms that are willing and able to pay for high limits often do not feel that their limits are adequate. Some firms feel the need for higher limits but are not willing or able to pay for them, and some find that higher limits are unavailable.

Given the problem of growing loss potential, insurance availability, and price, firms must coordinate their insurance purchasing decisions with careful consideration of all available alternatives. If a firm retains the smaller losses that are so costly to insure and concentrates its premium dollars on the purchase of the higher limits needed (which may be less expensive to insure), and if it implements effective loss controls, it should be in a much better position to obtain catastrophic protection at economically feasible costs. In short, a firm can get the most from insurance only when it is properly combined with noninsurance techniques.

## Summary

The maximum possible loss for liability loss exposures is difficult to estimate accurately. Organizations therefore generally want high limits of liability insurance. However, primary insurers typically offer limits of $1,000,000 per occurrence. To obtain higher limits, organizations usually must obtain additional policies, which come in two basic types: excess liability policies and umbrella liability policies.

Excess liability policies and umbrella liability policies both perform the following functions:

- Provide additional limits above the each occurrence limits of the insured's underlying policies
- Take the place of the underlying insurance when underlying aggregate limits are reduced or exhausted

In addition, an umbrella policy also covers some claims that are not covered by the insured's underlying policies, subject to a self-insured retention.

A true *following-form* excess liability policy covers excess losses subject to the same provisions in the referenced underlying policy. A *self-contained* excess liability policy is subject only to its own provisions. Some excess liability policies combine these two approaches. For example, they might incorporate the provisions of the underlying policy but modify those provisions with some additional conditions or exclusions in the excess policy.

Although an excess liability policy may apply over one or more underlying policies, an umbrella liability policy normally applies over primary CGL, commercial auto, and employers liability coverages. An umbrella policy may also provide excess coverage over watercraft, aircraft, liquor liability, or perhaps other primary policies.

There are no standard excess or umbrella liability forms. Each insurer drafts its own form. Thus, when an insured is buying excess or umbrella liability insurance, the prospective policy forms must be analyzed carefully to make sure that they meet the insured's needs.

An umbrella liability policy ordinarily has a comprehensive insuring agreement covering bodily injury, property damage, personal injury, and advertising injury. Those terms can be defined differently in each policy and are not always defined similarly to those used in the CGL policy. Defense costs may be covered within limits or in addition to limits. Umbrella policies ordinarily have an each occurrence/offense limit and one or more aggregate limits. The coverage trigger is usually occurrence but in some cases may be claims-made.

In drafting its policies, an umbrella insurer may omit, add, or modify the exclusions found in the underlying policies. Thus, an umbrella policy is often broader than the underlying policy in some respects and narrower in other respects.

Because of special conditions found in umbrella liability policies, insureds must keep the required underlying policies in effect throughout the umbrella policy period. Moreover, the inception and expiration dates of all underlying, excess, and umbrella policies of a single insured should be concurrent in order to prevent coverage gaps.

# Chapter Notes

1. This chapter is based in part on material in the text for INS 23, Bernard L. Webb, Arthur L. Flitner, and Jerome Trupin, *Commercial Insurance* (Malvern, PA: Insurance Institute of America, 1996).
2. Marie Reubi and Jill Foster, "Current Award Trends," *Personal Injury Valuation Handbook* (Horsham, PA: LRP Publications, Inc., 1994), p. 56.
3. For more comprehensive treatment and comparison of umbrella policy exclusions and other provisions, see *Commercial Liability Insurance* (Dallas, TX: International Risk Management Institute).

# Chapter 14

# Surety Bonds

A contract of suretyship, or **surety bond**, is a "contract whereby one party agrees to be answerable for debt, default, or miscarriage of another."[1] Such a contract involves three parties: the principal, the obligee, and the surety. The **principal** is obligated to perform in some way for the benefit of the **obligee**. The **surety** guarantees to the obligee that the principal will fulfill the underlying obligations. For example, one of the most common types of surety bonds, used in connection with construction projects, is called a performance bond. In a performance bond, the surety and the building contractor (the principal) jointly guarantee to the project owner (the obligee) that the building contractor will perform the construction contract according to plans and specifications.

The earliest form of suretyship dates back to biblical times and was personal in nature. Then, the surety was an individual who, because of wealth, stature, or friendship, was asked to support another person's promise to perform a contract or fulfill some other obligation if that person became unable to do so. Personal sureties often provided this form of support for no charge, although some required compensation for their services. Corporate suretyship—whereby a professional surety provides its services for compensation—started to gain recognition in the latter part of the nineteenth century.

Although contracts of personal suretyship have not disappeared entirely, in modern times the dominant contracts of suretyship are those under which insurance companies serve as compensated corporate sureties. To enhance the practical value of a principal's legal obligation to perform, a corporate surety issues a surety bond that guarantees the performance of the obligation—and backs its guarantee with its own name, reputation, and financial resources. In return, the surety is compensated by the premium it charges for the bond.

# Surety Bond Fundamentals

The sections that follow answer several fundamental questions about surety bonds:

- What are the general characteristics of surety bonds?
- How do surety bonds differ from insurance?
- How are surety bonds used as a tool of risk management?
- What are the basic types of surety bonds?

## Characteristics of Surety Bonds

Although many different types of surety bonds are used to address a wide range of situations, all surety bonds are similar in terms of their distinguishing general characteristics. In addition to the fact that surety bonds involve three parties (as described above), the characteristics are as follows:

1. The principal is primarily liable to the obligee.
2. The surety theoretically expects no losses.
3. A bond may be indeterminate in length and noncancelable.
4. A bond is often required and influenced greatly by regulation or statute.
5. The surety's obligation is limited to the amount stated in the bond.

### Principal Becomes Liable to the Surety

If the principal fails in the performance of its obligation to the obligee, the surety becomes answerable. The surety can fulfill that obligation or pay the loss up to the bond limit (also called the **penal amount**, penal sum, or penalty). However, the surety's performance does not extinguish the principal's duty to reimburse the surety. On the contrary, the principal is obligated to indemnify the surety. This right is granted to sureties at common law and need not be expressed in the bond or in the application. However, bond applications often contain indemnity agreements between principals and sureties.

### Surety Theoretically Expects No Losses

When a bond is issued, the surety is attesting to the principal's integrity, capability, trustworthiness, financial responsibility, or whatever qualities may be required for the undertaking. Therefore, a surety will not provide a bond unless in its judgment it is convinced that the principal has the qualifications necessary to perform the obligation guaranteed by the bond.

By prequalifying the principal through careful underwriting, and possibly through the use of collateral or joint control, the surety theoretically does not expect to sustain any losses. Although some losses do occur in practice, they are reduced by the exercise of the rights of the surety in the event of default, including the surety's right to recover its loss payments from the principal or other indemnitors through its subrogation and salvage efforts.

### Underwriting—The "Three Cs"

Bond underwriters must determine whether the principal has the necessary qualifications to be bonded. Such qualifications are considered in terms of the "three Cs":

1. **Character.** Does the bond applicant possess the traits of integrity, reliability, and leadership or drive necessary to accomplish goals in spite of difficulties?

2. **Capacity.** Does the bond applicant have the technical or professional ability to meet commitments necessary to perform the obligation to be carried out?

3. **Capital.** Does the principal have sufficient financial resources, financial strength, and credit standing to perform the obligation secured by the bond?

Before a surety bond will be issued, the surety's underwriter considers the three Cs to determine, to his or her own satisfaction, that the bond applicant is of such character, capacity, and capital that the obligation will be fulfilled.

### Collateral

Sureties occasionally require the principal to post collateral of a value equal to all or part of the bond penalty. Acceptable forms of collateral might include irrevocable letters of credit, certificates of deposit, treasury bills, certain high-quality stocks, and cash.

When the principal deposits collateral with the surety, the surety has access to the collateral should the surety be called on to pay in the event of a default, even though the principal's financial condition may deteriorate during the bond period. Usually, the use of collateral results in a premium credit, since it reduces the surety's loss exposure.

### Joint Control

Joint control may also be used to reduce a surety's loss exposure, particularly when fiduciary bonds are involved. Joint control means that the assets in an estate cannot be disbursed without the approval of the surety or, in some cases, the approval of the attorney who represents the fiduciary. For example, this makes it more difficult for a fiduciary administering a trust to divert some of the assets of the trust to the fiduciary's own benefit or to deploy the assets unwisely.

### Rights of the Surety If the Principal Defaults

If the principal is unable to perform fully, the surety must either do whatever is necessary to fulfill the undertaking or indemnify the obligee. However, if the principal defaults, the surety acquires no more of an obligation than the principal's original obligation, subject to the penal amount of the bond. If, for some reason, damages exceed the penal amount, the surety's obligation ceases once the penal amount is paid; but the principal's liability to the obligee for any default or damage may continue.

### Significance of Subrogation and Salvage

After fulfilling the principal's obligation, the surety is subrogated to the rights and remedies of the obligee, to the extent of any payment the surety has made. Through subrogation, the surety attempts to recover all of its loss payments from the principal. The surety may also be able to reduce its losses through salvage efforts, such as by demanding cash or other property from the principal at the time the surety becomes aware of the claim.

### Surety Bond Rates

Since surety losses do occur, despite underwriters' efforts to bond only qualified applicants, industry-wide premium and loss statistics are necessary for purposes of developing valid rates for surety bonds. To assist insurers in this regard, The Surety Association of America (SAA) collects data on premiums written and earned and losses incurred on the various classes of surety bonds. These data are used to calculate loss costs that SAA member companies can use in developing the rates they charge for surety bonds. To develop rates from loss costs, each insurer must add expense loadings (and perhaps profit loadings) to the loss costs. Expenses are usually a significant proportion of surety bond rates because of the extensive underwriting required for surety bonds.

## Indeterminate in Length and Noncancelable

Surety bonds usually terminate when the principal's obligations have been fulfilled, so a bond could involve performance taking place over several years.

For this reason, some surety bonds are considered to be indeterminate in length. This is especially true when the bond is noncancelable. However, not *all* surety bonds are noncancelable or terminate only when performance has been completed. Variations will become more apparent as specific bond types are analyzed later in this chapter.

## Influenced by Regulations and Statutes

Surety bonds can be statutory or nonstatutory in form.

- The obligation of a **statutory bond** is prescribed by a municipal ordinance or a federal or state regulation or statute. Because the law specifies the conditions of a statutory bond, the obligations of all three parties are controlled not by the bond provisions but by the law involved.
- The obligation of a **nonstatutory bond** is controlled by a contract between the principal and the obligee and by the bond provisions.

## Bond Limit

The penal amount is the amount for which the bond is written. It is similar to the limit of liability in an insurance policy. If, for some reason, damages exceed the penal amount, the surety's obligation usually ceases at the penal amount, although some bonds may specifically provide for payment of court costs and interest on judgments above the bond penalty, as do most liability insurance policies. Although the penal amount limits the obligation of the *surety*, the obligation of the *principal* for any default or damage may be unlimited.

# Suretyship Versus Insurance

Many authors and courts have attempted to distinguish between surety bonds and insurance policies. There are important distinctions between the two, but the differences have diminished somewhat over the years.

One often-cited distinguishing characteristic of suretyship, for example, is that many bonds are noncancelable. Most insurance policies can be canceled, but statutes now preclude the cancellation of many property-liability policies without good cause. Some insurance policies (such as an open cargo policy) are continuous until canceled; and a few, such as title insurance, provide protection as long as the insured continues to own the property, based on payment of a single premium. Noncancellation is neither a feature of all surety bonds, nor is it unique to surety bonds.

Another alleged point of difference is that statutes are virtually read into surety bonds. However, the same can be said of many insurance contracts. For example, financial responsibility laws are read into auto insurance policies, and workers compensation insurance provides the benefits prescribed by law.

Perhaps the greatest differences between surety bonds and insurance are the following:

| Surety | Insurance |
| --- | --- |
| • Surety bonds are three-party agreements involving the principal, the surety, and the obligee. | • Insurance contracts are usually two-party agreements involving the insurer and the insured. |
| • The surety is answerable to the obligee if the principal defaults. | • The insurer is primarily responsible to its own insured. |
| • The surety theoretically does not expect losses. | • The insurer expects some losses. |
| • The surety can reduce its net losses through subrogation *against its principal*. | • The insurer usually cannot subrogate against its own insured. |
| • The surety bond must be in writing as surety bonds are subject to the statute of frauds. A surety bond cannot be created under a binder (an oral agreement that puts coverage into effect). | • An insurance policy, although usually in writing, can be created through the issuance of a binder. |

## Suretyship as a Risk Management Method

From the standpoint of an obligee, requiring a surety bond can be thought of as a method of handling its exposure to a financial loss.

Under the provisions of the applicable statute, ordinance, or contract, the principal has a legal obligation to perform and to make good on losses caused by its failure to perform. However, if the principal fails to perform and is insolvent or otherwise unable or unwilling to provide full restitution, the loss would then fall upon the obligee, in the absence of a surety bond.

By requiring the principal to furnish a surety bond, the obligee is attempting to transfer the risk of loss to a professional risk bearer, the surety company. The transfer will be successful to the extent that the surety is solvent and the bond provides a large enough limit to cover the loss.

Requiring the principal to furnish a surety bond can also be thought of as a form of loss control. A well-managed surety company will not provide a surety bond unless the company is first convinced that the principal will be able to fulfill its legal obligation to perform. This prequalification process is a valuable loss prevention service, the cost of which is included in the insurer's premium.

## *General Types of Surety Bonds*

Many types of surety bonds are used to fulfill a variety of surety bonding needs. However, most surety bonds fall into the following categories:

1. **Contract bonds** guarantee the performance of public or private contracts. Examples of bonds within this category are bid bonds, performance bonds, and payment bonds.
2. **Federal noncontract surety bonds** guarantee compliance with federal laws or regulations, such as those concerning the payment of excise taxes and customs duties.
3. **License and permit bonds** are required by federal, state, or municipal governments as prerequisites to engaging in certain business activities. Among those who may need such bonds are contractors who work on public streets, plumbers, electricians, and automobile dealers.
4. **Public official bonds** guarantee the honesty and faithful performance of those who are elected or appointed to positions in government.
5. **Judicial bonds** are prescribed by statute and filed in either probate courts or in courts of equity. Probate courts deal with such matters as the appointment of guardians and the handling of deceased persons' estates. Courts of equity are concerned with disputes involving specific performance, or other equitable remedies, rather than money damages.

# *Contract Bonds*

Surety bonds are often required of those who have contractual obligations to perform work or service for others. All such bonds serve two broad purposes:

1. The surety's willingness to furnish the bond is evidence that in the surety's judgment the principal is qualified to fulfill the terms of the contract.
2. The surety guarantees that, even if the principal defaults, the obligations of the contract will be performed, or the surety will indemnify the obligee up to the penal amount of the bond.

Although the obligees of contract bonds may be either private or public entities, the latter are especially prevalent because governmental entities enter into many contracts for which the bonds are required by law.

Contract bonds are not confined to construction operations. For example, contract bonds might also be required by a municipality that advertises for bids from firms interested in handling the municipality's trash collections. However, contract bonds are used primarily for construction purposes, and contract bonds required in connection with construction projects generate most of the contract bond premium volume of insurers. Contract bonds used for construction purposes include bid bonds, performance bonds, payment bonds, and maintenance bonds. These contract bonds are summarized in Exhibit 14-1 and described in more detail in the sections that follow.

Surety bond forms are frequently promulgated by the obligee, although in some instances the obligee may specify a bond form that is available from an unrelated organization, such as the American Institute of Architects (AIA). The AIA is a national organization of architects that supports and encourages the use of contract bonds in private construction work. With the cooperation of the Surety Association of America, the AIA has developed standard bid, performance, and payment bonds. If the obligee does not provide the bond form or specify a particular bond form, the surety may have a form available that is acceptable to the obligee. The federal government has drafted and printed standard forms for statutory contract bonds required by the federal government.

## Bid Bonds

In a **bid bond**, the obligee to whom the bond is furnished is usually the owner of the proposed construction project. However, the obligee can also be a general contractor who requires subcontractors to give bonds for the general contractor's own benefit. The surety promises that the general contractor or subcontractor (principal) bidding for a contract will, if the bid is accepted, enter into a contract and furnish other necessary contract bonds. If the bid is accepted and the principal refuses to enter into the contract or fails to provide such bonds, the obligee in most instances is entitled to be paid (subject to the penal amount of the bond) the difference between the amount of the principal's bid and the next lowest bid that is finally accepted by the obligee.

Bids for public work are normally solicited through public advertisements. Although some statutes allow the alternative of furnishing either a certified check or a bid bond, bid bonds are more commonly used. Public work is usually awarded to the lowest bidder. On private work, the use of bid bonds or certified

**Exhibit 14-1**
Contract Bond Comparison

|  | Obligee | Principal | Guarantee |
|---|---|---|---|
| **Bid Bond** | The owner or the party calling for the bid | The bidder | The bidder will enter into the contract and provide a performance bond if the bid is accepted. |
| **Performance Bond** | The property owner or the party having the work done | The contractor | The contract will be performed by the contractor according to plans and specifications. |
| **Payment Bond** | Same as performance bond | The contractor | The project will be free of liens—that is, certain bills for labor and materials will be paid. |
| **Maintenance Bond** | Same as performance bond | The contractor | The work will be free from defects in materials and workmanship for a specified period. |

Adapted from *FC&S Bulletins,* Casualty & Surety vol. (Cincinnati, OH: National Underwriter Co.), p. Surety B-1, September 1990.

checks is purely a matter of discretion with the owner. Also, when private work is involved, the owner is under no legal obligation to accept the lowest bidder.

Generally, a claim against a bid bond arises only when, after being awarded the contract by the obligee, a contractor refuses to enter into the contract to perform the work or is unable to supply the required bonds. The contractor usually refuses for one of the following reasons:

1. The contractor determines that performance of the contract is virtually

impossible at the quoted price or finds another project that offers better profit potential.

2. Economic conditions change, increasing the cost of performing the work and making the bid price inadequate. Examples of such change in economic conditions include a sharp increase in interest rates and unexpected inflation bringing about substantial increases in wages and material prices.

3. The contractor discovers that a mistake was made in preparing the bid and does not make an effort to obtain relief from a court, or such effort fails.

Contractors sometimes make mistakes when preparing bids. Some mistakes involve purely clerical errors, while others are the results of poor judgment. When a bid mistake is discovered that would seriously impair the contractor's ability to perform the contract at a profit, the contractor should give serious consideration to withdrawing the bid. Depending on how quickly the mistake was discovered, the circumstances involved, and the type of error, the contractor may be able to withdraw the bid. If the project owner will not agree to the withdrawal of the bid, the contractor may be forced to seek relief in court.

Although some courts allow contractors relief after weighing certain criteria, these procedures for granting relief are not always followed. Even if they are, a contractor may not meet all such criteria. Moreover, some courts have ruled that no mistakes are excusable. Contractors must therefore exercise the utmost care in estimating costs and checking figures.

After a bid has been accepted, the contractor who is awarded the work must enter into a contract with the owner and also furnish any other bonds required to secure the contractor's performance of the work. These other bonds usually include a performance bond and a payment bond. A maintenance bond may also be required.

## Performance Bonds

A **performance bond** guarantees that the obligee will be indemnified for any loss resulting from the failure of the principal to perform the work according to the contract, plans, and specifications at the agreed price within the time allowed.

Performance bonds are generally structured to provide that the principal must have defaulted before the obligee can demand that the surety perform its obligation under the bond. Ordinarily, the performance bond form includes language that gives the surety a number of options if the principal has defaulted. Sureties tend to vigorously oppose bond forms or contract terms that limit their options in a claim situation, especially forms that compel the surety to complete the contract, which may expose the surety to a potential loss in excess of the penal amount of the bond. The surety can usually take any of the following actions and will attempt to select the action that has the best potential of mitigating its loss.

1. *Complete the contract using the existing contractor.* A surety sometimes uses the existing contractor when the reason for a problem is something other than the contractor's incompetence. Some circumstances of hardships that have led sureties to use existing contractors include a bank's refusal to grant any additional extension of credit, an improper and insufficient estimate of contract costs, delay brought about by modification of the contract, delay in receiving necessary equipment, and delay because of bad weather or labor disputes.

2. *Complete the contract using a replacement contractor.* Sureties have used other contractors to finish work when the original contractor defaulted because of incompetence, bankruptcy, suicide, or disappearance of the principal.[2] However, once the surety elects to complete the contract, it is obligated to do so even if the cost of completion proves to be greater than the penal amount of the bond.

3. *Have the owner for whom work is being done arrange for the completion of work, with the surety paying for the additional cost up to the penal amount of the bond.* Financial assistance by the surety will not always solve a performance problem. Sometimes, a surety will not opt to have the contract completed. It is then up to the owner or governmental entity to proceed with the completion of the project. Whether a surety may become obligated for any damages depends on the outcome of the completed work in terms of total, final costs. If the balance of funds retained by the obligee (the amount representing the unpaid balance that would have been paid to the original contractor had the work been completed) is sufficient to cover all costs of completion by others, there can be no claim against the surety under the performance bond. However, if the costs of completion exceed those originally estimated by the defaulting contractor, the excess represents the owner's loss and is payable by the surety, subject to the penal amount of the bond.[3]

4. *Pay the penal amount of the bond to the obligee.*

Whatever the outcome in the event of default, the surety always has the right to seek reimbursement from the principal. The surety can collect from the principal (1) by an assignment of the obligee's rights to the surety, (2) by reason of the written indemnity agreement (sometimes included in the bond application), or (3) through subrogation.[4]

## Payment Bonds

A **payment bond**—also referred to as a labor and materials payment bond—guarantees that bills incurred by a contractor for labor and materials will be fully paid at the completion of the project.

Before 1935, it was customary to issue a single performance bond guaranteeing both the performance of the contract and that certain laborers, material suppliers, and subcontractors would be paid. This arrangement led to conflicts when there was a contractor default involving both performance and unpaid bills. Usually, the project owner would demand that the performance obligation be given first priority even if this meant little or nothing was left for the other claimants. Moreover, the other claimants were often made to wait until the performance obligation was completed before they would receive any payment, a delay that could last several months or even years.

The Miller Act, passed in 1935, required that a separate payment bond be provided for federal work. Over the ensuing years, it has become common practice for construction project owners, both public and private, to require a separate payment bond, usually in an amount equal to 100 percent of the contract price.

This payment protection, whether obtained under a performance bond or under a separate payment bond, is especially important to private project owners because labor and material suppliers who go uncompensated usually can apply a mechanic's lien to the property. A **mechanic's lien** is a right granted by statute and is available to those who seek to secure the value of their work or services that have gone into the form of additions on real estate.[5] When a lien is placed on such property, the owner does not have clear title to the property until all debts are settled.

## Miller Act

The **Miller Act** is a federal statute, enacted by Congress in 1935, that governs contracts for the construction, alteration, or repair of any public buildings or public work for the federal government. This act states that when construction contracts exceed $100,000, a contractor must furnish a performance bond for the protection of the government and a payment bond for the protection of certain persons who supply labor and materials for the required work.

Effective October 1, 1995, the government contracting officers may specify that the prime contractor provide alternative payment protection on jobs between $25,000 and $100,000. Allowable alternatives to bonds could include escrow agreements, letters of credit, certificates of deposit, and deposits of other types of security.

The Miller Act does not provide for total payment to all creditors. Basically, two general categories of creditors are protected under the payment bond required by this act, provided, of course, the bond limit is sufficient:

1. Material suppliers, laborers, and subcontractors who deal directly with the prime contractor

2. Those who have a direct relationship with a subcontractor but who do not have a contractual relationship, expressed or implied, with the prime contractor who furnishes the payment bond

In order to have a right of action under the bond, creditors in the latter category must file written notice to the prime contractor within ninety days from the date on which such creditors last performed labor or furnished material for which claim is to be made under the bond.

## Maintenance Bonds

Many statutes, ordinances, and contracts require that a certain degree of care be exercised in the construction of property. In addition, construction contracts often specify that contractors must remedy any faulty work or defective materials discovered within a specified period of time. To comply with these laws and contractual specifications, contractors must usually provide obligees with a **maintenance bond** to guarantee that faulty work will be corrected and defective materials will be replaced.

Generally, a performance bond includes this maintenance guarantee, without additional premium, for a period of one year after completion of performance. Even when a separate maintenance bond is required along with a performance bond, there usually is no additional charge by the surety for a maintenance bond, provided the duration is one year or less. When a contractor does not have to furnish a performance bond but still has to produce a maintenance bond, or when the contractor must guarantee certain work and materials for longer than one year, the maintenance bond requires an additional charge.

Sureties often are reluctant to provide maintenance guarantees for over one year. After a lapse of time, determining the cause of defects becomes more difficult. The defects could be caused by the contractor, by faulty specifications, by abnormal use of the property by the owner, by failure to perform necessary maintenance, or by some combination of reasons. And, finally, the reluctance of sureties to extend lengthy guarantees can be attributed to liberalizations in the law permitting property owners to recover from contractors for defects in completed work.

## Miscellaneous Contract Bonds

Bonds are also used to secure a variety of contracts other than construction contracts. The purposes for which such bonds may be required include the following:

- The rental of mechanical equipment with or without operators
- The transportation of school children
- The removal of snow and garbage
- The cleaning of streets

Two of the more common types of miscellaneous contract bonds—subdivision bonds and supply bonds—are described below.

### Subdivision Bonds

Land developers and real estate firms often desire to subdivide tracts of property for housing developments. Developers must agree to construct all improvements—such as streets, storm sewers, sidewalks, and streetlights. They must also provide proper sewage disposal systems, a water supply, and other utilities. Before construction can begin, developers are usually required to obtain permits and to provide subdivision bonds to the local governmental authority. A **subdivision bond** guarantees the local governmental authority (obligee) that the developer (principal) will complete the subdivision in accordance with approved proposals and at the developer's expense.

Developers are exposed to a variety of risks that may cause them to run out of the funds needed to complete the promised subdivision improvements. For example, costs can escalate, original estimates can be too low, financing arrangements can fail to close, other ventures can consume cash, or properties may not sell as planned. Largely because of such hazards, a subdivision bond is difficult for developers to procure unless they can provide the type of qualifying credentials required by the surety.

### Supply Contract Bonds

A *supply contract* involves an agreement for furnishing and delivering materials or supplies at an agreed price. Most such contracts take place between private enterprise and federal, state, or local governmental entities, but some involve private parties only.

Those who wish to obtain supply contracts from purchasers invariably must submit bids. Typically, the lowest bidder is selected. When a successful bidder fails to furnish the required supplies according to the contract specifications, the purchaser stands to suffer a loss equal to the difference between the bid price and the higher cost of buying supplies in the open market. Although the bidder can ultimately be held liable for this amount, purchasers often require their suppliers to be bonded so that compensation by the defaulted bidder will be guaranteed.

The appropriate bond for this situation is a **supply contract bond**. The bond guarantees that the supplier (principal) will perform the designated supply contract according to specifications. Because, for the most part, these bonds are required by the government, they are usually statutory.

## Surety Bond Guarantee Program for Small Contractors

Many small contractors lack some of the capital necessary to meet sureties' underwriting requirements for surety bonds. Assistance in obtaining surety bonds is available to such contractors through the Small Business Administration (SBA) under its **Surety Bond Guarantee Program**.

The program is intended to give small, less-experienced contracting firms the opportunity to be bonded so that they can compete for bonded jobs and prove themselves by profitably performing work to specifications. A history of successful performance may, in turn, enable such firms to secure surety bonds for future jobs based on their own reputation and financial ability.

The SBA program is limited to bonds listed in the contract bond section of the *Manual of Rules, Procedures and Classifications* published by The Surety Association of America. However, work requiring another type of bond is sometimes permissible if that bond is written in conjunction with a contract bond. For example, a license or permit bond required of a construction contractor working on a public highway may be included under this program, since it is considered to be incidental to a contract bond. The SBA program will not accept bonds for contract amounts in excess of $1,250,000.

Under this program, the SBA does not issue surety bonds. It merely guarantees to reimburse a participating surety for a stipulated portion—such as 70, 80, or 90 percent—of any loss sustained. In addition to issuing the required bond or bonds, the participating surety must pay the SBA a fee for guaranteeing the bonds that are written.

If a contract is breached by a contractor bonded under the SBA program and a claim or suit is brought against the surety, the SBA must be notified within a reasonable time. Even though the SBA requires notification of any breach, the surety is still responsible for handling all phases of the claim before being reimbursed by the SBA.

# Federal Noncontract Surety Bonds

In addition to contract bonds required under the Miller Act, the U.S. government requires various parties that are subject to federal laws or regulations to provide statutory surety bonds. Manufacturers of alcoholic beverages, tobacco manufacturers, importers, federally licensed warehouses, and grain dealers are examples of those who must provide federal noncontract surety bonds. These bonds guarantee that the regulated parties will perform in accordance with federal laws or regulations. Two examples of federal noncontract surety bonds are described below and summarized in Exhibit 14-2

**Exhibit 14-2**
Summary of Excise Bonds and Customs Bonds

|  | **Obligee** | **Principal** | **Guarantee** |
| --- | --- | --- | --- |
| **Excise Bond** | Federal government | Manufacturers of alcohol or tobacco products | Principal will account for and remit excise taxes. May also guarantee compliance with federal regulations or reporting of statistical information to government agencies. |
| **Customs Bond** | Federal government | Importers of goods subject to customs duties | Principal will pay customs duties and comply with data reporting requirements. |

## Excise Bonds

Federal excise taxes are levied on certain commodities such as alcohol and tobacco. A firm that manufactures such commodities must provide an **excise bond** guaranteeing that the principal will account for and remit excise taxes due to the federal government. These bonds may also guarantee federal regulation compliance, or the full, adequate, and timely reporting of statistical information to various government agencies.

## Customs Bonds

The federal government imposes taxes called customs duties on goods imported into the United States. In addition, importers may be required to report data to governmental agencies. Organizations importing goods subject to customs duties and data reporting requirements are required to provide customs bonds. A **customs bond** guarantees that the principal will pay customs duties as required and comply with data reporting requirements.

# License and Permit Bonds

Many enterprises need licenses to operate. *Licenses* provide special privileges entitling their holders to do something that they would otherwise not be entitled to do.[6]

Licenses are required by states, counties, cities, and political subdivisions, for two primary reasons:

1. They are a source of revenue.
2. They may help in the regulation of license holders through statutes, regulations, or ordinances that exist for the safety and general welfare of the community.

Among those who may be required to obtain licenses are auctioneers, auto dealers, barbers, owners or operators of laundromats, commission merchants, electricians, plumbers, demolition contractors, fumigators, owners of gas stations, vendors of alcoholic beverages, grocery store proprietors, operators of parking lots, photographers, ticket brokers, and warehousers.

*Permits* are somewhat like licenses. They, too, must be obtained from political subdivisions. They also serve as a means of regulation and as sources of revenue. Often they are needed as prerequisites for performing special functions that are incidental to business operations. Some examples are as follows:

- A business may need a permit before it can use public property to park customers' autos.
- Permits are often required when signs or canopies extend over public property, as well as for sidewalk elevators (for freight handling) on public walkways.
- Truckers with oversized loads often need permits before they can legally use public roadways.
- Contractors who work on streets, sidewalks, and public sewer systems need permits.

- Individuals and businesses who make structural alterations or improvements to their properties require building permits.

Whatever the type, licenses or permits frequently are not issued until those who are in need of them furnish a license bond or a permit bond to the appropriate public entity.

License and permit bonds are usually written for a one-year term, although they can terminate sooner, or run indefinitely until cancelled, depending upon the reasons for their use. Because the bonds are statutory, the laws are read into these bonds. Thus, whether these bonds may be cancelable depends on the law for which they are issued or on the cancellation provision in the bond form. Many laws do permit cancellation.

A license or permit bond may provide any of a number of guarantees. The guarantees can be grouped into five categories:

1. Compliance guarantees
2. Good faith guarantees
3. Credit guarantees
4. Financial guarantees
5. Indemnity guarantees

These guarantees are described below and summarized in Exhibit 14-3.

**Exhibit 14-3**
Summary of Guarantees in License and Permit Bonds

| | |
|---|---|
| **Compliance Guarantee** | Principal will comply with the laws that apply to the activity for which principal is licensed. |
| **Good Faith Guarantee** | Principal will perform in good faith. |
| **Credit Guarantee** | Principal will conduct its business in the best interests of others and provide an honest accounting of all funds in its possession. |
| **Financial Guarantee** | Principal will pay taxes as required or will make payment for products recieved from others. |
| **Indemnity Guarantee** | Third parties injured by the principal's activities are given a right of action against the surety. |

## Compliance Guarantees

Consistent with their statutory nature, all license and permit bonds begin with the basic guarantee that principals will comply with the laws that apply to the activities for which they are licensed. Licensed electricians and plumbers, for example, are required to adhere to certain building code specifications when installing wiring, electrical units, plumbing, and other fixtures. Public inspectors usually check all such work to determine whether, in fact, the work meets the required specifications.

## Good Faith Guarantees

Some license and permit bonds, in addition to guaranteeing compliance with the law, also carry the guarantee that principals will perform in good faith, thus protecting the public against any harm that might result from unfair business practices. For example, statutes in many jurisdictions require that used car dealers be licensed as such and also furnish bonds. These bonds benefit persons who sustain losses arising out of any unlawful act of the used car dealer, whether criminal in nature or merely a tort.

## Credit Guarantees

Principals required to furnish bonds providing credit guarantees essentially promise to conduct their business affairs in the best interests of others and to provide honest accountings of all funds in their possession. Auctioneers and dealers in agricultural products are among those who must obtain bonds with guarantees of this nature.

## Financial Guarantees

Some license or permit bonds provide financial guarantees promising that the principal will pay certain taxes as required or will make payment for products received from others.

Manufacturers, wholesalers, and retailers of goods, as well as service firms, are almost always required to collect taxes at the time of sale. For example, amusement and sales taxes are required under the laws of municipalities, and tobacco and gasoline taxes are imposed by federal, state, and local laws.

The responsibility for collecting and recording those taxes inevitably requires some additional bookkeeping expense for businesses. Some of the additional expense can be overcome through the profitable use of tax money until it is due. However, this is where problems may develop. If the business uses tax money for its own purposes, it may be unable to pay those taxes when due. The appropriate bonds guarantee payment of those taxes, and when they cannot be paid, the surety is obligated to pay them.

## Indemnity Guarantees

Bonds that provide indemnity guarantees are distinguishable in one important respect from those that do not. Bonds, such as those obtained by merchants under various tax obligations, directly benefit only public entities. In contrast, bonds that provide indemnity guarantees directly benefit not only public entities but also third parties. Third parties, in other words, are given a right of action against sureties of those bonds if the third parties sustain damages because of bodily injury or property damage caused by the acts or omissions of the bond principals.

Bonds with indemnity guarantees are usually required of those who must obtain permits from public entities before commencing certain activities or before using public property. Among those who must obtain permits and bonds with indemnity agreements are contractors who work on public streets, walkways, and utility systems; contractors who must perform structural alterations, improvements, demolition, or blasting in areas of public exposure; truckers conveying excessively wide or heavy loads on public roadways, including house movers; merchants who attach to their buildings signs or awnings that overhang public thoroughfares; those who construct billboards on public property; and those businesses that use sidewalk freight elevators.

Bonds providing indemnity guarantees should not be confused with liability insurance policies, despite the apparent similarities. If a surety is required to indemnify a third party, it will later seek to recover the sums it has paid from the principal. Under a liability insurance policy, in contrast, the insurer promises to pay on behalf of the insured and cannot subrogate against the insured. Sureties usually require verification that satisfactory liability insurance is in force before they will issue a bond providing indemnity guarantees.

## Public Official Bonds

Individuals who are appointed or elected to positions of public office have the obligation to faithfully discharge their duties to the best of their abilities and otherwise to protect the public interest. The duties of public officials vary with the position in government and the applicable law. However, most public officials are obligated to act in good faith. When they hold public funds, they also have the duty of accounting for them and turning them over to their successors in office. With few exceptions, laws generally hold public officials personally accountable for losses, shortages, or damage to public property. Some officials are even held responsible for the acts and omissions of their subordinates.

All such obligations are affirmed by public officials when they take an oath of office, which is one condition precedent to acting in their official capacities. Another requirement is that these individuals furnish public official bonds.

## Nature of the Guarantee

A public official bond guarantees the public or governmental entity that the official who has been bonded will uphold his or her promise to faithfully and honestly perform all of his or her official duties. Any public official who fails to fulfill these promises must make restitution to the extent of his or her liability. If the official is unable to do so, the surety then becomes answerable up to the penal amount for any damages. Interest on any judgments incurred may be payable by the surety in addition to the penal amount.

It would be nearly impossible to list all the kinds of public officials who must be bonded. However, public officials who must be bonded encompass members of the three broad groups listed below:

1. Those whose primary duties involve handling public funds—tax collectors and treasurers, for example.
2. Those whose primary duties are administrative, such as assessors, insurance commissioners, and judges.
3. Those whose duties involve direct exposure to members of the public, such as constables, sheriffs, and notaries public.

## Noncancelable and of Indeterminate Length

Public official bonds are generally noncancelable because they are coextensive with the officials' terms of office. Thus, the bonds terminate only when successors are appointed or elected and take office.

In any case, the succeeding official should see to it that the necessary arrangements are made for the transfer of office—including the full accounting for all transactions, funds, and other property. When a new public official takes office, an independent audit of the predecessor's office is often advisable. This prevents the new official from being held responsible for acts of a predecessor.

When an official is reappointed or reelected, a new bond is required for the new term of office. Sometimes individuals hold an office for an indefinite period. In these cases, bonds are written without expiration, but subject to annual premiums.

## Relationship to Public Employee Dishonesty Insurance

Public entities can obtain employee dishonesty insurance for their nonbonded employees under the public employee dishonesty coverage forms of the commercial crime insurance program jointly administered by the SAA and ISO. These crime coverage forms *exclude* any employees of the insured governmental entity who are required by statute to post bond as a condition of taking office. This exclusion prevents the crime insurance policy from duplicating sums payable under surety bonds on bonded public officials. The public employee crime coverage forms are described in the text for CPCU 3.

# Judicial Bonds

A judicial bond guarantees that a person or organization will faithfully perform certain duties prescribed by law or by a court or show financial responsibility for the benefit of another until the final outcome of a court's decision. If the principal fails to meet such obligations, the surety must answer for damages. Judicial bonds are usually noncancelable and continuous. They are prescribed by statute and are filed in probate court or in courts of equity.

A *probate court* (or a surrogate's court, as it is sometimes called) deals with settlements of estates and appointments of guardians for minors and incompetent persons. Each county has a probate court that administers the transactions occurring in that county.

A *court of equity* is primarily concerned with arguments involving specific performance or other situations in which money damages would not provide an adequate remedy. For example, a court of equity is used when someone seeks an injunction against another or when someone seeks to regain possession of property being held by another. (Many states no longer have separate courts of equity, but they do continue to provide equitable remedies.)

The two general classes of judicial bonds are court bonds and fiduciary bonds.

A **court bond** generally arises out of litigation—as opposed to an action in probate court concerning faithful disposition of property of others. The primary purpose of a court bond is to permit someone to seek a remedy in court while at the same time protecting the other party against whom a claim is made for any damages sustained if the person seeking the remedy does not prevail.

A **fiduciary bond** is required of a person who is selected by a probate court to administer the property or interests of others according to the specifications laid down by the court. It also is used in equity proceedings involving receivers and liquidators of property, among others.

## Court Bonds

There are many different varieties of court bonds. However, the various types can usually be classified as corresponding pairs of plaintiff bonds and defendant bonds.

A person who commences an action against another in order to obtain some type of equitable remedy—such as the performance of a certain act, the repossession of certain property, or the fulfillment of some monetary obligation—may need to give a particular type of plaintiff bond before the court will proceed with the action. This type of bond guarantees, if it is ultimately determined that such action was wrongfully taken, that the plaintiff will pay any damages sustained by the defendant as the result of such action.

If the defendant desires to continue performing a certain act or to retain the property in question during the court proceedings, he or she may be required to give a defendant bond. If the court decides in favor of the plaintiff, the defendant must then refrain from performing the act in question, return the property sought, and/or pay damages sustained by the plaintiff.

Two pairs of corresponding plaintiff and defendant bonds are described below as examples of court bonds. These bonds are also summarized in Exhibit 14-4.

## Attachment Bond

Before a court will attach property (take it by legal authority) at the request of another, the plaintiff must give the court an **attachment bond**. This bond guarantees that, if the court decides against the plaintiff, the defendant will be paid any damages as the result of having such property attached. If the court decides in the plaintiff's favor, the bond automatically terminates.

## Release of Attachment Bond

After property of a defendant is attached, it can be released back to the defendant pending final outcome of the court's decision if the defendant gives the court a **release of attachment bond**. This bond guarantees that the defendant will return the property in question and pay any damages and court costs if the court should decide in the plaintiff's favor. The defendant is *required* to furnish a release of attachment bond only if the defendant desires to maintain possession of the property until the dispute is settled. To secure the bond, the defendant must satisfy the surety that he or she is financially responsible. Liability insurance policies commonly agree to pay the premiums for release of attachment bonds required in any suit for damages covered by the policy.

## Appeal Bond

An **appeal bond** is required of a plaintiff who did not obtain the remedy that was sought and desires to appeal an adverse decision to a higher court. The bond, when posted, guarantees payment of all court costs on the appeal.

**Exhibit 14-4**
Summary of Selected Court Bonds

| | Obligee | Principal | Guarantee |
|---|---|---|---|
| **Attachment Bond** | The court, for the benefit of defendant | Plaintiff requesting attachment of property | If court decides against plaintiff, plaintiff will pay any damages sustained by defendant as a result of having property attached. |
| **Release of Attachment Bond** | The court, for the benefit of plaintiff and court | Defendant who wants to regain possession of property that has been attached by plaintiff | If court decides in plaintiff's favor, defendant will return the property and pay any damages and court costs. |
| **Appeal Bond** | The court | Plaintiff who desires to appeal an adverse decision to a higher court | Plaintiff will pay all required court costs on the appeal. |
| **Defendant's Appeal Bond** | The court, for the benefit of plaintiff and court | Defendant who desires to appeal an adverse decision to a higher court | If higher court sustains initial judgment, defendant will pay the entire judgment plus court costs and interest. |

## Defendant's Appeal Bond

When the *defendant* desires to appeal a case to a higher court, a **defendant's appeal bond** (or a supersedeas bond, as it is sometimes called) is required. The bond guarantees the plaintiff that the defendant will pay the entire judgment, plus court costs and interest, should a higher court sustain the initial judgment in favor of the plaintiff. Defendants' appeal bonds are another type of bond that liability insurers typically agree to pay the premium for when such bonds are required of their insureds in a covered lawsuit.

## Fiduciary Bonds

The word "fiduciary" refers to persons or legal entities such as administrators, guardians, and trustees who are appointed by a court for purposes of managing, controlling, or disposing of property of others. Like court bonds, fiduciary bonds are a type of judicial bond used for a variety of purposes. Fiduciary bonds generally guarantee that persons entrusted with the care of property belonging to others will exercise their duties faithfully, account for all property received, and make good any deficiency for which a court may hold such fiduciaries liable.

Governed by statutes or by directives of probate and equity courts, fiduciary bonds usually hold the principals and the sureties jointly and severally liable to obligees for the faithful performance of specified duties. They are continuous instruments requiring no renewal, although premiums are charged annually. Moreover, they are noncancelable—usually running until the proceedings are completed and the sureties and fiduciaries have been released from further obligation.

Both individuals and corporations can be selected to act as fiduciaries. Among the fiduciaries who are frequently bonded are (1) guardians, (2) administrators and executors, and (3) receivers and trustees in bankruptcy proceedings.

### Guardians

A *guardian* is anyone who legally has the care of a person or a person's property (or both) because of the inability of that person to manage his or her own affairs. A guardian is often appointed by a probate court to look after the affairs of a minor or other person suffering a legal disability. The minor or incompetent person is called a ward of the court. The one appointed to act as guardian can be a parent, a relative, or some other competent person. The "guardian of the property" is usually responsible to see to it that the ward is properly supported and educated.

A *curator* or "guardian of the property" is a guardian who controls property of a ward. Thus, it is not uncommon for a ward to have two guardians, although an individual guardian can fill both roles. A *conservator* or a *committee* is a guardian selected by a court to manage the affairs of a person deemed to be legally incompetent.

All jurisdictions have statutes that safeguard the rights and interests of minors and legally incompetent persons. Those statutes require that a guardian give a bond before assuming the role of fiduciary for a minor or incompetent. The bond guarantees that the fiduciary will faithfully perform all duties, observe all directives of the court, and provide an accounting of all money and other property when required by the court to do so. Failing this, the fiduciary is liable to the court for all damages. The surety is secondarily liable, up to the penalty of the bond. However, a surety might be required to pay, in excess of the penal amount, any court costs and interest that has accrued from the time any judgment is rendered against the fiduciary.

## Administrators and Executors

An *executor* is one named in a will to administer an estate. When a person dies intestate (without leaving a will), a court will appoint an *administrator* to settle the estate of the decedent.

The duties and obligations of administrators and executors are generally the same, but there are distinctions. For example, administrators settle estates according to the directives of the courts, whereas executors settle estates as specified in the wills, subject to approval of the courts. The duties and responsibilities of both types of fiduciaries include collecting all assets of the estate and preserving them from loss, paying all debts that were incurred by the decedent, and providing the court with an accounting of all transactions. Upon the court's approval of such accounting, the fiduciary is obligated to distribute the remaining assets as specified in the will or by the statute in question. After satisfactorily completing these duties, the fiduciary is discharged by the court.

When a court requires an administrator or an executor to post a bond (the latter may be excused from doing so if the will so specifies), the bond guarantees the fiduciary's faithful performance as dictated by law or by the court. The surety also may require, as a prerequisite to writing a bond, that it or a responsible third party (such as an attorney) be given joint control, along with the fiduciary, over the disbursement of certain assets.

A bond furnished for an executor or an administrator of an estate is noncancelable and terminates with the court's acknowledgment that all duties required of the fiduciary have been properly discharged. Although the fiduciary is liable to the full extent of any losses, the surety must, if the fiduciary defaults, answer only to the extent of the bond limit. In some cases, the surety may also be responsible, in addition to the bond limit, for court costs and interest that accrues on any judgment rendered against the principal.

## Trustees in Bankruptcy Proceedings

In situations involving bankruptcy, the United States trustee appoints and supervises a panel of private trustees who are available to serve as trustees in cases under Chapters 7 and 11 of the bankruptcy code. These trustees supervise the administration of cases, and the United States trustee establishes the penal amount. The law also allows the trustee to establish a blanket bond in favor of the United States conditioned on the faithful performance of official duties by the panel of trustees. Such blanket bonds often include a "per case" limit and an aggregate limit per trustee.

In a Chapter 7 liquidation, the trustee reduces any assets to cash and determines the priority of payment among the creditors for the final distribution of these assets. In a Chapter 11 reorganization case, the trustee supervises and monitors the administration of the case to ensure that appropriate actions are taken and that money received is properly deposited or invested. In general, bonds written for trustees guarantee faithful performance of all their official duties.

## Common Causes of Loss

Although courts usually exercise care in selecting guardians, administrators, and other fiduciaries, and even though sureties also try to ascertain the qualifications of the same people, losses still occur. Most problems involving fiduciary bonds deal with administrators of estates and with guardians of minors and incompetents. Claims involving administrators range from allegations of simple failure to perform to charges of mismanagement of estates' affairs because of ignorance, negligence, or dishonesty.

Administrators and executors are obligated to exercise reasonable care in notifying all heirs of an impending probate proceeding. That is not always done, and estates are sometimes settled without notification of all heirs. Courts have held administrators and their sureties accountable in cases when all heirs could have been notified if the administrators had exercised reasonable care.

Administrators and executors are also obligated to give public notice of the estate proceedings for a certain period, usually six weeks, in order to give creditors of the estate an opportunity to file claims against the estate. Problems arise when fiduciaries begin to close the estate before the expiration of this period. Related to this are cases in which fiduciaries do not make payments to secured creditors and general (unsecured) creditors in proper order of priority.

Administrators who are direct heirs sometimes conceal funds or other property of the estate so that those funds are not included in the distribution among other heirs, and fiduciaries sometimes do not make a proper accounting for tax purposes—leading to subsequent suits by the government.

Guardians of minors and conservators of incompetents can experience difficulties for a number of reasons, including the following:

1. Expenditures are improperly made.
2. Funds are misappropriated.
3. Funds or property are mismanaged.
4. Records are inadequate.

# *Financial Guarantee Coverages*

Until the late 1970s, a financial guarantee bond was generally thought of as a bond given to secure the payment of a sum or sums of money and with no other alternative. These traditional financial guarantee bonds were used in a wide variety of situations. Examples are bonds given to guarantee the payment of highway tolls and bonds given to secure the payment of utility bills for power, water, or gas.

Starting in the late 1970s, the term "financial guarantee" began to take on an additional meaning as demand arose for bonds such as those used to secure the promissory notes given by investors in limited partnerships. At about the same time, issuers of municipal bonds (which are not surety bonds, but debt instruments issued by governmental entities) discovered that they could save substantial amounts of interest expense if they obtained a surety bond to guarantee that the municipal bond investors would receive their interest payments as promised and get their principal back at maturity. With a surety bond in place, a higher investment grade would apply to the entire issue, allowing the municipality to sell its bonds at a lower rate of interest.

Once these new "credit enhancement" types of surety bonds caught on, premium volume began to soar. Eventually, this activity was noticed by state insurance departments, and they became concerned about the catastrophe potential should the country suffer a major economic downturn. In some states, this realization led to legislation restricting the writing of the new "credit enhancement" financial guarantee bonds to specialty licensed monoline companies. It also compelled the National Association of Insurance Commissioners to create a new line of business code just for credit enhancement financial guarantee bonds.

By the early 1990s, financial guarantee annual written premiums exceeded $1 billion, with the five largest monoline writers accounting for about 90 percent of the market.

## Summary

In a surety bond, the surety (which is usually an insurance company) guarantees that the principal will perform certain obligations for the benefit of the obligee. If the principal fails to perform its obligations, the surety becomes answerable to the obligee. However, unlike a liability insurance policy, a surety bond permits the surety to seek reimbursement of its loss from the principal that has defaulted.

Insurers do not issue surety bonds unless they believe that the principal is capable of performing as promised. The underwriting process for surety bonds therefore ascertains whether the bond applicant has the character, capacity, and capital required to perform the underlying obligations to the obligee.

Contract bonds guarantee the performance of contracts, most commonly construction contracts. The main types of contract bonds are bid bonds, performance bonds, payment bonds, and maintenance bonds, which guarantee various contractual obligations made by builders and other contractors.

Federal noncontract bonds guarantee compliance with federal laws or regulations. Examples of such bonds are excise bonds and customs bonds.

License and permit bonds are required by federal, state, or municipal governments as prerequisites to engaging in certain business activities.

Public official bonds guarantee the honesty and faithful performance of those who are elected or appointed to positions in government.

Judicial bonds include court bonds and fiduciary bonds. Court bonds are frequently required in disputes seeking equitable remedies. Fiduciary bonds are required of individuals serving as guardians, executors, administrators, or trustees.

Various financial guarantee coverages resemble surety bonds. These coverages include municipal bond insurance and various other contracts in which an insurer guarantees certain specified results between two parties.

## Chapter Notes

1. *Black's Law Dictionary*, 6th ed. (St. Paul, MN: West Publishing Co., 1990), s.v. "Suretyship, contract of."
2. *Contract Bonds: The Unseen Services of a Surety* (New York: The Surety Association of America, 1973), pp. 41-56.

3. Luther E. Mackall, *Surety Underwriting Manual* (Indianapolis, IN: The Rough Notes Co., 1972), p. 103.
4. Ronald C. Horn, *Subrogation in Insurance Theory and Practice* (Homewood, IL: Richard D. Irwin, 1964), p. 228.
5. *American Jurisprudence*, 2d ed. (Rochester, NY: Lawyers Cooperative, 1993), Section 1, p. 512.
6. *Am. Jur.* 2d, Section 1, p. 89.

# Chapter 15

# Advanced Risk Management Techniques[*]

Some risk management problems require solutions beyond the scope of conventional insurance. A common term for this body of additional solutions is the "alternative market." However, no singular insurance market offers these solutions. Some of the techniques identified with the alternative market are available from conventional insurers, operating either directly or as reinsurers, and others are available only from organizations that have been formed solely for the purpose of providing these alternative techniques. In fact, some of the alternative techniques are offered by a "non-market"—the insureds themselves—as they form captive insurance companies that obtain services and reinsurance from conventional insurers.

Another term that collectively identifies the array of alternative solutions is "advanced risk management techniques." That term connotes techniques based on the fundamental techniques of risk control and risk financing, but in such a way as to be more comprehensive, more complex, or more suited to an organization's unique situation.

[*]This chapter is adapted from *The Alternative Market* (Dallas, TX: International Risk Management Institute, Inc., 1994), a research project of the Golden Gate Chapter of the CPCU Society. The adapted material is used with the permission of International Risk Management Institute, Inc.

Advanced risk management techniques vary in degrees of formality, ranging from informal, nonfunded plans to fully regulated insurance entities. Most advanced risk management programs involve a significant degree of risk retention—paying part or all of one's own losses instead of transferring them to insurers or other parties.

The current estimate of the size of the alternative market is approximately one-third of the U.S. commercial insurance market and about one-quarter of the global insurance market. The alternative market expands rapidly during the "hard market" cycles of the insurance industry but does not contract as quickly when the market turns "soft." Many of those organizations that have left the traditional market are reluctant to return, or perhaps some of the traditional market sellers are reluctant to take back the secessionist buyers.

This chapter serves as an introduction to the alternative market by reviewing the following major categories of advanced risk management techniques:

1. Self-insurance
2. Large deductible plans
3. Captive insurers
4. Fronting
5. Retrospective rating plans

In practice, the boundaries between some of these categories are indistinct. At times, identifying a pure form of any of these techniques is difficult, since one of their key advantages is their flexibility in application to unusual situations.

## Self-Insurance

In the context of advanced risk management techniques, **self-insurance** is used to mean the planned retention of risk by the entity having the exposure. The term "retention" encompasses both self-insurance and unplanned or unconscious retention of one's own risks. Thus, self-insurance is a form of retention marked by a conscious decision-making process.

A self-insurance program can be as simple as an organization's going without physical damage insurance on its automobile fleet and paying for all auto repairs out of cash flow. At the other extreme, a self-insurance program can have a written coverage document as lengthy and detailed as an insurance policy and loss reserves set aside in accordance with actuarial projections.

Likewise, handling of losses can be simple or complex, depending on the loss exposure being self-insured. First-party losses, such as fleet physical damage, can be managed by the self-insured's clerical staff. Third-party liability and workers compensation claims generally involve contracting for professional claims management services. Program oversight may include annual audits by Certified Public Accountants (CPAs), claim consultants, and state regulators.

Few organizations have the ability to fully retain their loss exposures. Therefore, self-insurance plans often include excess insurance to cover losses exceeding the organization's self-insured retention. A distinct commercial market serves the various needs of self-insured organizations seeking excess insurance for property, liability, and workers compensation risks. Each insurer has its own policy form, and variations in coverage and terms can be substantial. The most common types of excess insurance used in connection with self-insurance plans are specific excess policies, aggregate excess policies, and policies that combine those two approaches. These types of excess insurance were described in Chapter 13.

## *Constraints on Self-Insuring*

Organizations self-insure usually because their managers believe that risk costs can be reduced by eliminating the insurer's overhead, profit, and premium tax loadings. Occasionally, organizations are forced into self-insurance because commercial coverage is unaffordable or unavailable. Sometimes, however, even if an organization wants to self-insure, it may be unable to do so because of various constraints.

Restrictions may be imposed externally by clients, lenders, or others. For example, a contractor may be able to charge to a client all insurance costs pertaining to a project, but not self-insurance reserves. Such a restriction might make purchasing insurance more feasible than self-insuring. For another example, a loan agreement might require the lender to provide insurance, thus precluding the use of self-insurance. Similarly, a service organization's key customers might require the service organization to provide them with certificates of insurance from recognized commercial insurers.

An organization's ability to use self-insurance might also be affected by regulatory constraints. For example, most states require employers to obtain state permission before self-insuring workers compensation obligations. Some states also regulate self-insurance of auto financial responsibility statutory obligations.

Finally, the excess insurance market may not support the levels of self-insurance a firm desires. For example, no excess insurer may be willing to write coverage over a specified retention without an intervening layer of insurance written by an insurer sophisticated in analyzing self-insurance programs.

## Tolerance for Risk

Even when no barriers would prevent an organization from self-insuring, the organization may not be able or willing to tolerate the risk of self-insurance. Therefore, a study of self-insurance feasibility typically considers the organization's financial ability to bear risk. Further, the organization must study its psychological ability to bear risk. Some entities are psychologically more able than others to assume significant levels of risk.

### Catastrophic Loss

The probability and potential severity of catastrophic loss are important considerations. The mere fact that a large loss has not occurred before does not mean that it cannot occur in the future.

### Variability of Results

Some types of loss are more predictable than others. For example, an employer might expect a certain average annual cost for workers compensation losses over time. However, the actual cost for any given year can fluctuate materially from year to year. In this situation, the organization's risk is not the predicted average amount of loss, but the annual variation from the predicted amount.

Stabilization of self-insured loss costs from year to year can often be accomplished by self-insuring multiple loss exposures. An organization that self-insures only one major loss exposure could experience an unacceptable fluctuation in loss costs from year to year. In contrast, an organization that self-insures several major exposures in one overall program can stabilize overall results for the program. A bad year in one exposure area may be offset by good results for the year in another area.

### Financial Outlook

An organization's future financial situation is also an important consideration in a self-insurance study. An organization that has huge cash reserves today may intend to apply those reserves toward other business purposes, such as a major plant expansion. Thus, the organization may be cash-poor in the future. Moreover, if the overall prospects for the organization or its industry are poor in the long term, it may be a bad idea to self-insure significant loss exposures as funds may not be available in the future to pay self-insured losses.

## Support Services

A self-insurance program requires a number of services. The most commonly needed services are for loss control, claims handling, and claims audits. The least expensive claim is the claim that is prevented, or, if not prevented, that has its consequences controlled. After the claim is presented for settlement, control of costs through efficient, proper claims handling is required. Finally, financial audits of claim trust accounts and technical reviews of claims administration and legal work complete the cost control measures.

## Loss Control

A self-insured organization must replace the loss control services formerly provided by the insurer. The organization can develop internal loss control expertise or hire external specialists. External services are available from a wide range of sources, including insurance brokerages, risk management consulting firms, and loss control consulting firms.

## Claims Handling

Someone must investigate, adjust, and administer the self-insured claims. When an organization retains risk through a high deductible, rather than a self-insurance program, the insurer provides claim services, pays out losses, and then seeks reimbursement from the insured for the amount of the deductible. A possible disadvantage of this arrangement is that the insurer controls claims falling within the deductible amount. In contrast, when an organization retains risk through a self-insurance program, the organization is responsible for managing claims falling within the self-insured retention.

Management of the claims process through a self-insured retention allows the organization to customize legal defense arrangements and claims adjusting procedures. For example, a manufacturer of a specialized product may choose one defense firm to coordinate all products liability cases, so that the law firm develops expertise in the technical issues involving the product. Likewise, the client may desire unusually high standards of claims adjusting services to conform to its own public image of customer service.

Theoretically, an organization can hire its own staff to administer claims and use its own legal department for defense work. Most self-insured organizations, however, prefer to hire an independent contractor, known as a **third-party administrator (TPA)**, to manage their claims. The choice of internal or external administration may be based on cost and efficiency considerations. External forces may impose some restrictions. For example, if excess workers compensation or liability coverage is purchased, the insurer may demand that claims be handled by a professional administrator approved by the insurer. Moreover, in most states, workers compensation claims must be handled in accordance with state law by licensed claims administrators.

In the absence of outside pressures, the organization may prefer external claims administrators for qualitative reasons. For example, the organization may be reluctant to deny claims brought by customers or by employees. An external administrator provides the appearance of an insurance company and can more easily deny a claim without arousing adverse reactions against the self-insured organization itself. The use of an external administrator also overcomes personnel and payroll restrictions that may be appropriate for the organization's overall needs but inappropriate for claims handling.

Another reason to consider external claims arrangements is that even if the volume of claims is sufficient to justify internal staff, a third-party administrator may be more efficient at supporting the claims administrators with up-to-date hardware and software, continuing education, and qualified supervisors.

### Claims Auditing

Many self-insured organizations obtain periodic audits of their self-insurance programs. Accounting audits of claim trust accounts are generally performed by a CPA at least annually. Technical reviews of the claims administration and legal work may be done at intervals of three years or less. The reviews include examination of (1) reserving practices and adequacy, (2) staff qualifications and caseloads, and (3) the adequacy of procedures and protocols.

## Tax Issues

One of the desirable financial aspects of conventional insurance is that the policyholder is entitled to a federal income tax deduction for all sums it pays as insurance premiums during the current tax year. For example, if Acme Manufacturing Company pays $400,000 in premiums for conventional insurance in the current year, Acme will be able to deduct all $400,000 from its gross income in determining its taxable income *for the current year*.

Some advanced risk management plans receive less favorable tax treatment. Consequently, in deciding whether to use a particular plan instead of conventional insurance, organizations normally seek to ascertain the tax treatment that a proposed plan would receive. Taxation of advanced risk management plans is a complex subject that depends largely on court interpretations, which change over time as new cases are decided. Competent tax counsel should be involved in the evaluation of any advanced risk management plan being considered.

Unlike premiums for conventional insurance, the sums that a self-insured organization pays into its own loss reserves during a particular year generally are not tax-deductible for that year. However, losses and loss-related expenses that are actually paid during a particular year are tax-deductible for that year. In other words, an organization with conventional insurance receives a tax deduction on its premium payments in the current tax year, whereas a self-insured organization does not receive a tax deduction until it actually pays losses (even though it paid an equal sum into its loss reserves in a prior tax year).

Large liability losses are often not actually paid until many years after the self-insured organization has established loss reserves. The inability of the self-insured organization to take a tax deduction when its pays money into reserves can therefore be a significant disadvantage of self-insurance plans in comparison to conventional insurance plans. Of course, certain advantages of self-insurance may outweigh the disadvantage posed by the tax deductibility issue.

## Advantages and Disadvantages

To summarize the major points explained above, the advantages and disadvantages of self-insurance are listed below.

### Advantages

1. *Reduced Cost.* Insurance premiums are intended by insurers to cover all loss costs, insurer expenses, taxes, and profits. Self-insurance costs include only loss costs and loss adjusting costs. Self-insurance eliminates all transaction costs, such as the insurer's profit, sales commissions, and state premium taxes.

2. *Improved Cash Flow on Loss Payments.* Insurers typically collect premiums before losses occur, often at the beginning of the policy term. Insured losses may not be paid out for months or years after the premium is collected. Self-insurance allows the organization to retain control of loss funds until they are actually expended for loss payments.

3. *Greater Emphasis on Loss Control.* Self-insured organizations may be more motivated to control losses, since managers realize that losses are paid directly from the organization's assets, rather than from the assets of an insurance company.

4. *Improved Control Over Claims.* Self-insurance allows greater flexibility in developing claims programs that are customized to the organization's needs. Self-insured organizations also maintain that the absence of insurance can have a positive influence in liability settlement negotiations.

5. *Improved Scope of Excess Insurance.* Organizations that are willing to accept substantial retentions often find that excess insurers will write a broader scope of coverage than the insured might get in a primary program with no deductible or a low deductible.

## Disadvantages

1. *Narrow Market for Excess Coverage.* Although excess policies may provide a broader scope of coverage, the insurers offering these excess policies are substantially fewer than those offering traditional "primary" policies. Further, many of these insurers are surplus lines insurers, and, as such, are less likely to be within the protection of state guaranty funds.
2. *Greater Reliance on Effective Loss Control.* Unless the greater emphasis on loss control is maintained at a high level of effectiveness, the self-insured program may suffer significant losses.
3. *Market of No Return.* After an organization has become self-insured, it may find a return to the traditional insurance market is difficult because of insurers' perceptions regarding reliability of data and commitment.
4. *High Level of Management Commitment Required.* The effectiveness of a self-insurance program can only be judged over a period long enough to take into account yearly fluctuations in loss experience. Management must have a high level of commitment to the self-insurance concept to avoid bolting at the first sign of trouble or raiding the program funds when it is successful. American business, with its emphasis on short-term results, does not often exhibit a willingness to undertake long-term projects.
5. *Tax Deductibility.* The self-insured organization does not receive a federal income tax deduction until losses are actually paid.

# Large Deductible Plans

A **large deductible plan** is an insurance plan in which the insured is responsible for reimbursing the insurer for claims up to a relatively large dollar amount (such as $250,000) and the insurer is responsible for paying claims in excess of the deductible amount. Typically, the insurer provides all administrative services, including claims administration and the issuance of insurance certificates.

Large deductible plans resemble self-insurance plans that include excess insurance. Under both types of plans, the insurer provides coverage in excess of the retention amount. However, under a self-insured retention plan, the insurer normally is not responsible for losses or claims administration or filing certificates of insurance for coverage within the retention layer. Under a large deductible program, the insurer has all of these responsibilities. Moreover, the insurer under a large deductible plan is responsible for the payment of losses even if the insured fails to reimburse the insurer for the losses within the deductible layer.

Large deductible programs for liability and property insurance coverages have existed for many years, but their use for workers compensation programs was prohibited until recently. Since 1990, states have begun to allow bureau-promulgated plans or have passed enabling legislation permitting insurers to file deductible plans. Currently, over 30 states allow insurer-developed large deductible workers compensation plans for employers meeting certain minimum annual premium requirements, generally $500,000 or more, and for insurers meeting certain financial requirements. Although the minimum deductible under the plans usually is $100,000, a $250,000 deductible is more common.

State-promulgated deductible plans tend to vary from state to state, and they may apply to medical payments only, disability payments only, or both medical and disability payments. The insurer-promulgated plans tend to be similar on a state-to-state basis, but they vary a great deal among insurers. Insurer-promulgated plans typically apply to all types of workers compensation claims. The state-promulgated plans typically feature smaller deductibles than insurer-promulgated plans.

## *Tax Issues*

Large deductible insurance programs have some of the same characteristics as both conventional insurance programs and self-insurance programs. For instance, to the extent that actual premium payments are made to the insurance company for losses in excess of the deductible, the payments are treated in the same manner as premium payments for a conventional insurance program. Also, to the extent that funds (or securities) are placed in escrow to guarantee future payments for the deductible portion of the program, the escrow funding cannot be deducted for income tax purposes, as is also the case with self-insurance reserves. However, any reimbursements to the insurer for actual claim payments are tax-deductible in the year paid.

## *Advantages and Disadvantages*

The advantages and disadvantages of large deductible plans are summarized below.

### *Advantages*

1. The major advantage is that the employer is able to receive many of the benefits of self-insurance without having to obtain approval to become a qualified self-insurer. Such a benefit is magnified greatly if the employer has business operations in more than one state (assuming that deductibles are allowable in the states in question).

2. The employer is able to receive many of the benefits of self-insurance without incurring the costs of internal administration.
3. Employers willing to accept responsibility for a large deductible may find greater market access than if they were seeking "first-dollar" coverage.
4. Large deductible workers compensation programs may be more advantageous than self-insurance programs for employers with difficult property or liability placements, as they offer the possibility of additional premium income to insurers.
5. For privately held employers, a large deductible plan does not require the public disclosure of financial information, as may be required for self-insurance.
6. In contrast with first-dollar insurance, large deductible plans provide a greater incentive to invest in safety and loss control programs because they can measure directly the benefits of favorable loss experience.
7. A large deductible plan can be a good stepping stone to self-insurance.
8. Should the need arise, exiting from a large deductible program is less difficult than exiting from a self-insurance program.

## Disadvantages

1. Without an aggregate cap, multiple losses could adversely impact earnings. (This disadvantage can be overcome by obtaining an aggregate cap on the amount that the insured must pay in deductibles.)
2. A large deductible plan, unlike self-insurance, gives the insurer ultimate control over claims management.
3. Large deductible plans require more administration by employers than traditional insurance programs.

# Captive Insurers

There are several acceptable definitions of the term "captive" or "captive insurer." For purposes of this chapter, a **captive** is any insurance company that is owned by one or more organizations (called "parents") and that insures only the owners of the company. This definition is very close to the definition of a mutual insurance company, the difference in practice being that the owner/policyholders in a captive are fewer in number and have made significant capital contributions to the captive insurance company.

The use of captive insurers is not a new idea. Early examples of captives that evolved into traditional insurance companies include the members of the Factory Mutual System and county farm mutuals in the Midwest. From the

1950s to today, the number of captives has increased from several hundred to over 3,000 writing over $14 billion in premiums.

## *Types of Captives*

Captives can be grouped according to general characteristics. A single-parent captive, or pure captive, is a wholly-owned subsidiary of its parent and insures only the loss exposures of the parent and its affiliates. A captive owned by two or more parents, who are usually in the same business, is referred to as a multi-parent captive, a multi-owner captive, or a group captive. A captive that is owned by an association, called an association captive, technically is a single-parent captive, because it is owned by a single entity (the association). However, since the association members own the association as a homogeneous group, some consider association captives to be group captives.

Captives can also be classified as direct or indirect. A **direct captive** issues policies directly to its insureds. In many cases, a direct captive purchases reinsurance to cover losses in excess of its desired retention. In other cases, a direct captive might not purchase reinsurance if the purpose of the captive is to fund large deductibles or self-insured retention programs. An **indirect captive** operates as a reinsurer, often reinsuring its parent's loss exposures through the services of a fronting insurer. (Fronting is described in more detail in a later section of this chapter.)

Still another way of classifying captives is by domicile (the jurisdiction under whose laws the captive is organized). From an American perspective, onshore captives are those domiciled in the United States or its territories. Offshore captives are those domiciled outside the United States and its territories. Offshore captives are often divided into two categories: those with Western Hemisphere domiciles and those with Eastern Hemisphere domiciles. Western Hemisphere domiciles include the Bahamas, Barbados, Bermuda, British Columbia, the British Virgin Islands, the Cayman Islands, Curacao, and the Turks and Caicos islands. Eastern Hemisphere domiciles include Gibraltar, Guernsey, Ireland, the Isle of Man, Jersey, Luxembourg, and Singapore. Eastern Hemisphere domiciles are commonly used by European, Australian, and Japanese parent corporations.

## *Risk Retention Groups[1]*

Some captives can be classified as **risk retention groups**. The term "risk retention group" originated in the federal Risk Retention Act of 1981, which was passed in response to a "products liability crisis" that arose from the rising costs and decreasing availability of products liability coverage from commercial insurers during the 1970s. This act was written to help organizations in any industry meet their products liability risk financing needs by (1) forming their own mutual risk financing organization (a risk retention group) or (2) establishing a buyers' cooperative (a purchasing group) to secure insurance in regular commercial markets for the group on a more efficient and favorable basis than could an individual member. In response to the liability crisis of the mid-1980s, the act was expanded in 1986 to include all types of liability insurance except workers compensation and personal liability.

A risk retention group must insure all of its owners, and all owners must be insureds. As a federal act, the Liability Risk Retention Act of 1986 only requires that a risk retention group be licensed in one state in order to underwrite risks in all states. Thus, a risk retention group can be organized as either a group captive with capital stock or a mutual insurer licensed under the laws of a single state.

## Tax Issues

A detailed discussion of tax issues concerning captives is beyond the scope of this text. However, the following general points are noteworthy:

- Federal income tax deductibility for the insured parent is complex, depending on elements of risk-shifting or transfer and risk-distribution. Issues are constantly litigated, with results differing case by case.
- Premiums are subject to state premium tax or federal excise tax, depending on the state of domicile and state of insurance operations, including claim settlement activity.
- Income earned by captives is subject to federal and state income taxation. Exceptions as to what constitutes taxable income differ by domicile and the nature of the captive's operations.

Taxation of captives is an extremely complex matter, and advice of competent tax counsel is highly recommended.

## Advantages and Disadvantages

The major advantages and disadvantages of captives are summarized below.

### Advantages

1. *Control.* Management of the captive is in the hands of the parent, not the insurance market.
2. *Policyholder Needs.* A captive can provide insurance coverage tailored to meet the parent's specific insurance needs. In some cases, the captive may

even provide coverages that would not otherwise be available from traditional insurers. The captive can also negotiate reinsurance according to the parent's specialized needs, changing limits and attachment points in accordance with the reinsurance market and contract terms.

3. *Cost Stabilization.* The use of a captive can achieve long-term stabilization of ultimate insurance costs, since the captive is insulated from hard market turns in the insurance cycle. Although market forces in the reinsurance market still affect captives, the captive can control reinsurance costs by altering limits and attachment points, changing the net retention of the captive and thus of the parent.

4. *Cost Reduction.* Profit, contingency, and sales commission expenses are removed. Further reductions are possible through improved operating efficiency.

## Disadvantages

1. *Organizational Costs.* The initial costs of starting-up a captive can be substantial, particularly if the captive is a group captive.

2. *Capitalization Costs.* Minimum capital requirements can be substantial, depending on domicile. However, the minimum capital requirements are only minimums; capital and surplus adequate to support the risk assumed by the captive are likely to be higher than the statutory minimums.

3. *Organizational and Operational Complexity.* Single-parent captives are easier to organize than group captives for the obvious reason that a smaller number of decision makers are involved. Once organized, captives have to be managed like any other company. Because the management expertise of the parent is generally outside the realm of insurance, management responsibility is contracted to an outside captive management company, but the parent remains responsible for major decisions, including analysis of audited financial statements.

4. *Outside Business.* In order to achieve tax deductibility of the parent's premiums, some captives accept outside business (i.e., insure entities other than the parents). Although relatively few captives have failed, the acceptance of outside business is cited as being a key factor in those failures that have occurred.

# Fronting

**Fronting** most commonly refers to the practice of a nonadmitted insurer (an insurer that is not licensed to do business in a particular state) contracting with a licensed insurer to issue an insurance policy for regulatory or certification purposes. The licensed insurer, or fronting company, reinsures from 90 to 100 percent of the policy limit with the nonadmitted insurer.

Sometimes a self-insured organization that needs evidence of commercial insurance will have a policy issued by a fronting company, signing an indemnity agreement that promises to reimburse the fronting insurer for any claims paid. For example, if an entity wants inspection services, but not insurance, from a boiler and machinery insurer, the insurer can issue a policy with a deductible equal to the limit, thereby eliminating any net transfer of risk.

## History

The technique of fronting encompasses a number of practices that have been used for many years. If "fronting" is defined to include programs in which the policy-issuing company has retained 0 to 10 percent of the exposure on a net basis, most insurance companies have engaged in fronting.

The term "fronting" has often created problems with regulators who have expressed concern about their loss of control over the transaction and over the ability of the fronting insurer to bear the risk. To reduce the perceived stigma, many other names for fronting have been suggested, but "fronting" remains the term used most widely.

In the 1970s and 1980s, fronting insurers often ceded 90 percent or more of their policy limits to reinsurers. Frequently, the coverage was ceded to thinly capitalized offshore reinsurers. Some insurers perceived the fronting fees as a way to expand rapidly without much risk and gave too much underwriting authority, with little or no oversight, to independent managing general agents. Compounding the problem, the fronting insurers did not obtain adequate security from their policyholders. At best, the letters of credit and trust funds used as security were equal only to the outstanding loss reserves. The large-scale failures of some of these insurers have resulted in a more conservative stance today, both by regulators and insurance companies.

The federal Liability Risk Retention Act preempts some state regulatory functions and has thus eliminated the need for fronting arrangements in many instances in which they were formerly needed to satisfy state insurance regulators. However, other governmental regulators or insurance certificate-holders may still require a traditionally licensed and regulated insurer. For example, a state department of motor vehicles or public utilities commission could reject a risk retention group filing. Thus, there is still a need for fronting arrangements.

## Uses of Fronting

In the context of alternative risk financing, the most significant uses of fronting are for self-insurers and captive insurance companies.

*Self-insurers* find a fronting program useful to do the following:

1. Comply with financial responsibility laws and other state laws
2. Meet requirements of mortgagees, governmental bodies, and other entities for evidence of insurance
3. Obtain claims or loss prevention services from a particular insurer

*Captive insurance companies* use fronting to do the following:

1. Allow the captive to write business in a state that requires admitted insurance
2. Comply with financial responsibility and other state laws
3. Meet requirements of mortgagees, governmental bodies, and other entities for evidence of insurance

Fronting is also used by insurance companies that wish to provide insurance in states in which they are not licensed. Such an insurer can engage in business in that state if an admitted, properly filed insurance company issues the policy and reinsures losses to the nonadmitted reinsurer.

## Insurers' Concerns About Being Fronting Companies

Although fronting has been used for many years, it still causes some concerns for insurers that anticipate serving as fronting companies. Some of the most common concerns have to do with security, fees, and claims handling.

### Security

Fronting insurers commonly require the captive insurer or self-insured entity to provide security for payment of claims. A common type of security provided for fronting insurers is a letter of credit provided by a bank. Another popular type of security is a trust fund, also called a custodial trust account or New York State 114C trust.

Letters of credit are only as strong as the ability of the issuing bank to honor them. Recent banking regulations have stiffened the reserving requirements for banks issuing letters of credit, which provides a greater degree of protection but also significantly increases the fee for the letter of credit.

Under a trust fund plan, a bank holds the insured's assets in an amount determined by the fronting company and generally based on probable claims.

*246   Commercial Liability Insurance and Risk Management*

Although the investment income accrues to the insured, the fronting company has direct access to the funds.

### Fronting Fee

The fronting company charges the insured a fee for its services. The fronting fee charged must be adequate. The amount of the fee is determined by the scope of the services provided. The typical range is 5 to 25 percent of the insurance premium. In addition to covering the fronting services, the fronting fee must be sufficient to cover the additional risk that the reinsurer (often a captive owned or controlled by the insured) might default on its reinsurance obligations, thus making the fronting company liable for the entire loss.

### Claims Authority

Determining claims settlement authority often is a difficult problem to resolve. The parent of the captive generally understands that the majority of any claim payment is the captive's money. Similarly, the fronting insurer generally understands that liability for bad faith claims or judgments in excess of policy limits may fall on the fronting company. In many fronting arrangements, the parties agree that the fronting insurer has final claims authority and that the captive must pay settlements promptly.

### Tax Issues

As in most advanced risk financing arrangements, the tax question is controversial and complex. In general, premiums paid to a fronting insurer are not deductible to the extent that they are reimbursable to the taxpayer, on the basis that no risk-shifting or risk-distribution occurs.

## Advantages and Disadvantages

Fronting can be advantageous to risk managers, insurers, and reinsurers. When used advantageously, fronting can do the following:

1. Provide coverage not otherwise available.
2. Open doors to reinsurance markets that would otherwise be closed.
3. Satisfy those who demand certificates of insurance from the insured.
4. Provide conventional insurers and reinsurers the flexibility they need to participate in markets where they otherwise would be shut out as nonadmitted.

Fronting can also have disadvantages, as summarized below:

1. Security, often in the form of letters of credit, may be expensive or not recognized by regulators as adequate, thus prohibiting the fronting carrier from taking credit for the ceded reinsurance.
2. Fronting arrangements may hide the inadequacies of loss reserves or the need for more security or collateral.
3. Fronting may avoid regulation and encourage fraud.

# Retrospective Rating Plans

A **retrospective rating plan** can be defined as a rating plan "in which the final premium is based on the insured's actual loss experience during the policy term, subject to a minimum and maximum premium, with the final premium determined by a formula . . . guaranteed in the insurance contract."[2]

Retrospective rating plans first became popular in the 1940s. Initially, the plans were used by defense contractors in connection with cost-plus government contracts. They gained popularity with workers compensation insurers as underwriters sought a means to exercise some of the same underwriting judgment and rating flexibility that were possible with other lines of insurance. Until the introduction of retrospective rating plans, underwriters and insureds were limited to the use of manual rates and experience modification factors (based on loss experience during past periods). Both fell short of projecting the actual losses to be expected during the current policy period.

Just as underwriters sought greater assurance that losses during the policy period would not be worse than expected losses, insureds sought greater rewards for their loss control efforts. Many insureds, especially large ones, thought that they could limit their losses to a lower level than the premium being charged under their guaranteed cost plan. Retrospective rating plans gained popularity primarily because they offered something for both parties: a form of "cost-plus" contract whereby the insured paid its actual losses (subject to a minimum and maximum) plus certain agreed-upon expenses.

For the same reasons, retrospective rating plans ultimately were extended beyond workers compensation to encompass general and automobile liability and even automobile physical damage, crime, and glass insurance. In many states, retrospective rating programs can be used either separately for a single coverage or under a plan combining several coverages.

## Comparison to Prospective Rating Plans

A **prospective rating plan** is one in which the premium for the coming policy period is calculated at the inception of the policy and is not subject to adjustment for the actual loss experience during the policy period. Prospective rating plans include (1) guaranteed cost rating plans and (2) experience rating plans.

In a **guaranteed cost plan**, the policy is rated at the beginning of the policy period using an estimated exposure basis (such as payroll or sales) that reflects the insured's predicted exposures during the policy term. The term "guaranteed cost" is somewhat of a misnomer because the rate, rather than the final cost, is what is guaranteed. The premium will be adjusted, if necessary, based on a premium audit made at policy expiration to determine the actual exposure base. Thus, the premium will be adjusted in accordance with the actual exposure basis—sales, payroll, and so on—once they are known, but losses incurred during the policy period will not affect the premium for that policy year.

**Experience rating** adjusts the premium of an insured for the *coming* policy period to recognize the loss experience of the insured during *past* policy periods. Thus, under experience rating, insureds that maintained favorable loss levels in the preceding years receive a premium reduction, and those with poor past loss experience are charged an increased premium. Experience rating relies on the premise that the insured's past loss history indicates what its future experience will be.

In contrast to a prospective rating plan, a retrospective rating plan bases the final premium on the insured's loss experience *during* the policy period. Therefore, retrospective rating plans are said to be "loss sensitive." Subject to a minimum and a maximum premium, the final premium varies directly with the insured's current loss experience, as illustrated in Exhibit 15-1.

## How Retrospective Rating Plans Work

The elements of a typical retrospective rating plan consist of the following:

1. The basic premium, which consists of the following:
    - The insurer's acquisition costs. Acquisition costs are the sales commissions that the insurer pays to its agents or brokers.
    - The insurer's operating expenses. Operating expenses include expenses for underwriting, loss control services, premium auditing, and general administration.
    - An "insurance charge." The insurance charge represents the difference between the charge for a maximum premium limitation and the credit for a minimum premium.

**Exhibit 15-1**
The Operation of a Retrospective Rating Plan

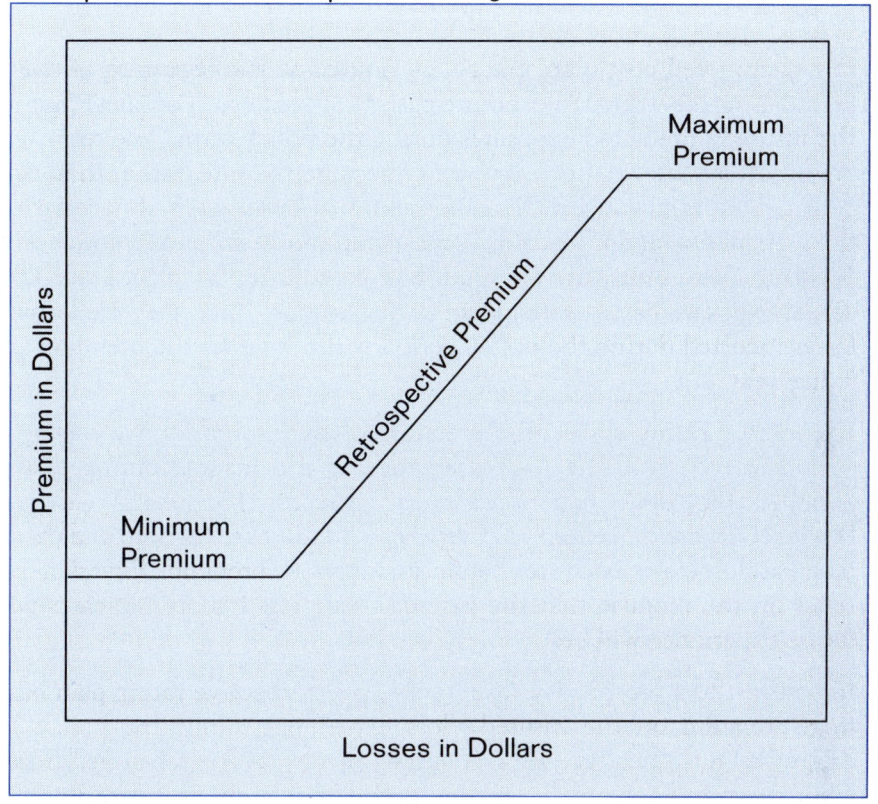

*[Graph showing Premium in Dollars on y-axis and Losses in Dollars on x-axis. A line labeled "Retrospective Premium" rises diagonally between a horizontal "Minimum Premium" segment at the lower left and a horizontal "Maximum Premium" segment at the upper right.]*

- An allowance for profit. Most insurers that seek to make a profit from their underwriting operations include an allowance for profit in their rates, and the same practice is followed in setting the basic premium for a retrospective rating plan.

2. Incurred losses. Incurred losses include actual losses paid, loss reserves, subrogation expenses, interest on judgments, and in some cases, allocated loss adjustment expenses. (Some retrospective rating plans use *paid* losses rather than *incurred* losses. Paid loss retrospective rating plans are discussed in a later section.) In the retrospective rating formula, incurred losses are multiplied by a loss conversion factor, which increases the incurred losses to allow for the insurer's loss adjusting expenses.

3. A tax multiplier. The tax multiplier reflects state premium taxes, licenses, fees, and miscellaneous assessments that the insurer must pay on the premium it collects.

Given these elements, the retrospective premium is determined using the following formula:

Retrospective premium =
[Basic premium + (Incurred losses × Loss conversion factor)] × Tax multiplier

In addition to the elements shown above, most retrospective rating plans include the following:

1. A *maximum* premium limitation, which caps the amount of premium the insured must pay, even if the retrospective premium, as determined using the formula shown above, exceeds the cap. Few insureds would be willing to enter into an insurance plan with no limit on their possible cost.
2. A *minimum* premium, which the insured must pay even though the indicated premium is calculated as a lower amount.

The difference between (1) the charge made for putting a maximum premium into the plan and (2) the credit given for imposing a minimum premium is referred to as an "insurance charge" and may be included in the basic premium or may be stated separately.

Insureds that meet certain minimum premium criteria ($100,000 or more, in many states), may also limit the chargeable amount of a single loss in the retrospective premium calculation. For example, at the $100,000 premium level, the chargeable amount of a single loss might be limited to $25,000. The premium charge for the loss limitation is determined by applying additional factors to the rating formula.

When used for workers compensation insurance, the rating formula is revised further in states that assess insurers for the operation of a workers compensation assigned risk pool. The charges assessed to the insurers are referred to as a residual market loading and may be added either to the loss conversion factor or the tax multiplier or charged as a separate item inside or outside the retrospective rating formula.

The retrospective premium is first calculated at the beginning of the policy period, when the appropriate exposure bases are used to calculate an initial deposit premium. After the policy expires, premiums are calculated periodically, at which time losses are factored into the formula. The payment of retrospective premiums after the policy has expired is described in more detail below.

## Paid Loss Alternative

A retrospective rating plan can use paid losses instead of incurred losses. A

**paid loss retrospective rating plan** offers the insured cash flow features that are absent from incurred loss retro plans.

The retrospective rating formula used with a paid loss retro plan is identical to that of an incurred loss retro plan except that it calculates the retrospective premium on the basis of *paid* losses rather than *incurred* losses. During the often extended period of time between loss events and actual payment of claims, the insured holds the unpaid premium and unpaid loss reserves and thus can use them to generate income. In other words, the insured holds funds that would have been held by the insurer under incurred loss retro plans or guaranteed cost plans. These funds are eventually paid to the insurer, when needed to pay claimants, but the insured holds them until then.

The premium paid at the beginning of a paid loss plan is usually significantly less than the premium paid at the beginning of an incurred loss plan. The initial premium paid under an incurred loss plan is typically the full standard premium or the full retrospective premium based on expected losses. (The "standard premium" is the insurer's manual premium, as modified by the applicable experience rating factor.) In contrast, the initial paid loss retrospective premium is sometimes only one-tenth or one-twelfth of the estimated annual premium. Some states permit the initial premium deposit for a paid loss plan to be the basic premium plus a few months of expected losses. Some states even permit the deposit premium to be based only on the basic premium, without a loss fund. A cost, however, is associated with these variations: the cost that the insured incurs to post security for future premium payments.

Typically, under a paid loss plan with one of the cash flow advantages described above, the insurer requires the policyholder to provide security or collateral guaranteeing the policyholder's payment of the difference between the deposit premium and the standard premium or expected eventual payout. Such security costs incurred by the insured might include, for example, premiums for surety bonds or bank fees for letters of credit that guarantee the eventual payment of the final premium at some time in the future.

Cash flow advantages can be added to an *incurred* loss plan by altering the method of payment of the initial deposit premium. The policyholder may wish to defer payment for a number of months and negotiate for a spread of the estimated retrospective premium over the policy term (and occasionally beyond expiration). This variation is called a **deferred pay-in plan**. Another variation occurs when the insurer allows the policyholder to "depress," or understate, the exposure base on which the initial premium is computed, with its final determination to be made by audit shortly after expiration but before the first retrospective adjustment. This variation is called a **depressed pay-in plan**.

## Payment of Premiums After Expiration

Regardless of the type of retro plan, after expiration of the policy period, the plans work in essentially the same way. About six months after expiration of the policy period, losses that are to be counted (incurred or paid during the policy period, according to the plan type) and applicable allocated loss adjustment expenses are tallied and factored into the retrospective rating formula. If the indicated premium exceeds the premium already paid, the insurer charges an additional premium.

At the next retrospective adjustment period, usually twelve months later, total losses and allocated loss adjustment expenses are again tallied and factored into the formula, with another premium adjustment. The retrospective premium is recalculated at the end of additional periods as agreed on by the insurer and the policyholder. The process continues until all losses are closed or the final adjustment, as agreed to in the negotiations, is made.

In the case of paid loss plans, security adjustments are also made at each retrospective adjustment; however, the principal sum of surety bonds or amounts of letters of credit rarely decrease over time, as the renewal of the retrospective rating plan has added a new set of losses into the security mechanism. Thus, over time, the cost of collateral or security can be substantial, as year after year of unpaid losses are incurred. Paid loss plans often convert to incurred loss plans at some time after expiration, such as three or five years.

## Current Use of Retrospective Rating Plans

Although eligibility requirements and some plan elements differ, retrospective workers compensation rating programs are available for use in most states, even states with monopolistic state funds. The most common programs are the ones adopted by the states that subscribe to the National Council on Compensation Insurance (NCCI). Until 1991, NCCI offered a choice of four plans (known as Plans I, II, III, and IV), which applied only to workers compensation coverage.

These plans provided preset tables of factors (thus, they were commonly referred to as "tabular plans") that were calculated for a wide range of premium levels. The limited flexibility of the plans, due to their use of preset factors, and the increased use of a fifth plan (described below) led to their demise in all but three or four NCCI states.

In most states that subscribe to the NCCI, an insured can elect to include coverages other than workers compensation in a combined lines retrospective premium program (formerly called Plan V). The combined plan is the most flexible of the NCCI plans in that it allows considerable freedom of choice with regard to minimum and maximum premiums and loss conversion factors.

Since discontinuing the tabular plans, NCCI has also introduced a combined lines Large Risk Alternative Rating Option. The option requires a standard premium of at least $1 million and is available in many states that subscribe to NCCI.

## Tax Issues

Although retrospective rating bears some similarities to self-insurance, the IRS has not challenged retrospective rating plans in the same manner as it has challenged pure self-insurance or captive insurance companies. However, the IRS does carefully scrutinize cash flow and paid loss retrospective rating plans. The current test used is the so-called economic performance test, which, in simple terms, states that the economic performance test is not satisfied until premiums are actually paid to the insurance company.

## Advantages and Disadvantages

The advantages and disadvantages of retrospective rating plans are summarized below.

### Advantages

1. Retrospective rating favors insureds whose hazards of operation are lower than average for their rate classification.
2. Retrospective rating can benefit an organization with favorable loss experience when the experience modifier does not result in an adequate premium reduction.
3. Retrospective rating can benefit an insured that has an unfavorable experience modification due to circumstances, such as several bad losses, that are unlikely to be repeated.
4. A retrospective rating plan may make placement of insurance coverage easier for an insured that has had past loss problems because the underwriter can receive a higher premium than that developed by manual rating.
5. Retrospective rating may make placement of insurance coverage easier for the insured whose losses are subject to a great deal of variability.

### Disadvantages

1. Retrospective rating does not favor insureds whose hazards of operation are higher than average for their rate classification.

2. Retrospective rating can produce wide premium swings from one policy period to another.
3. Retrospective rating makes financial planning difficult because the final cost of insurance may not be known for several years after the end of each policy year.
4. Retrospective rating does not favor an insured that has had a low experience modification but now must cut costs through reduction in staff or reduction in loss prevention expenditures.
5. Some insureds with retrospective rating plans may perceive that the insurer is careless in settling claims because the money paid out is not the insurer's but, in fact, the insured's. Such perceptions sometimes lead to expensive lawsuits between insurers and their insureds.

## Summary

Advanced risk management techniques (also referred to as the "alternative market") provide solutions for risk management problems that go beyond the scope of the conventional insurance policies described in the other chapters of this text. The alternative market represents about one-third of the U.S. commercial insurance market.

Self-insurance plans involve the planned retention of risk. The self-insured organization pays losses, up to a certain predetermined amount, out of its own funds. The organization often carries excess insurance to pay losses above the self-insured retention.

In a large deductible plan, the organization retains a layer of losses by purchasing an insurance policy with a relatively large deductible. The main difference from a self-insurance plan is that the insurer administers and pays all claims. The policyholder then reimburses the insurer for the deductible amount.

A captive is any insurance company owned by one or more organizations (called "parents") that insures only the parents. Because the parent manages the captive, the use of a captive can help the parent achieve long-term stabilization of insurance costs as well as other benefits.

Fronting is a practice that enables a self-insured organization, a captive insurer, or a nonadmitted insurer to comply with regulatory requirements or to obtain needed certificates of insurance. The entity in need of such assistance contracts with a licensed insurer to issue an insurance policy. The licensed insurer, or fronting company, then reinsures 90 to 100 percent of the policy limit with the self-insured organization, captive insurer, or nonadmitted insurer.

Retrospective rating plans combine insurance and retention. Subject to a minimum premium and a maximum premium, the insured's final premium is based on the insured's actual loss experience during the policy period. In a retrospective rating plan, premiums can be calculated on the basis of either incurred losses or paid losses. Using paid losses can provide additional cash flow benefits to the insured.

# Chapter Notes

1. The description of risk retention groups is adapted from George L. Head, Michael W. Elliott, and James D. Blinn, *Essentials of Risk Financing*, 2d ed., vol. 1 (Malvern, PA: Insurance Institute of America, 1993), p. 129.
2. Richard V. Rupp, *Insurance & Risk Management Glossary* (Chatsworth, CA: NILS Publishing Co., 1991), p. 291.

# Bibliography

*American Jurisprudence.* 2d ed. Rochester, NY: Lawyers Cooperative, 1993.

*Black's Law Dictionary.* 6th ed. St. Paul, MN: West Publishing Co., 1990.

Bregman, Robert A., and Jack P. Gibson. *Professional Liability Insurance.* Dallas, TX: International Risk Management Institute.

Clapp, Wallace L., Jr. "Employment Practices Liability—Employers Respond to a Growing Need." *Rough Notes* (November 1993).

*Commercial Liability Insurance.* Dallas, TX: International Risk Management Institute.

*Contract Bonds: The Unseen Services of a Surety.* New York: The Surety Association of America, 1973.

Golden Gate Chapter of the CPCU Society. *The Alternative Market*: Dallas, TX: International Risk Management Institute, Inc., 1994.

Head, George L., Michael W. Elliott, and James D. Blinn. *Essentials of Risk Financing.* 2d ed., vol. 1. Malvern, PA: Insurance Institute of America, 1993.

Hersbarger, R.A., and M.L. Cross. 1979. "Nature and Major Provisions of Directors and Officers Liability Insurance." *CPCU Journal* 32 (1).

Horn, Ronald C. *Subrogation in Insurance Theory and Practice.* Homewood, IL: Richard D. Irwin, 1964.

"Insuring Your Fiduciary Liability Exposure." *John Liner Letter* (June 1993).

*IRMI's Workers Comp: A Complete Guide to Coverage, Laws, and Cost Containment.* Dallas, TX: International Risk Management Institute, 1995.

Levy, S. *Accountants' Legal Responsibility.* New York, NY: American Institute of Accountants.

Mackall, Luther E. *Surety Underwriting Manual.* Indianapolis, IN: The Rough Notes Co., 1972.

Markham, James J., ed. "Role of the Workers Compensation System." Chapter 1 in *Principles of Workers Compensation Claims.* Malvern, PA: Insurance Institute of America, 1992.

Monteleone, Joseph. "D&O Allocation: Problems and Solutions." *The Risk Report.* vol. XVIII, no. 8 (April 1996).

"Professional Liability and Claims Made Coverage." St. Paul, MN: St. Paul Fire and Marine Ins. Co.

"Prudential Sues Law Firms." *Journal of Commerce*, 2 October 1989.

Reubi, Marie, and Jill Foster. "Current Award Trends." In *Personal Injury Valuation Handbook*. Horsham, PA: LRP Publications, 1994.

Rupp, Richard V. *Insurance & Risk Management Glossary*. Chatsworth, CA: NILS Publishing Co., 1991.

*Statement of Financial Accounting Standards*, Nos. 35 and 36.

*Watson Wyatt D&O Liability Surveys*. Chicago, IL: Watson Wyatt & Co., 1993, 1994, 1995.

Webb, Bernard L., Arthur L. Flitner, and Jerome Trupin. *Commercial Insurance*. 3d ed. Malvern, PA: Insurance Institute of America, 1996.

# Index

## A

Above-ground and underground storage tank insurance, 160-161
Accident, workers compensation and, 9
Accident commission, industrial (workers compensation board), 14
Accountants, breach of contract and, 61
 common allegations against, 62-64
 loss control and, 67-68
 loss exposure for, 61
Accountants professional liability insurance, 61-68, 65
 exclusions to, 66-67
 insuring agreement of, 65
 limits and deductibles of, 67
 policy provisions of, 65-67
 who is insured under, 65-66
Accountants and tort liability, 61-62
Accounting services, common allegations against accountants and, 63
Acid rain exclusion, 145
Adequacy of excess limits, 197-198
Administration, workers compensation claim, 13-14
Administration and use of anesthetics or drugs, 52-53
Administrative errors, other, liability for negligent advice and, 95-96
Administrator, 226
 third-party (TPA), 235
Administrators and executors, 226
Advanced risk management techniques, 231-255
Advantages and disadvantages, captives, 242-243
 combined insurance forms, 159-160
 fronting, 246-247
 large deductible plans, 239-240
 retrospective rating plans, 253-254
 self-insurance, 237-238
Advice, business and investment, common allegations against accountants and, 64
 negligent, liability for other administrative errors and, 95-96
Aggregate excess policy, 174-175
Aggregate limits, effect of, 169-170
Aggregate and specific excess insurance, 174-175
Aggregate umbrella limits, 179-180
Aircraft and watercraft exclusions, 187
Alienated premises exclusion, 144
Allegations against accountants, common, 62-64
 accounting services and, 63
 audit services and, 62-63
 breach of fiduciary duties and, 64
 business and investment advice and, 64
 client counterclaims and, 63
 failure to detect embezzlement and, 63-64
 management advisory services and, 64

securities laws and, 64
tax services and, 62
Allegations against architects and engineers, common, 69-71
Allegations against physicians, common, 51-53
Allocation, arbitration/alternative dispute resolution, directors and officers liability insurance and, 91-92
   "best efforts," directors and officers liability insurance and, 91
   directors and officers liability insurance and, 91
   predetermined, directors and officers liability insurance and, 92
Amount, penal, 202
Anesthetics or drugs, use and administration of, 52-53
Anheuser Busch, Gediman v., 95
Appeal bond, 223-224
   defendant's, 224
Application process for environmental insurance, 163-165
Arbitration/alternative dispute resolution allocation, directors and officers liability insurance, 91-92
Architects and engineers, common allegations against, 69-71
   defenses in negligence cases against, 71
   loss control and, 74-75
   loss control and performance responsibilities of, 75
   loss control, management and personnel support, and, 74
   loss control, quality control, and, 75
   loss control, record keeping, and, 74
   loss exposure and, 68-71
   noninsurance transfers and, 75
Architects and engineers professional liability insurance, 68-75, 71
   exclusions of, 73-74
   insuring agreement of, 72
   policy provisions of, 71-74
   who is insured under, 72-73

Asbestos abatement contractors general liability insurance, 152
Asbestos and lead abatement contractors general liability insurance, 152-154
Assigned risk plans, 12
Assignment, WC&EL policy and, 33
Assumption of risk, employee and, 3
Attachment bond, 223, 224
Audit services, common allegations against accountants and, 62-63
Authority, claims, fronting and, 246

# B

Bankruptcy proceedings, trustees in, 226-227
Benefits, death, 11
   employee, nature and scope of, 94
   financing, methods of, state workers compensation laws and, 11-13
   workers compensation, injuries and diseases covered under, 8-9
"Best efforts" allocation, directors and officers liability insurance and, 91
Bid bonds, 208-210
Bodily injury, consequential, 27
Bond, appeal, defendant's, 224
   attachment, 223, 224
      release of, 223, 224
   nonstatutory, 205
   statutory, 205
   surety, rates for, 204
Bond limit, 205
Bonds, bid, 208-210
   contract, 207-215
      miscellaneous, 214-215
      supply, 214-215
   court, 222-224
   customs, 217
   ERISA, 97-98
   excise, 216
   federal noncontract surety, 207, 216-217
   fiduciary, 222, 225-228

common causes of loss and, 227-228
judicial, 207, 222-228
license and permit, 207, 217-220
maintenance, 213
payment, 212
performance, 210-211
public official, 207, 220-222
  nature of guarantee and, 221
  noncancelable nature and indeterminate length of, 221
subdivision, 214
supply contract, 214-215
surety, 201-230
  characteristics of, 202-205
  fundamentals of, 202-207
  general types of, 207
  indeterminate in length and noncancelable, 204-205
  regulations and statutes influencing, 205
Breach of contract, accountants and, 61
Breach of fiduciary duties, common allegations against accountants and, 64
Broad-as-primary endorsement, 191
Buffer layer, 195
Bumbershoot policy, 188
Business and investment advice, common allegations against accountants and, 64
Business judgment rule, 82

# C

"Cs," the three underwriting, 203
Cancellation, WC&EL policy and, 33
Capacity, 203
  dual, 27
Capital, 203
Captive, 240
  direct, 241
  indirect, 241
Captive insurers, 240-243
Captives, advantages and disadvantages of, 242-243

tax issues and, 242
types of, 241
Care, custody, or control, 188-189
Care, duty of, employer's, 2-3
Care and loss of services, 27
Catastrophic loss, 234
Causes of loss, common, fiduciary bonds and, 227-228
CGL insurance policy, 1970 pollution exclusion in, 132-133
CGL insurance policies, professional liability coverage under, 42-43
  subsequent, pollution exclusion in 1986 and, 134-135
CGL/EIL insurance policies, combined, 162
Character, 203
Characteristics of environmental loss exposures, 130-131
Characteristics of excess and umbrella liability policies, basic, 170-171
Characteristics of surety bonds, 202-205
Claims, third-party, 14-15
Claims auditing, self-insurance and, 236
Claims authority, fronting and, 246
Claims handling, self-insurance and, 235-236
Claims or suits covered under employers liability insurance, other types of, 27-28
Claims-made coverage, site-specific EIL insurance and, 141-142
Claims-made provisions, fiduciary liability insurance, 102
Claims-made trigger, directors and officers liability insurance and, 86
Clean Air Act (CAA), 117-118
Clean Water Act (CWA), 116-117
Cleanup coverage in commercial property policies, 138-139
Client counterclaims, common allegations against accountants and, 63
Collateral, 203
Combination excess policy, 174

Combined CGL/EIL insurance forms, 161-162
Combined CGL/EIL insurance policies, 162
Combined insurance forms, advantages of, 159-160
Combined insurance policies available, types of, 160-163
   menu-style, 163
Combined pollution coverage forms, 158-163
Commercial property policies, cleanup coverage in, 138-139
Common allegations against accountants, 62- 64
   accounting services and, 63
   audit services and, 62-63
   breach of fiduciary duties and, 64
   business and investment advice and, 64
   client counterclaims and, 63
   failure to detect embezzlement and, 63-64
   management advisory services and, 64
   securities laws and, 64
   tax services and, 62
Common allegations against architects and engineers, 69-71
Common allegations against physicians, 51-53
Common causes of loss, fiduciary bonds and, 227-228
Common characteristics of professional liability policies, 44-48
Common features of compensation laws, 6-14
Common law, employers liability under, 2-4
Common-law defenses, employer and, 3-4
Common pollution coverage extensions in standard liability forms, 137-138
Comparative negligence, 4
Compensation, workers, 1
Compensation laws, common features of, 6-14
Compensation laws, federal, 15-21

Competitive state funds, 12
Compliance guarantees, 218-219
Comprehensive Environmental Response, Compensation, and Liability Act (CERCLA or "Superfund"), 123-126
Concurrency, 193
Condition, maintenance of underlying insurance, 192
Conditions, WC&EL policy, 32
   assignment, and, 33
   cancellation, and, 33
   inspection, and, 32
   long-term policy, and, 33
   sole representative, and, 33
Consent, informed, 51, 54
   lack of, 52
Consequential bodily injury, 27
Conservator, 225
Constraints on self-insuring, 233
Contract, liability assumed under, employers liability insurance and, 29
   supply, 214-215
Contract actions, 41
Contract bonds, 207-215
   miscellaneous, 214-215
   supply, 214-215
Contract versus tort actions, 41
Contractor, independent, 7
Contractors environmental impairment liability (EIL) insurance, 146-148
Contractors limitation endorsement, 191-192
Contractors, small, surety bond guarantee program for, 215
Contractual duty, 40-41
Contractual liability exclusion, 144
Contractual obligations, 114
Contributory negligence, 3-4
   physicians and, 54
Control, joint, 204
Control, care, or custody, 188-189
Corporate reimbursement coverage, directors and officers liability insurance and, 84-85

Corporation, duty of loyalty to, 80
Corporations, professional, 41-42
Court, probate, 222
Court bonds, 222-224
Court of equity, 222
Coverage, claims-made, site-specific EIL insurance and, 141-142
   corporate reimbursement, directors and officers liability insurance, and, 84-85
   defense, 183-184
   drop-down, 176
   entity, directors and officers liability insurance and, 92
   foreign voluntary compensation, 34-35
   individual, directors and officers liability insurance and, 84-85
   layering of, 168-169
   layers, problems in, 197
   need for, employers liability insurance and, 26-27
   prior acts, 86
   stop gap, 31
Coverage endorsement, maritime, 35-36
   voluntary compensation maritime, 35-36
Coverage form, asbestos abatement contractors general liability insurance policy, 153-154
Coverage forms, combined pollution, 158-163
Coverage under professional liability policies, defense, 46-47
Coverage territory, professional liability policies and, 48
   umbrella liability insurance and, 194
Coverage triggers, professional liability policies and, 47-48
   occurrence and claims-made, 183
Coverages, financial guarantee, 228
Covered acts and consequences under professional liability policies, 44-45
Credit guarantees, 219
Crew members, laws applicable to, 20

Cross liability, umbrella liability policy and, 191
Curator, 225
Cure, maintenance and, 20
Current use of retrospective rating plans, 252-253
Custody, care, or control, 188-189
Customs bonds, 217

# D

D&O liability insurance. *See* Directors and officers liability insurance
Damage to the insured site, exclusion of, 144
Damages, punitive, umbrella liability policies and, 190
Death benefits, 11
Deductibles, accountants professional liability, 67
   directors and officers liability insurance and, 90-91
   large, 238-240
   site-specific EIL insurance, 145-146
Defendant's appeal bond, 224
Defense Base Act, 19
Defense coverage, 183-184
   under directors and officers liability insurance, 87-88
   under professional liability policies, 46-47
Defenses, common-law, employer and, 3-4
Defenses for negligence action against physician, 53-54
Defenses in negligence cases against architects and engineers, 71
Deferred pay-in plan, 251
Delegation, physicians and, 50-51
Deliberate noncompliance with environmental laws, exclusion of, 143
Depressed pay-in plan, 251
Derivative and nonderivative suits, 82-83
Diagnosis, improper, 52

## 264 Index

Difficulties in managing environmental exposures, overcoming, 131-132
Diligence and abandonment, physicians and, 51
Direct captive, 241
Directors and officers, duties under ERISA and, 81
  duty of care and, 80
  duty of disclosure and, 81
  indemnification of, 83-84
  major responsibilities and duties of, 79-81
Directors and officers (D&O) liability insurance, 77, 78-93
  allocation and, 91
  arbitration/alternative dispute resolution allocation and, 91-92
  "best efforts" allocation and, 91
  claims-made trigger and, 86
  corporate reimbursement coverage and, 84-85
  deductibles and, 90-91
  defense coverage under, 87-88
  individual coverage and, 84-85
  insuring agreements of, 84-92
  limits of liability and, 90
  "loss" and, 85
  loss control and, 92
  loss exposure and, 78-84
  persons insured under, 87
  policy provisions of, 84-92
  predetermined allocation and, 92
  types of, 92-93
  "wrongful act" and, 85-86
Directors and officers liability insurance exclusions, 88-90
  insured versus insured and, 88-89
  maintenance of insurance and, 89
  outside directorships and, 89-90
  severability of interests and, 90
Directorships, outside, directors and officers liability insurance exclusions and, 89-90
Disability, permanent partial, 10
  permanent total, 10
  temporary partial, 10
  temporary total, 10
Disadvantages. See Advantages and disadvantages
Disclosure, duty of, directors and officers and, 81
Discrimination, 105
Drop-down coverage, 176
Drugs or anesthetics, use and administration of, 52-53
Dual capacity, 27
Duties under ERISA, directors and officers and, 81
Duties if injury occurs, your, WC&EL policy and, 31-32
Duties of professionals, 40-42
Duties and responsibilities of directors and officers, major, 79-81
Duty, contractual, 40-41
  tort-related, 41
Duty of care, directors and officers and, 80
  employer's, 2-3
Duty of disclosure, directors and officers and, 81
Duty of loyalty to corporation, 80
Duty of loyalty to stockholders, 80-81
Duty of referral, specialists and, 50

## E

Each occurrence limit, 169-170
EBL insurance. See Employee benefits liability insurance
Effect of aggregate limits, 169-170
EIL insurance. See Contractors environmental impairment liability insurance and Site-specific environmental impairment liability insurance
Employee, 7
  assumption of risk and, 3
  fellow, negligence of, 4
Employee benefits liability (EBL) insurance, 77, 98-101

loss control and, 103-104
loss exposures and, 93-98
Employee Retirement Income Security
    Act of 1974 (ERISA), 81
    bonds for, 97-98
    fiduciary liability under, 96-98
Employer, common-law defenses and, 3-4
Employer's duty of care, 2-3
Employers liability insurance, 1-38. *See
    also* Workers compensation and
    employers liability insurance
    exclusions of, 143
Employers liability under common law, 2-4
Employment practices liability (EPL)
    insurance, 78, 104-108, 106
    loss control and, 108
Employments and persons covered under
    state workers compensation laws, 6-8
Endorsement, broad-as-primary, 191
    contractors limitation, 192
    LHWCA coverage, 35
    maritime coverage, 35-36
    United States Longshore and Harbor
        Workers' Compensation Act, 35
    voluntary compensation, 33-34
    voluntary compensation maritime
        coverage, 35-36
Endorsements, coverage, other, 36-37
    following-form, 192
    WC&EL policy and, 33-37
Enforcement of environmental laws, 126-127
Engineers and architects, common
    allegations against, 69-71
    defenses in negligence cases against, 71
    loss control and, 74-75
    loss exposure and, 68-71
    noninsurance transfers and, 75
Entity coverage, directors and officers
    liability insurance and, 92
Environmental exposures, overcoming
    difficulties in managing, 131-132
Environmental insurance, 111-166

Environmental laws, exclusion of deliberate noncompliance with, 143
Environmental liability, legal basis for, 112-128
Environmental loss exposures, characteristics of, 130-131
Environmental management decisions,
    executive accountability for, 127-128
Environmental professional errors and
    omissions (E&O) liability insurance,
    148-152
    exclusions of, 150-152
Environmental remediation insurance,
    154-156
Environmental risk management, 128-132
Environmental statutes, 115-128
EPL insurance. *See* Employment practices
    liability insurance
Equity, court of, 222
ERISA. *See* Employee Retirement Income
    Security Act of 1974
Error, surgical, 52
Errors, administrative, other liability for
    negligent advice and, 95-96
Errors and omissions (E&O) liability
    policies, 45
Excess and umbrella liability insurance,
    167-200
Excess liability insurance, 172-175
    specific and aggregate, 174-175
Excess liability policy, 170
    combination, 174
    following-form, 172
    self-contained, 173-174
Excess limits, adequacy of, 197-198
Excess policy, aggregate, 174-175
    specific, 174
Excess or umbrella liability coverage, need
    for, 167-170
Excess workers compensation insurance,
    13
Excise bonds, 216
Exclusion, 1970 pollution, CGL policy
    and, 132-133

1986 pollution, subsequent CGL policies to, 134-135
   acid rain, 145
   alienated premises, 144
   contractual liability, 144
   known pre-existing conditions, 143
   nuclear liability, 144
   products and completed operations, 144-145
   punitive damages, 143
   transportation exposures, 145
   war, 145
Exclusion of damage to the insured site, 144
Exclusion of deliberate noncompliance with environmental laws, 143
Exclusions, accountants professional liability insurance, 66-67
   aircraft and watercraft, 187
   architects and engineers professional liability policies, 73-74
   contractors EIL policy, 147-148
   directors and officers liability insurance, 88-90
   EBL insurance, 100-101
   employers liability insurance, 28
   environmental professional E&O liability insurance, 150-152
   environmental remediation insurance policy, 155
   fiduciary liability insurance, 103
   other, WC&EL policy and, 29
   physicians professional liability policy, 56-57
   pollution, 132-139
   professional liability policies, 48
   site-specific EIL policy, 142-145
   umbrella, underlying insurance and restrictions of, 189
   umbrella liability insurance, 184-185
   workers compensation and employers liability, 143
Executive accountability for environmental management decisions, 127-128

Executor, 226
Experience rating, 248
Exposure, professional liability insurance and, overview of, 40-48
Exposures, environmental, overcoming difficulties in managing, 131-132
   loss, environmental, characteristics of, 130-131
*Exxon Valdez* oil spill, 130

# F

Failure to detect embezzlement, common allegations against accountants and, 63-64
Features of compensation laws, common, 6-14
Federal compensation laws, 15-21
Federal Employees' Compensation Act, 21
Federal Employers' Liability Act (FELA), 15
Federal noncontract surety bonds, 207, 216-217
Fee, fronting, 246
Fellow employee, negligence of, 4
Fiduciary, 96
Fiduciary bonds, 222, 225-228
Fiduciary duties, breach of, common allegations against accountants and, 64
Fiduciary liability insurance, 77, 101-102
   exclusions of, 103
Fiduciary liability under ERISA, 96-98
Financial guarantee coverages, 228
Financial guarantees, license and permit bonds and, 219
Financial outlook, self-insurance and, 234
Financing benefits, methods of, state workers compensation laws and, 11-13
Following-form endorsements, 192
Following-form excess policy, 172
Foreign voluntary compensation coverage, 34-35

Fronting, 243-247
Fronting companies, insurers' concerns about being, 245-246
Fronting fee, 246
Funds, state, 12

# G

Gediman v. Anheuser Busch, 95
Good faith guarantees, 219
Good Samaritan statutes, 54
Guaranteed cost plan, 248
Guarantees, compliance, 218-219
   credit, 219
   financial, 219
   good faith, 219
   indemnity, 219-220
Guardians, 225

# I

Improper diagnosis, 52
Improper tests, 52
Indemnification of directors and officers, 83-84
Indemnity guarantees, 219-220
Indemnity payments, 9-10
Independent contractor, 7
Indirect captive, 241
Individual coverage, directors and officers liability insurance and, 84-85
   physicians professional liability insurance and, 55
Industrial accident commission (workers compensation board), 14
Informed consent, 51, 54
   lack of, 52
Injury, 9
   bodily, consequential, 27
   occupational, 8
Injury outside United States or Canada, 29
Inspection, WC&EL policy conditions and, 32

Insurance, accountants professional liability, 61-68, 65
   architects and engineers professional liability, 68-75, 71
   asbestos and lead abatement contractors general liability, 152-154
   contractors environmental impairment liability, 146-148
   directors and officers (D&O) liability, 77, 78-93
   employee benefits liability (EBL), 98-101
   employment practices liability (EPL), 104-108, 106
   environmental, 111-166
   environmental professional errors and omissions (E&O) liability, 148-152
   environmental remediation, 154-156
   excess liability, 13, 172-175
   excess and umbrella liability, 167-200
   fiduciary liability, 101
   layers of, 168
   other states, 30
   physicians professional liability, 48-60
   private, 11-12
   professional liability, 39-76
      continued, 77-110
   remediation stop-loss environmental, 156-158
   self-, 12-13, 232-238
   site-specific environmental impairment liability, 139-146
   suretyship versus, 205-206
   umbrella liability, 175-195
   underground storage tank (UST), 160-161
   underlying, 168
   workers compensation and employers liability, 1-38
Insured site, damage to, exclusion of, 144
Insured versus insured, directors and officers liability insurance exclusions and, 88-89

Insurers, captive, 240-243
Insurers' concerns about being fronting companies, 245-246
Insuring agreement(s), accountants professional liability insurance, 65
　architects and engineers professional liability insurance, 72
　contractors environmental impairment liability policies, 147
　directors and officers liability insurance, 84-92
　EBL insurance, 99
　environmental impairment liability policies, 147
　environmental professional errors and omissions liability policy, 149-150
　environmental remediation insurance policy, 154-155
　fiduciary liability insurance, 101-102
　physicians professional liability policy, 55-56
　site-specific EIL insurance, 140-141
　umbrella liability insurance, 180-181
　　definitions and, 181-183
Intentional torts, 113-114
Interests, severability of, directors and officers liability insurance exclusions and, 89-90

## J

Joint control, 203
Jones Act, 20
Judicial bonds, 207, 222-228

## K

Known pre-existing conditions exclusion, 143

## L

Lack of informed consent, 52

Large deductible plans, 238-240
　advantages and disadvantages of, 239-240
Law, common, employers liability under, 2-4
Laws, environmental, enforcement of, 126-127
　exclusion of deliberate noncompliance with, 143
　securities, common allegations against accountants and, 64
　workers compensation, 4-21
Laws applicable to crew members, 20
Layer, buffer, 195
Layering of coverage, 168-169
Layers (of insurance), 168
　working, 195
Legal basis for environmental liability, 112-128
LHWCA. *See* United States Longshore and Harbor Workers' Compensation Act
Liability, cross, umbrella liability policy and, 191
　employers, common law and, 2-4
　limits of, WC&EL policy and, 30
　professional, 39
　statutory, accountants and, 62
　strict, 114
Liability assumed under contract, employers liability insurance and, 29
Liability for negligent advice and other administrative errors, 95-96
Liability program, structuring the, 195-198
License and permit bonds, 207, 217-220
Lien, mechanic's, 212
Limit, bond
　each occurrence, 169-170
　underlying, 181-182
Limits, aggregate, effect of, 169-170
　aggregate umbrella, 179-180
　excess, adequacy of
　required underlying, 178-179

Limits of liability, accountants professional liability insurance, 67
  directors and officers liability insurance, 90
  EBL insurance, 99
  fiduciary liability insurance, 101-102
  site-specific EIL insurance, 145-146
Locality rule, physicians and, 50
Longshore and Harbor Workers' Compensation Act (LHWCA). *See* United States LHWCA
Loss, catastrophic, 234
  directors and officers liability insurance and, 85
  maximum possible, 167-168
  ultimate net, 181
  variability of results and, 234
Loss control, accountants and, 67-68
  architects and engineers and, 74-75
  directors and officers liability insurance and, 92
  employee benefits and fiduciary liability insurance and, 103-104
  employment practices liability insurance and, 108
  performance responsibilities of architects and engineers and, 75
  physicians and, 57-60
  self-insurance and, 235
Loss exposure, accountants, 61
  architects and engineers, 68-71
  directors and officers liability insurance, 78-84
  employee benefits and fiduciary liability insurance and, 93-98
  environmental, characteristics of, 130-131
  physicians and, 49
Loss of services, care and 27

# M

Maintenance bonds, 213
Maintenance and cure, 20
Maintenance of insurance, directors and officers liability insurance exclusions and, 89
Maintenance of underlying insurance condition, 192
Management advisory services, common allegations against accountants and, 64
Management and personnel support, architects and engineers, loss control, and, 74
Managing environmental exposures, overcoming difficulties in, 131-132
Maritime coverage endorsement, 35-36
Maximum possible loss, 167-168
Mechanic's lien, 212
Medical professionals, other allegations against, 53. *See also* Physician(s)
Menu-style combined insurance policies, 163
Methods of financing benefits under state workers compensation laws, 11-13
Migrant and Seasonal Agricultural Worker Protection Act, 20-21
Miller Act, 212-213
Miscellaneous contract bonds, 214-215
Monopolistic state funds, 12
Motor Carrier Act of 1980, 120-122

# N

National Council on Compensation Insurance (NCCI), 21
Nature and scope of employee benefits, 94
Nature of guarantee, public official bonds, and 221
Need for employers liability insurance, 26-27
Need for excess or umbrella liability coverage, 167-170
Negligence, 112-113
  comparative, 4
  contributory, 3-4
    physician and, 54

Negligence action against physicians,
   defenses against, 53-54
   statute of limitations for, 53-54
Negligence cases against architects and engineers, defenses against, 71
Negligence of fellow employee, 4
Negligent advice, liability for other administrative errors and, 95-96
Nonappropriated Fund Instrumentalities Act, 20
Noncancelable and of indeterminate length, public official bonds being, 221
Noncompliance with environmental laws, deliberate, exclusion of, 143
Nonderivative suits, 82-83
Noninsurance transfers, architects and engineers and, 75
Nonstatutory bond, 205
Nuclear liability exclusion, 144
Nuisance, intentional torts and, 113

## O

Obligations, contractual, 114
   statutory, 28-29
Obligee, 201
Occupational injury, 8
Occurrence, 182-183
Occurrence and claims-made coverage triggers, 183
OCSLA (Outer Continental Shelf Lands Act), 19
Officers and directors, duties under ERISA and, 81
   duty of care and, 80
   duty of disclosure and, 81
   indemnification of, 83-84
   major responsibilities and duties of, 79-81
Oil Pollution Act of 1990 (OPA), 119-120
Oil spill, *Exxon Valdez*, 130
Organization coverage for physicians, 55-56

Organizations and persons covered under EBL insurance, 99-100
Organizations and persons insured under fiduciary liability insurance, 102
Other insurance, directors and officers liability insurance exclusions and, 88
Other states insurance, 30
Outer Continental Shelf Lands Act (OCSLA), 19
Outside directors liability policy, 89
Outside directorships, directors and officers liability insurance exclusions and, 89-90

## P

Paid loss retrospective rating plan, 251
Pay-in plan, deferred, 251
   depressed, 251
Payment bonds, 212
Payments, indemnity, 9-10
Penal amount, 202
Performance bonds, 210-211
Performance responsibilities of architects and engineers, loss control and, 75
Permanent partial disability, 10
Permanent total disability, 10
Physician, contributory negligence of, 54
   defenses for negligence action against, 53-54
   statute of limitations for negligence action against, 53-54
Physicians, common allegations against, 51-53
   delegation and, 50-51
   diligence and abandonment and, 51
   individual coverage for, 55
   locality rule and, 50
   loss control and, 57-60
   loss exposure for, 49
   organization coverage for, 55-56
   standard of care for, 49-50
Physicians professional liability insurance, 48-60
Pollution, 189-190

Pollution coverage extensions in standard liability forms, common, 137-138
Pollution exclusion in 1986 and subsequent CGL policies, 134-135
Pollution exclusions, 132-139
Pollution exclusions in other liability policies, 136-137
Pre-existing conditions exclusion, known, 143
Predetermined allocation, directors and officers liability insurance and, 92
Premium, WC&EL policy and, 32
Principal liable to surety, 202
Principles of workers compensation law, 5-6
Prior acts coverage, 86
Private insurance, 11-12
Probate court, 222
Problems in layering coverage, 197
Products and completed operations exclusion, 144-145
Professional corporations, 41-42
Professional liability, 39
Professional liability coverage under CGL policies, 42-43
Professional liability exposure and insurance, overview of, 40-48
Professional liability insurance, 39-76
    accountants, 61-68, 65
    architects and engineers, 68-75, 71
    common characteristics of, 44-48
    coverage territory of, 48
    coverage triggers in, 47-48
    covered acts and consequences under, 44-45
    defense coverage under 46-47
    exclusions of, 48
    physicians, 48-60
    who is covered under, 46
Professionals, duties of, 40-42
Prospective rating plans, 247-248
Public employee dishonesty insurance, public official bonds and relationship to, 221-222

Public official bonds, 207, 220-222
Public official bonds and relationship to public employee dishonesty insurance, 221-22
Punitive damages, umbrella liability policies and, 190
Punitive damages exclusion, 143

## Q

Quality control, architects and engineers, loss control, and, 75

## R

Rates, surety bond, 204
Rating, experience, 248
Rating plans, prospective, 247-248
    retrospective, 247-254
Record keeping, architects and engineers, loss control, and, 74
Referral, duty of, specialists and, 50
Regulations and statutes, surety bonds influenced by, 205
Rehabilitation services, 10-11
Release of attachment bond, 223, 224
Remediation stop-loss environmental insurance, 156-158
Representative, sole, WC&EL policy and, 33
Resource Conservation and Recovery Act (RCRA), 118-119
Responsibilities and duties of directors and officers, 79-81
Retention, self-insured, 176, 178
Retrospective rating plans, 247-254
    advantages and disadvantages of, 253-254
    paid loss, 250-251
    prospective rating plans compared to, 247-248
    tax issues and, 253

Rights of surety if principal defaults, 204
Risk, assumption of, employee and, 3
    tolerance for, 234
Risk management, environmental, 128-132
Risk management method, suretyship as, 206-207
Risk management techniques, advanced, 231-255
Risk plans, assigned, 12
Risk retention groups, 241-242

# S

Seaworthiness, vessel owner's warranty of, 20
Securities laws, common allegations against accountants and, 64
Security for fronting insurer, 245-246
Self-contained excess policy, 173-174
Self-insurance, 12-13, 232-238
    advantages and disadvantages of, 237-238
    claims auditing and, 236
    claims handling and, 235-236
    financial outlook and, 234
    loss control and, 235
    support services and, 234-236
    tax issues and, 236-237
Self-insured retention, 176, 178
Self-insuring, constraints on, 233
Services, rehabilitation, 10-11
    support, self-insurance and, 234-236
Severability of interests, directors and officers liability insurance exclusions and, 89-90
Sexual harassment, 105-106
Significance of subrogation and salvage, 204
Site-specific environmental impairment liability (EIL) insurance, 139-146
Small contractors, surety bond guarantee program for, 215

Sole representative, WC&EL policy and, 33
Specialists and duty of referral, 50
Specific and aggregate excess insurance, 174-175
Specific excess policy, 174
Standard of care for physicians, 49-50
State funds, 12
State workers compensation laws, 4-15
    benefits provided under, 9-11
    choice of law and, 6
    methods of financing benefits under, 11-13
    payments for medical services under, 10
    persons and employments covered under, 6-8
Statute of limitations for negligence action against physician, 53-54
Statutes, environmental, 115-128
    Good Samaritan, 54
Statutory bond, 205
Statutory liability, accountants and, 62
Statutory obligations, 28-29
Stockholders, duty of loyalty to, 80-81
Stop gap coverage, 31
Strict liability, 114
Structuring the liability program, 195-198
Subdivision bonds, 214
Subrogation and salvage, significance of, 204
Suits, derivative, 82
    nonderivative, 82-83
Superfund (CERCLA), 123-126
Supply contract bonds, 214-215
Supply contract, 214-215
Support services, self-insurance and, 234-236
Surety, 201
    principal liable to, 202
    rights of, if principal defaults, 204
Surety Bond Guarantee Program, 215
Surety bond rates, 204
Surety bonds, 201-230

characteristics of, 202-205
fundamentals of, 202-207
general types of, 207
noncontract, federal, 207, 216-217
Surety theoretically expects no losses, 202-204
Suretyship as risk management method, 206-207
Suretyship versus insurance, 205-206
Surgical error, 52

# T

Tax issues, captives and, 242
    fronting and, 246
      large deductible plans and, 239
      retrospective rating plans and, 253
      self-insurance and, 236-237
Tax services, common allegations against accountants and, 62
Temporary partial disability, 10
Temporary total disability, 10
Termination, wrongful, 105
Territory, coverage, umbrella liability insurance and, 194
Tests, improper, 52
Third-party administrator (TPA), 235
Third-party claims, 14-15
Third-party-over, 27
Tolerance for risk, 234
Tort actions, 41
    contract versus, 41
Tort liability, accountants and, 61-62
Tort-related duty, 41
Torts, 112-114
    intentional, 113-114
Toxic Substance Control Act (TSCA), 122-123
Transfers, noninsurance, architects and engineers and, 75
Transportation exposures exclusion, 145
Trespass, intentional torts and, 113-114
Trustees in bankruptcy proceedings, 226-227

# U

Ultimate net loss, 181
Umbrella and excess liability insurance, 167-200
    basic characteristics of, 170-171
    need for, 167-170
Umbrella liability insurance, 170, 175-195
    basic functions of, 176-178
    coverage territory of, 194
    cross liability and, 191
    exclusions of, 184-185
    insuring agreement of, 180-181
    other provisions of, 192-194
    punitive damages and, 190
Underground and above-ground storage tank insurance, 160-161
Underground storage tank (UST) insurance, 160-161
Underlying insurance, 168
Underlying limit, 181-182
Underwriting—the "three Cs," 203
United States Longshore and Harbor Workers' Compensation Act (LHWCA), 15, 17-20
    coverage endorsement, 35
UST (underground storage tank) insurance, 160-161

# V

Vessel owner's warranty of seaworthiness, 20
Voluntary compensation coverage, foreign, 34-35
Voluntary compensation and employers liability coverage endorsement, 34
Voluntary compensation endorsement, 33-34
Voluntary compensation maritime coverage endorsement, 35-36

## W

War exclusion, 145
Warranty of seaworthiness, vessel owner's, 20
Watercraft and aircraft exclusions, 187
Workers compensation, 1
   procedure for obtaining benefits for, 13
Workers compensation benefits, injuries and diseases covered under, 8-9
Workers compensation board (industrial accident commission), 14
Workers compensation claim administration, 13-14
Workers compensation and employers liability insurance, 1-38
Workers compensation and employers liability (WC&EL) policy, 21-37
   assignment of, 33
   cancellation of, 33
   conditions and, 32
   endorsements of, 33-37
   information page of, 22-23
   inspection and, 32
   limits of liability in, 30
   long-term policy and, 33
   other exclusions of, 29
   other states insurance and, 30
   policy form of, 24-33
      employers liability insurance and, 26-30
      general section in, 24
      workers compensation insurance and, 24-26
   premium and, 32
   sole representative and, 33
   your duties if injury occurs and, 31-32
Workers compensation laws, state, 4-15
   federal, 15-21
Working layers, 195
"Wrongful act," directors and officers liability insurance and, 85-86
Wrongful termination, 105

## Y

Your duties if injury occurs, WC&EL policy and, 31-32